CHANGING TIMES

The Millennium Story of the People of Bolton, Westmorland

Written & Compiled by Barbara Cotton

This book is dedicated to the people of Bolton

HAYLOFT

First published 2001

Hayloft Publishing,
Great Skerrygill, South Stainmore,
Kirkby Stephen, Cumbria, CA17 4EU.

Tel. 017683 42300 or Fax. 017683 41568
e-mail: dawn@hayloft.org.uk
website: www.hayloft.org.uk

' 2001 Bolton Millennium Association and Barbara Cotton

ISBN 0 9540711 3 1

A catalogue record for this book is available
from the British Library

Design & production by Hayloft

Cover illustration by Bolton Primary School pupils

Foreword

The seed of an idea to produce some kind of written record about the village of Bolton was sown at the first meeting of the newly formed Millennium Association in 1999. Then, in the knowledge that we would need a decent computer system to assist with the compilation and retention of information and data, a successful grant application was made to the Lottery Millennium Festival Awards Scheme and we were ready to go.

Various ideas and plans were discussed regarding the methodology of collecting information including the content, style and format of the intended publication but it was not until Barbara Cotton was invited to join the group that things really began to happen.

Barbara threw herself wholeheartedly into the project, researched archives, interviewed countless people, investigated facts with a detective s zeal, even threw her home open to the public in order to gather informationand with the help of Pam Metcalf s newly acquired computer skills, the book you hold in your hands today was produced, the final presentation of which has been beautifully put together and printed by Hayloft Publishing of South Stainmore.

This book constitutes a record of social and economic change, which we hope will attract the attention of academics and historians and every one with an interest in the dynamic life of a country village.

But above all it is a testimony to the people of Bolton past, present and future, to whom this book is dedicated.

Alan Kingston
Chairman
Bolton Millennium Association

Acknowledgments

I would like to thank the following people for their help, enthusiasm and encouragement: firstly Pam Metcalf for help with the word processing, Mr McCreedie headmaster, Eden Grove School, Audrey and David Dent, Revd Tony Dent, Kathleen Creighton nee Bellas, Sue Mounsey, Margaret Jones at Staveley and Margaret and Andy Jones, Whinfell View, Elizabeth Barker, Barbara Davis, Frank and Alison Baxter, Anne and Ken Shepherd, George Ellwood, Wilf and Mary Allinson, Eleanor Hayton, Thelma and Philip Jackson, David and Linda Fox, Christine and Richard Birkbeck, Liz and Chris Gilroy, Linda and John Campbell, Pat Macnulty, Edith Stockdale, Claire Hudson, Fiona Young, John Cotter, Barbara and Alan Kingston, Annie Kirkup, Doug and Charlotte Wills, Harry Bell, Val and Dan Bromley, Anita and David Woods, Hazel and Arthur Bird, Roger Bird, Mr and Mrs Richardson, Bolton Lane Ends, May Forrester, Ada Addison, Maisie Parkin, Padget Richardson, Marion Richardson, Ella Wilson and Joanne Mounsey for lending me her school project *My Settlement* and Helen McWilliam for lending hers *All Saints Bolton*, Charlotte and Doug Wills, Bob Thwaites, John Bainbridge, Jo Bennett, Billy Howe and Revd David Wood, Enid Page, Brian Lamont, Chris Butterworth and Elisabeth Hodgson. Lastly, my daughter Catherine for help with the research at Kew and my husband Derick for finding me the job!

Not forgetting thanks to the staff at the County Archives, Kendal, the Castle, Carlisle and the staff at Kew Record Office, London.

This book would not have been possible without the help of so many people and I would also like to thank any one I may have inadvertently left out. There are many people that there just was not the time to visit or contact.

The information available about the village to be researched certainly has not been exhausted. So if the information herein enclosed has whetted your appetite there is plenty left to fill another book.

Barbara Cotton

Contents

Bolton

In former times, local inhabitants spoke their own dialect. With the passing of time, few locals now do so. Annie Kirkup who features elsewhere in the book composed the following dialect poem:

We've just hed oor Millennium si
Wi thowt wid rite a byiak
Ah hope yer nut ower thrang ter sit doon en hev a lyak
Yerl finned it varra interestin wi tyals lang sen ter noo
We've got sum gay gud fotoes si wi thowt wed print a few
Boltons set int Eden Valley, a bonnier spot yerl niver finned.
Wid luvly vyoos ert Pennines, but wi dunt like t cold Helm Winnd.
We've gota nice old Norman Kirk en a nice laal chapel nar.
We've a villidge hoe en a modern skiel where oor bonny kids o ga.
Then farther on doont villidge we've got a friendly pub
Where thirsty fwook can hev a beer ent best erv country grub.
Ort t gardens er a picture set oot wi cullers breet.
Oor fwerk er warm en frendly,therl welcome yer awreet.
Si git yersels ter Bolton in hev a nice day oot
It l nut be lang till yer back agen ev that ther is nea doot.

Annie Kirkup
May 2001

Introduction

Some tasks you take on and enjoy and complete. Some you take on and regret but somehow muddle through while some you start and then wonder what made you ever think you could do this. The last goes some way to describe my feelings of sheer horror faced with a book to complete. A book that relates directly to my friends and neighbours, the good people of Bolton. A book that in its final stages appears like the north face of the Eiger would appear to novice climbers because I ve never written a book before and I ll probably never write one again.

Fundamentally this book is about people. Specifically the people of Bolton and their forefathers and their forefathers forefathers, all the way back to the Middle Ages. In fact Bolton became Bolton in real terms when the church was built sometime in the 13th century. The history of the village comes alive through the history of the people, their lives and events, the births, marriages and deaths cause the interaction that ultimately at village level becomes our history.

This book aims to put into print the social, geographic and historical context of the village in such a way that anyone, be they Bolton born and bred, or simply a visitor to Cumbria will be able to read a small bit of what brought the village to the Millennium s celebrations of the year 2000.

I have long had a desire to discover the history of my house, Glebe House, its occupiers, owners and hopefully deliciously juicy past. To take on the whole village has more than satiated my appetite. For very good logistical reasons this book is more a series of sketches that briefly light up sections of the past. Shining a torch on little spots of our collective memories that enable a broader canvas to be brushed. But time and tides are against me and I can only show a little of who, why, what and when. I do hope you enjoy this snapshot and do not judge me as a writer but rather as a researcher and collator. It is a journey I have been glad to make but am also glad the journey is over and that normal life can begin again.

For Bolton I am sure that another willing volunteer will appear in the next Millennium all I know is that it will not be me.

Barbara Cotton

The Building of Bolton

In ancient times Bolton was written Boelthus, Boeltum, Bovelthus and Botheltum. In dialect it is pronounced Bowlton. The suggested meaning of the name is enclosure with buildings or the village proper.

The village lies about a mile and a half from the A66 in the appropriately named Eden Valley, four miles from Appleby to the south, and nine miles from Penrith to the north. The Pennines lie to the east with a good view of High Cup Nick on a clear day. The fells are an ever changing scene depending on the weather pattern. To the west can be seen the tops of the Lakeland hills. It is a peaceful place to live but not lonely as it is still a working village and there is a lively community supported by the village school, pub, two churches, a shop and the Memorial Hall. The economy of the village has been founded on agriculture since time immemorial.

With a church dating back to the 12th century and houses to the 17th century it is perhaps useful to review the history of building. With the invasion of the Anglo Saxons came the house carpenter. Every settlement appears to have had someone who knew how to square logs and build with them. The science of house building began its development with the invention of the pit saw. One man stood on the log and pulled the blade up and the other one stood in the pit and pulled it down. The trade of sawyer became very important in the Anglo Saxon community and he learned to use other tools to fix the wood together.

As a tradesman the wright as he was known had to be paid for his skill so

Greystone House, then known as Marle Cottage

Orchard House

his services could only be employed for building by those who could afford him. The principal contribution of the Anglo Saxon house builder was the introduction of the ground set. Prior to this the poles of the house would have been planted in the earth. This was not a good practice as the water would rise up the timber and rot it. The posts were to carry the roof timber and were not intended to form part of the walls.

The first walls were made of stones picked up from the moor or plough land. Later ragstone perhaps dug out of Bolton quarry was used with a mortar of clay.

The first English stone quarries were probably discovered in the Bath region and opened by craftsmen at the beginning of the 8th century. These men learned how to dress stone, burn limestone to make lime and mix it with sand to make a good mortar. They then trained apprentices from the local area and they in turn spread the knowledge to others throughout the country.

In the centuries which followed it was the church that reaped the benefits of the craft of the masons in the building of churches and monasteries. In order to know how big to make a building some system of measurement had to be devised. Medieval measurement was very simple. Sixteen men were gathered in the churchyard and asked to place their right feet together one behind the other to set out the length of the village pole. This model represented stall room for a yoke of four plough oxen and became the basis for measuring a furlong, ie the length of a furrow and then a mile. Used for square measure it produced the rood and the acre.

During the Middle Ages clothiers came from the continent and introduced the cloth yard - the distance between the finger tips and the end of the nose with the head turned away. This eventually took the place of the Anglo Saxon yard. The pole then had to be divided into five and a half yards with further changes to the mile and acre. At the beginning of the 17th century the size of the minimum house was 16 feet by 30 (one pole by two).

At the beginning of the second millennium the English layman was banned from building two storey houses because of the lack of masons. Once again it was the church that had the monopoly and was able to build abbeys and monasteries. At the beginning of the 12th century the great churches were almost completed but by the middle of the century house building was being neglected because of the building of castles during the long reign of Henry II. It was not until the end of the 12th century that private people began to build houses themselves, with the majority being town houses built by very rich merchants. The upper middle class would have had rubble and stone laid by the local waller who would then call on a skilled mason to build the corners and frame the openings. Proper walling was an expensive luxury - framing enabled the panels to be filled up with wattle daubed with mud (wattle and daub). The joinered timber we know today did not appear until Elizabethan times. The upper storey was reached by a ladder or a steep spiral stone staircase which continued to be built well into the 17th century.

During the Middle Ages there were three types of domestic building:

¥ The home-made huts of the peasants

¥ In towns and villages the middle class houses built by the village carpenter

¥ The manor house of a large landowner

There are very few medieval houses or cottages remaining in England and those that do are nearly all remnants of a much larger building.

Spiers Jackson sitting by his fire at Broom Cottage

CHANGING TIMES

Greystone House

The 14th century would have seen Bolton as a village of hovels huddled around the church. The houses would have been little more than barns.

In 1349 the whole of England was swept by plague and half the population died resulting in a shortage of labour. The few remaining peasants were able to make a reasonable living hawking their services around the country seeking the highest prices. The large landowners realised they would not be able to restore their livelihood and a law was passed preventing the peasants from leaving the village. However the peasant had experienced a new freedom because of the virtual breakdown in government during the plague. He was not going to be dependent on the Manor again. The landowners had to find a new way to support their livelihoods and so they converted their arable land to pasture and started to graze sheep. This proved to be a good decision, as many of them became very rich. Many of the sheep farmers had been men who owned small manors and their peasants had had to work very hard to scratch a living. The new rich were forming a middle class between the hereditary nobles and the peasants - this was a true middle class.

The new middle classes were called yeomen and became important customers of the builders. This period saw the setting out of the village as we know it today. Where there was a large manor house and parish church the settlement could become a township and a township attached to a rich manor would attract the itinerant traveller selling such necessities as cloth and other household goods.

The small manor houses became the first farmhouses. The yeoman farmers in Tudor times built their houses in the township and their land was scattered in strips throughout the great common fields of the day. A yeoman held freehold property which was not subject to manorial custom and could be disposed of

Glebe House in 1900

without restriction. The houses were often designed to look like the squire's house and evidence can be seen of this in Bolton at North End where the architecture of the farm houses resemble that of Eden Grove. It was not until the 18th century when fields were arranged into more compact strips that farmers began to build farmhouses on their land.

During the 17th century the long house became distributed throughout the northern counties. The free masons of medieval times were being replaced by the bricklayer.

Travellers in Cumbria in the late 17th century describe the Cumbrian cottages as consisting of one room built of dry stone walls, long and low and often joined to the end of the farm buildings. The whole range would have been covered in roughly hewn slate from the local quarry. If slate was not available the houses were thatched with heather or rushes. In Bolton the last house to have its thatch replaced by tiles was probably Greystone House. Spiers Jackson could remember carting the thatch away and tipping it near to Luz Beck. At the time Greystone House was just one storey.

In the 16th and 17th centuries many of the smaller houses were built round a cruck construction. Pairs of naturally arched cruck timbers would be pegged together at the top and raised to support a ridge beam and a series of rough hewn rafters onto which the roof would be fixed. The walls were often built so as to hide the crucks. In many English villages cottages can still be seen today with crucks in their gable end. A difficulty, which had to be overcome, was how to lift the rafter feet from their anchorage in the ground without them sliding away causing the roof to collapse. By the middle of the 12th century the crucks solved this problem well. We may call these buildings cottages but they would have been built for farmers and small-holders. Bolton can boast a house with crucks in the gable end at Orchard House.

There are several old houses in Bolton but they will have been considerably altered from when they were first built. Many have features of 17th century building but it is difficult to say what they would have been like prior to this time; perhaps they were single storey and thatched. The middle of the 17th century was the time when the architecture of the houses began to change and a period of re-building and alteration took place. Evidence of this remains at Glebe House where it can be seen that the roof has been raised by some fifteen inches (people were much smaller then than they are today) and the outline of much smaller windows are evident in two of the bedrooms. Windows were a nuisance. They let in the wind and the rains, were expensive to glaze and meant easy entry for robbers. Few people could read and so no-one needed light to read by and during day light hours it was time to be out of doors. 1698 saw the start of the window tax. Richard Bellas is noted as assessor of window tax in 1777 for Bolton.

The Black Death which started in the south swept throughout the country. It was everyone s belief that the plague was carried by a south wind and so whenever possible the houses were built north and south so that a narrow windowless end was set towards the pestilence. Bolton s houses are set almost north to south.

From the middle of the 17th century a common style emerged and one of the features was a hallan or passage which ran from the front to the back of the house, dividing it into two. This style can be seen in the old houses of Bolton. One part became the service area or down house and the other was the fire house or living area. There were variations depending on the wealth of the family. The door leading into the hallan was low with an oak beam known as

Applegarth

Croft House

the threshwood let into the floor and fixed to the walls either side of the door. The hallan was about four feet wide and acted as a convenient storage space. The wall dividing the hallan from the fire house was built of stone and the opposite wall of wattle and daub or wicker. Opposite the threshwood and at the end of the hallan were two doors, one opening into the down house and the other opening into a short passage known as the mell. The mell passage commonly led off the hallan into the living area and was about six feet long to shield the fireplace from any draughts. William Rollinson says there is some confusion about the terminology here as some authorities refer to the short passage as the heck . Others refer to the partition as being the heck and the passage as being the mell.

The hearth occupied most of the stone wall partitioning the house from the hallan. The hearth stone was slightly raised from the floor and above would have been a great funnel like chimney. A huge hood extended out into the middle of the room about six feet and narrowed as it ended in a flue in the loft. The hood was made of either wicker-work daubed with clay or cow dung or lath and plaster. The remains of the old flue can also be seen at Glebe House and at the time the floor was removed a large ash area was found in the middle of the earth floor.

The area under the canopy would have been warm and the best place to sit; this would have been the social area of the house where folk would sit and card wool or knit. Carding is a process that removes all the impurities from wool, teasing the stiffer fibres apart and softening them so that they would spin smoothly. The carding was done with teasel heads (later short metal spikes) mounted on wooden boards.

It was not a very clean place to sit as a black liquor of soot and water trickled down the side in wet weather and stuck to everything it touched. It was known as the hallan drop . Meat would be hung to dry in the smoke. A rannel-balk or randle tree was a long beam placed on two beams projecting from the wall to the fire hood. This could be moved backwards and forwards and cooking utensils hanging on chains from it could be adjusted over the fire. Sometimes ratten crooks, adjustable iron pot hangers were fitted instead. On one side of the fireplace would have been a cupboard built into the wall to store the household salt and spices to keep them dry. The spice cupboard at Glebe House was discovered when the plaster was renewed on the wall. A small beam remained above the cupboard and the shelf was still in place. It had just been filled with rubble and plastered over. Sadly the door of the cupboard was missing because apparently these often bore the date of the house and the initials of the owner. The cupboard has been opened up again.

The dwellings must have been very dark because, as stated previously, there were few windows. There would be a small window to light the hearth and above this a small shelf for the family bible. The largest and most impressive piece of furniture was the bread cupboard made of carved oak and often bearing the date of the building and the initials of the owners. This cupboard usually formed part of the partition dividing the chamber and the buttery from the firehouse and would have been fitted into the fabric of the house. The room would have been very simply furnished with one or two wooden chairs, a large oak table and a sconce. This was a fixed wooden bench under which the kindling was stored. Opposite the fire may have been a settle which often had elaborate carving and the space beneath the seat may have been used to store clothes.

South View Farm

The painted date stone at Glebe House

The date stone at Greystone House, previously known as Marle Cottage

The date stone on the building to the north of the cross roads on the east side. The T of TOB has worn away

On either side of the cupboard would be a door leading through a wattle and daub wall. One led to the best bedroom and the other to a buttery. The down house was often open to the rafters and was the area where the washing, baking, brewing and preserving were done. It would also have been used for storage of things like wood and peat.

Access to the loft was by a flight of stairs or a ladder leading from the firehouse. The loft was where the servants and children slept. It was open to the rafters and must have been very cold and wet. What would have been the loft area at Glebe House appears to have extended across the fire room, the hallan and the down house because the thick old oak floor boards stretch continuously in some parts under the later dividing partitions.

The sanitary arrangements were most unsatisfactory as the door opened directly upon the midden stead subjecting new tenants to a midden fever. It was no use their complaining for: *Wha iver heard o cow muck making a body badly?*

Style changed again in the 18th century when the position of the main door was altered to make entry directly into the house with often a porch being built to protect the door from the elements and to draught proof the house. The down house was converted perhaps into a kitchen. The main bedroom was moved to the loft which now had a ceiling. The great hooded canopies were removed and cast iron ranges installed. Windows were

The bank barn at Glebe House

R. A. beneath.

Broom Cottage has T. L. 1728. The 1937 survey states that Peatgate house about one and a quarter miles WNW of the church was rebuilt in the 18th century but incorporates a lintel with the initials and date I. S. 1607 or 1667. Unfortunately because of foot and mouth disease it has not been possible to record this photographically.

With the exception of the date stone at Broom Cottage and Glebe House all the above are listed in the Westmorland Survey and Inventory by the Royal Commission on Historical Monuments.

The house next to the church has a different style of date stone - a shield engraved into the stone work with J. S. 1878 inscribed in it - possibly the home of John Spedding. There is a similar shield on the wall at Pennine View farm with reads Pennine View 1897.

The barns, cow houses and stables can be seen to be very much a part of the old houses in Bolton. From old documents that still survive for some of these houses they appear to be as important as the dwelling house itself. Some of the barns in the village are joined to the houses. As farms have ceased to exist and technological developments have been made in farming, many have become obsolete. Some have been converted into houses or into extra living space for the adjoining house.

There are examples of the bank barn in the village at Glebe House, Croft House, Luz Beck House and the Hermitage. This style of barn is confined to Cumbria and the Yorkshire Dales. As the name implies, this is a barn built on a natural or artificial slope. On the upward side of the building is a ramp leading to an upper storey where hay would be stored. On the opposite side of the barn

19

Looking east from the cross roads, showing the old blacksmiths shop and the barn which is now the Memorial Hall.

is an entrance or entrances to the cow house and stable. Trap doors enabled fodder to be dropped to the animals below.

On the upper floor was an area where corn was threshed and deeted. Opposite the big ramp entrance doors was a winnowing door. This was opened to allow a strong through draught. After flailing, the grain was tossed into a shallow dish made of sheep skin and known as a weyt and in the through

Hillcrest

Dents Cottage

draught the chaff would be carried away.

Many of the houses had small enclosed gardens with pot herbs and a sheltered area for the bees. Some of the grander houses had orchards that are still in evidence today. These orchards grew Victoria plums, damsons, cherries, pears and varieties of apples including Carlisle Codling, Bramley, Newton Wonder, Lanes, Prince Albert, Laxton, Fortune, Laxton Superb, Golden Spire, Allington Piper, Warners King, Ellisons, Orange Pippen and a Peasgood Nonsuch raised by a Mr. Peasgood from a seed planted in 1858. Some of these trees must be at least a hundred years old and specimens can still be found around the village.

Edith & Elsie Savage at West View

Chapel Street

Information about the people who owned or rented these homes can be gathered from old documents which still survive and from census returns. Date stones can also enable former occupants to be identified.

As we explore old houses we can trace their history. We may see where a spiral staircase once wound its way up to the second floor or see on old floor joists grooves indicating a vanished jetty. We may observe old doorways and old windows or centuries old timbers, all that remains of a medieval roof. We may uncover hidden cupboards and beneath lath and plaster we may see the great posts of a house frame.

At the beginning of the 18th century rural England was a scattering of open fields of arable land on which individual holdings were scattered in unrelated strips. The second half of this century saw the Georgian Commissioners beginning to complete the redistribution of these by gathering them together to form self-contained holdings which are the farms we see today. The squire took the opportunity to surround his home with a tree filled park. Hedgerows were planted along the boundaries of these new fields and many wealthy farmers abandoned their homes in the village and built Georgian farmhouses on their new holdings.

The new enclosures meant that farmers could improve their breeding stock to increase productivity. The Napoleonic Blockade brought further pressure to increase agricultural production. Many of the smaller farmers were unable to afford the cost of the fencing required for enclosures and had to sell out to adjoining more affluent land owners.

Some of the abandoned 17th century long houses in the village were con-

The New Crown Hotel now the Eden Vale Inn

verted into cottages by adding new doorways and new staircases. Today these old farmhouses are in disguise as rows of cottages for example those in Silver Street, School View . Other owners ruined by the Enclosure Acts might try to make extra income by opening an alehouse. Many country pubs have their origins in this way. Another diversification was to open a village shop in the parlour, for example at Greenside and Wayside.

The beginning of the 19th century saw the building of terraced houses by speculative builders, such as those in Chapel Street, built by the Bland family.

Whinfell Road

Marmion

The Victorian era also brought the building of classic heavy fronted houses such as the Old Rectory. Hawthorn House is also from this era. It was built by Willie Wilson of Bolton for Willie Harrison who married Wilson s daughter. Willie Wilson was the father of John Wilson who owned the New Crown Inn. Today it is the home of Liz and Chris Gilroy who have lived in the village since 1976. Chris comes from the north east and Liz from Appleby and both work as teachers.

Chris has taught Information and Design Technology at Appleby Grammar

Willowways, home to Harry & Margaret Hancock

Thornthwaite with George Ellwood in the garden

School for many years - he has seen many of his ex-pupils grow into adults and is now teaching some of their children. Liz teaches infants and juniors at St. Catherine s School, Penrith. Hawthorn House has been in Liz s family since it was built. Her father s mother was a Wilson who married an Arnison. It was her father who told Chris about the history of the house. It was built in 1870 at the time of the building of the Settle-Carlisle Railway. The front of the house is of sandstone, the same as that at Lowther Castle, and the back is made from stone from Bolton Quarry. The bricks around the windows at the back came from Culgaith brickworks.

In the early 1920s Padget Richardson s parents built Windygarth at North

Nos. 1 & 2 Eden Rigg

Elm Close

End. The house stands up on a hill and has the most magnificent views across to the Lake District.

Since then newer 20th century houses have been built throughout the village. Whinfell Road, a small estate of bungalows was built in the early 1980s on Billy Birkbeck s field by Cumbria Construction, with the exception of the Mounsey s home which was designed by them and built by Frank Moses of Renwick. Richard Birkbeck s was a Woolaways and Fred Brown, a builder, built his own. They were sold for between £38,000 and £42,000 each. From Whinfell going south towards the crossroads on the left hand side of the main street is:

Staveley a wooden clad house, built for Harry and Ada Jones. Mr. & Mrs. Shaw s house Cedarcroft is the same model and Richard Gelder from Long

The Council Houses

Mr & Mrs Holdsworth s bungalow on the site of Will Cherry s cycle shop

Marton erected these two dwellings.

Cecil Chapman from Brough built Marmion for £3,500 - Barbara and Philip Davies live there now.

Byways was built by Harvey Lowthwaite who was in partnership with Jack Kirkup, Annie s late husband, while Willowways was built by Jack Martin from Penrith for Mr. Ellwood.

Mr. Chapelhow from Cliburn built David and Pat Heath s home Conifers originally for a Mr. & Mrs. Greenwood. There have been several occupants since.

Thornthwaite George Ellwood s home has been up for ten years as has Holmlea , Margaret and Allen Fleming s house. Both were built by H. and W. Holmes - Henderson and Walker of Penrith.

Then we approach Overdale , just past the school and up a long driveway which was built for Thelma and Philip Jackson about 15 years ago by Frank Moses of Renwick.

The house between Greystone House and the Charltons, the home of Mr. Donald and Mrs. Ann Coward was at one time a plastics factory where plastic toys were made and painted; several people from the village were employed there. Ann Shepherd cycled from Kings Meaburn to work there when she first left school. The factory operated in the village for several years. Donald Coward was a postman delivering letters in the area before going into Appleby to be postmaster of the Post Office there.

Number 1 Eden Rigg, Noreen and Colin Charleton s home was built in 1939 for Noreen s parents. Mr. Chatworthy, who was a schoolmaster, lived next door

Jubilee Cottages

at No. 2 Eden Rigg before he left the village to go and live in Wales. It is now the home of June and Brian Hodgeson.

Turning to the left at the crossroads towards Penrith on the left is Elm Close, a development of small flats built for the Two Castles Housing Association.

North End Cottage

CHANGING TIMES

Garth End with Frank Taylor in the garden

There is then a row of council houses, built just after the war. The first two were designated as homes for agricultural workers and Harry Bell was the first to move in. The others could be let to anyone who applied. In later years the occupants were able to buy their homes if they so wished.

Back to the crossroads and turn left towards North End and the first new house is that of Mr. & Mrs. Lawrence Holdsworth. This was built on the site of Jack Kirkup s workshop and prior to that it was where Will Cherry mended cycles and watches. He also had a shop selling pop and fancy goods . He lived in the Larches, now home to Mike and Ann Graham. George Ellwood can remember that Will had some cows further down the village and after they had been milked the milk would be carried back in buckets hanging from great wooden yolks worn across the shoulders.

The bungalow next to Jubilee Cottage was built for Miss Gentry and Miss Thwaites but for some reason they never moved into it. Arthur Tatters lives there now. The next bungalow was built by Arthur Tatters and was where Geoff and Irene Tatters lived before they moved to Penrith.

In about 1945 Meadow View, Mrs. Stone s house was built for Mike Smith by Beacon Builders of Penrith. Turning back south towards the crossroads, Eden Grove farmhouse belonged to the Tatters and at the time was just a barn with byres underneath. It was converted into a house in about 1940. Jeanette Atkinson now runs a Bed & Breakfast business there.

Hubert Lines built Craiglands for Jean Bone and it is now the home of David and Doreen Ridehaugh. New North End Graham White built for himself

Braemore

and it is now the home of Kathleen and John Bainbridge.   North End Cottage is where George Ellwood was born. His grandparents lived there when his grandfather worked for Squire Graham.

At the crossroads turning left towards the church there is a new development of terraced cottages on the site where David Hayton s garage used to be. They were started in 2000 and built by a building firm from Shap for the Haytons. On the opposite side of the road is a small estate of new houses built by Russell Armour of Kendal, started in 1997, and called Eden Fold.

In Sycamore Drive Jimmy Ludgate built Clifford House for his family and Kevin Taylor built Barret House. Edenhills, a bungalow, was built in local stone

Stephensons Croft

Whiteriggs

by Wilkinsons of Brough and is the home of Mike and Helen Gerrish. Garth End was built in local stone in the 1990s for Frank Taylor when he retired as licensee of the New Crown Inn.

In 1963 Jack Kirkup built the bungalow next to the pub. The next bungalow was built for a retired RAF dentist who has since left the village. Turning left past the Post Office into Silver Street is Mary Sowerby s home which was pre-

Bolton Lane End cottages on the Kings Meaburn road.

Eden Fold

viously the home of Ada Longmire. Mary extended and modernised the cottage when she moved from Applegarth. The next new house is Sycamore House built for Hazel and Derek Mullen.

Just before Stephensons Croft is a bungalow Braemor built by Gelders for the Coles at Eden Grove School as a home for Mr. & Mrs. Gunn who worked at the school. Mr. & Mrs. Wilkinson moved from Darlington to live there in t he

Highfield House

late 1990s. It had been the home of the late Frank Graves, Mayor of Appleby from 1999-2000. Frank was just beginning his second term of office when he died. Standing well back from the road is another house built for the Mullens in the mid-1990s.

There is a small estate of bungalows built on land and with money bequeathed by the late Norman Stephenson from Croft House for housing to be built for the poor of Bolton. However times and needs change and the original criteria of the poor is obsolete and anyone in need of housing may apply. They were built by Barry Owen from Appleby and were initially managed by the Parish Council but now by the Carlisle Diocese. It is known as Stephensons Croft.

Edenholme was built for Mr. Frank Baxter s parents and is now home to Ann and Ken Shepherd. It was built by Frederick Potts of Appleby. Just past the public footpath to Bolton Mill is Ray and Margaret Fothergill s home Lindisfarne built on the site of an old barn belonging to Prospect House where Margaret and Ray had previously lived. Next to Holly House is Whiteriggs built for the Baxter s cowman by Fred Potts. Now it is let to Eden Grove School.

Almost at the end of the village, again going south, is the home of Geoff and Lorriane Forster, pharmacists at Appleby. The architects were Architects Plus from Carlisle and the builder Paul Richardson from Appleby. Building was started in 1999 and Mr. & Mrs. Forster and their daughter moved in in July 2000. Finally we approach Windyridge built for Mr. & Mrs. Jones of Eden Grove.

Going out of the village towards Penrith to the T-junction known as Bolton Lane Ends, on the junction of the left is the home of Mr. & Mrs. Harrison. At one time it was a row of farm cottages but has now been converted into one residence. This and Rose Cottage opposite, and the row of houses turning left at the junction were built for Crossrigg estate workers. These houses and Peatgate Farm all belong to the Crossrigg Estate. Near to Crossrigg Hall is Crossrigg House built for Mrs. P. Henly who now owns and runs the Crossrigg Estate. Birdby opposite to Crossrigg Hall is the home of the Bird family. It is a Grade II listed building and has been in their family for generations. It is a good place to observe the features of a 16th century Cumbrian house. There is reference to the house in the Morland Church records of 1538.

From Birdby towards Bolton take the first turn left towards Temple Sowerby and just before going over the River Eden on the right is Ousenstands, referred to in old documents as Oxenstands, and home to the Kelsey family today. In 1851 it was home to Edward and Isabella Cherry and their six children. The house appears to have served as a farm labourers cottage in earlier times.

Some houses and their inhabitants

WAYSIDE COTTAGE

From documents of Wayside House it can be recorded that in 1755 Wayside Cottage was owned by Mr Henry Fletcher of Hutton in the Forest and Walter Vane of London (part of the Fletcher/Vane manor). It was let for a yearly rent of £9 to Thomas Lambert. Wayside was sold to William Monkhouse by indenture on the 16 July 1755 for the sum of £220. However before this could happen a bond for the *Performance of an Indenture of a release of a messuage and Tennament at Bolton from Henry Fletcher and others To Mr William Monkhouse* had to be made. This was for a fee or fine to be paid by Mr Monkhouse. It seems that the Lamberts went on living there and Thomas Lambert husbandman is listed in the 1787 census as living in Bolton but there are no Monkhouses. William may have bought the tenement as an investment.

The house, land and outbuildings were left to Elizabeth the daughter of John Monkhouse for the remainder of her life and after her decease it was to go to his son George Monkhouse. Elizabeth is later described as a spinster living in Hindwell where her sister Mary lives with her husband. She either found it too lonely, or was too infirm to live in Bolton or she may have been encouraged to move by her family.

On 13 December 1814 a letter of attorney was sent from Joseph Monkhouse to his brother in Penrith: *Joseph Monkhouse late of Penrith but now the Island of Jamaica in the West Indies planter and one of the Grandchildren of John Monkhouse aforesaid gentleman deceased and one of the ?? in remainder named in the will of John Monkhouse appoint my brother John Monkhouse of Stowe in the county of Brecon Gentleman and my brother Thomas Monkhouse of Budge Row London my attorneys and Mary Monkhouse wife of Thomas Hutchinson and the four children of the said George.*

Perhaps both George and Elizabeth were by then deceased. On the 2 February 1815 Wayside was sold to Thomas Nicholson for £870. Joseph Monkhouse in Jamaica is now a bookkeeper. The deed describes the property and the surrounding area:

All the messuages, out houses, garden, croft and garth to the North west of the lands of John Chappelhow. All on towards the south the lands of Anne Stephenson and on towards the east by the road through Bolton village containing by admeasurement seven acres nine perches by the same more or less. Also all that close or enclosure lying in the townfield of Bolton called Hurrigg close containing by admeasurement 5 acres and 11 perches.Towards the south of the lands of John Chappelhow and all towards the south of by the lands of Thomas

CHANGING TIMES

Barton together with all and singular houses, outhouses, edifices, buildings barns, byres, stables, orchards, garth, gardens ways, paths, passages, water, watercourses, easements, profits, privileges and advantages.

On 11 April 1863 an agreement is made between:

John Nicholson of Stallsteads in the parish of Dufton farmer and Mary Nicholson of Kings Meaburn spinster farmer whereas Thomas Nicholson of Peatgate in the Township of Bolton Farmer being seized for an estate fee simple of the herediments hereinafter conveyed in his last will and testament in writing 26th November 1847 duly executed and attested as by law is required for the devise of freehold estate where by after bequeathing certain legacies the residue of his real and personal estate to his wife Elizabeth Nicholson for her use and benefit during her natural life and then to his son John Nicholson and his daughter Mary Nicholson their heirs equally share and share alike.

Elizabeth was by now dead and John contracts with Mary for sale to her of *his individual moity for £265.*

The property is described as being bounded on the north and west by the lands of John Thompson and to the south by lands of Mary Thompson. Richard Birkbeck remembers petrol was sold and cars repaired at the property before his father s time.

David and Linda Fox came from the north east to live at Wayside about eight years ago. David uses the barn at the side of the house as a workshop and works at Fairfield Marine and the Yacht Club on the shores of Lake Ullswater. Linda is a teacher and commutes from Bolton over to Stockton on Tees each day to work. In the year 2000 she was voted Teacher of the Year for the area where she works and went to London to the National Finals.

The house was extended in 2001 to make more living accommodation.

WHYBER

Whyber is the home of Christine and Richard Birkbeck. It used to be called Fell View when Richard s parents Elsie and Billy lived there. The property is a landmark in the village because Richard does car and agricultural repairs and sells petrol from there. They also have a small number of acres on which they farm. Christine s interests are her goats. She breeds British Alpines and British Toggenburgs and in 2000 she won Skelton, Crosby Ravensworth and Dufton show with them.

Ada Addison can remember when she was a little girl it being a shop and belonging to a Mrs Robinson. Richard and Christine know some thing of the history of the house from some old deeds they have.

May 14th 1874 *Indenture of conveyance of this date made between Mary Burrels and John Thompson and Ann Steel.*

Elsie & Billy Birkbeck outside Fell View, now Whyber

July 26th 1902 *Indenture of conveyance of this date made between William Wappett, John Richardson and George Hewetson.*

February 1907 *Indenture of conveyance between Constance Leversage George, Gertrude Emily George, George Hewetson and William Graham.* What was William Graham doing buying property when he was already in trouble financially? He soon has to sell it again.

On the 18th of May 1907 William Graham of Eden Grove sold the house to Thomas Robinson senior, a stone mason for the sum of £175. The money was for: - *The messuage or dwelling house and shop with the garden and orchard and out buildings there unto adjoining and belonging situate in the village of Bolton.*

On the 4th of July 1925 *Joseph Robinson of the Bungalow Dunton Bassett Rugby, School Master sold the house to Nathan Bland, Tailor for £435. To include the freehold cottage, garden, orchard and out buildings.*

Thomas Robinson senior had made out his will dated 1 June 1907 appointing his wife Elizabeth and his son to be executors. He gave all his real and personal estate to his wife for the term of her natural life. After her death his son Joseph was to inherit.

Thomas Robinson senior died 18 October 1909. Elizabeth his wife died on 8th April 1925. Nathan Bland died a bachelor in 1925. Presumably Billy and Elsie bought the house shortly afterwards and we know that when Billy and Elsie died Richard and Christine moved in.

GLEBE HOUSE

A short while after Barbara and Derick Cotton moved into Glebe House Mrs. Nancarrow s daughter called and asked if they would like the old deeds that she had found amongst her mother s belonging when she died. They were only too pleased to have them as they revealed a great deal of history about the house.

From an indenture dated 23rd February 1760 it is noted: *that an agreement was made between John Brougham of the Town and County of Newcastle upon Tyne Merchant and Joseph Bellas yeoman of Bolton to sell the property for a sum of £396. This included a dwelling house, 2 barns and byres and stables and garth and orchard behind the dwelling house and the close or enclosure behind the house and 3 acres commonly called the Croft. William Browns to the east and Thomas Lambert to the west and a parcel of arable or meadow ground about 1 acre known as the Butts at the lower end of the enclosure called the croft and 2 closes about 9 acres known as Grimesburrows Top adjoining to the ground of Thomas Carlton Esq to the east and the said Joseph Bellas to the west and one other close about 4 acres known as Mill Flatt adjoining the ground of Samuel Gibson to the East and John Smith to the West and one other close or meadow ground about one acre laying in a place called Peatmire adjoining the ground of George Smith to the west now owned by John Brougham his under-tenant and are subject to the payment of the yearly free rent of 7/9d to Henry Fletcher Esq and one and seven pence halfpenny Neatgold yearly to the Rt. Hon Sackville Earl of Thanet Island*

In 1760 John Brougham wanted to sell the house to Joseph Bellas and Matt Henrick was appointed to assemble the legal documents. He had to search for the information for the said documents and issued the following:

12 and 13 March 1711 - By indenture of Lease and Release of this date respectively and the release made between John Blaymire of Bolton in the parish of Morland Gentleman and Henry Brougham of Kirby Kendall in the county of Westmorland Son in law of the said John Blaymire. The said John Blaymire as well as and in consideration of the natural love and affection which he hath and shows for the said Henry Brougham his son in law as also for and in consideration of the sum of Two Hundred and Five Pounds paid by the said Henry Brougham and also for divers other good causes and considerations him thereunto moving, gives grants bargains sells releases and confirms unto the said Henry Brougham (amongst other lands and tenements at Bolton aforesaid) The Dwelling House Housing and Lands hereafter more particularly mentioned and described with the appurtuances To Hold the same with the appurtuances unto the said Henry Brougham his heirs and assigns to the only proper use and behoof of him the said Henry Brougham his Heirs and Assigns forever -

The Lease And Release above are in the hands of a purchaser of other Premises thereby conveyed.

SOME HOUSES & THEIR INHABITANTS

Outside the dairy at Glebe House - milk churns being loaded onto the wagon to be taken and deposited outside Greystone House for collection by Express Dairy. From left to right - Willie Tennant, Doug Wills and Jackson Bellas.

The said Henry Brougham continued in possession of the premises - hereafter more particularly mentioned and described from the date of the above Deeds until the time of his death which happened about Twenty Five years ago when John Brougham his only son entered and inherited the same.

There is an addition at the end of the document what appears to be a verification of Matt Henricks search:

I (M Mousne !!) have compared the above abstract of the deed 23 Feb 1760 in the original deed and do certify that the same is a true abstract thereof and do believe that such deeds of Lease and Release of the 12 and 13 March 1711 were searched to the pinpoint of observation but those Deeds being in the hands of a purchaser of other premisis I have not had the opportunity of seeing the originals and though the greatest part of the premisis comprised in the deed of 1760 are intended to be purchased yet the Vendor is unwilling that the Deed be sent up because he does not sell the whole premisis-

I do believe it to be true that Henry Brougham the ? in the Deeds of 1711 continued in possession of the premises now to be purchased, from the date of those deeds till his death and that John Brougham his son inherited the same was in possession when he conveyed to Bellas in 1760 as above mentioned. And I am of the opinion that Joseph Bellas and Elizabeth his wife may by levying a fine make a good Title of the premisis intended to be conveyed.

38

CHANGING TIMES

To the general Words an addition may be made of Pews or seats in the parish Church of Morland or Chapel of Bolton aforesaid belonging to the aforesaid Messuage or Dwelling House. (See Chapter on Bolton Chapel)

One would expect that parishioners would all be equal in God s eyes regardless of social status. However some were more equal than others and could choose where to sit in the chapel. If they were a churchwarden then they could tell other people where to sit. The lay or ecclesiastical rector responsible for financing the chancel repairs had the principal seat and he could allocate seats to others, for example the vicar and his family, but not to a perpetual curate. Because the church would be needed for other social activities there would be a need for a spacious area where religious plays could be performed or ale brewed for church funds and so parishioners would use rubble or stone seats against the walls to sit on during services.

The Lord of the Manor and estate owners who believed they would be rewarded in heaven for their generosity towards the church would perhaps build an aisle and maintain it if they and their family could sit there during their lifetime and once they were dead their heirs could continue to do so. This privilege would be granted to the family whilst they remained parishioners but it was usually attached to their residence and so became an appertenance which passed to subsequent owners and their heirs. If the land was sold but the house retained the new landowner did not have the right to sit in the pew. However if he built a new house on the land as a ratepayer he could apply to build a pew in respect of the new house. Any principal rate payer, i.e. owner or tenant of a large house or farmhouse would be entitled to a pew in the church.

When John made his agreement with Joseph was there something underhand taking place?

The dates of the Blaymires and Broughams life cycles do not appear to fit with the dates of the search and there appears to have been some resistance to producing the original deed by Henry s son John.

When property changed hands within the manor of Bolton whether it was for sale, rent or had been inherited a fine had to be paid to the Lord of the Manor. The rents for houses in Bolton paid to the Lord of the Manor were very low and had been for many years. Because the fines were so high they subsidised the rents and his Lordship didn t lose. Did John Blaymire senior only rent the property to his son in law and the money paid was a fine ? It was usual at the time for the eldest son to inherit any property and at the time of his death John Blaymire had a 20 year old son who does not appear to be married and a daughter Mary who remained a spinster.

SOME HOUSES & THEIR INHABITANTS

An undated schedule of Mr John Brougham s estate is as follows: -

Place	Acres	Yearly value
Backside Croft	3	£3 — 0 — 00
Butts	1	1 — 0 — 0d
Grimsborough	10	8 — 0 — 0d
Mill Flatt	4	4 — 4 — 0d
High Croft and Hocking Garth	3	3 — 0 — 0d
Bitts Close	3	2 — 15 — 0d
Outhwaites	3	3 — 0 — 0d
St Johns Close	4	4 — 0 — 0d
Huckworth Close	4	3 — 10 — 0d
Out Huckworth	4	0 — 12 — 0d
Water Riddings	1	0 — 0 — 0d
Bull Ings	1 ?	0 — 0 — 0d
?Ellens	1	0 — 14 — 0d
Lowfitt	2	0 — 14 — 0d
Crooks	?	0 — 12 — 0d
Peatmire	1	0 — 3 — 0d
Ings	?	0 — 10 — 0d
Speddings	1 /3	0 — 2 — 6d

Total £36 — 5 — 6d

12? Grasses on Low Moor   2 — 10 — 0d
4 Horse Baitings in Low Willows

The sale goes ahead and the house and lands are sold in 1760 to Joseph Bellas and Elizabeth his wife for the sum of £396. It appears from the 1787 census that they then went to live with their son and daughter in law. Joseph lived to the age of 59 years and died in 1772. His wife Elizabeth lived to the great age of 80 years dying in 1791, Elizabeth is described in the parish register as *the Relict of Joseph Bellas* .

The Bellas family were descended from Bellas of County Durham and the pedigree of the family at Long Marton began with a George Bellas who died in 1704. Several members of this family have lived in Bolton over the years.

Joseph and Elizabeth only owned the property until 25 April 1763 when it was purchased by the curacy of Bolton for the sum of £400. The curate at the time was Thomas Kilner.

The property became known as Old Vicarage Farm and in the 1851 census Samuel Robinson farming 45 acres lives there with Alice his wife and son Sam and daughter Elizabeth.

The property stays in the possession of the church until 25 April 1925 when it was sold again for £1000. An agreement was made between the Revd

CHANGING TIMES

Carmichael, vicar of Bolton, the governors of the Bounty of Queen Anne for the Augmentation of the Maintenance of the Poor Clergy, Henry Herbert Bishop of the Diocese, Revd Thomas Procter Hartley, vicar of Morland and the Right Honourable Cosmo Gordon, Lord Archbishop of York and David Hodgeson of Croft House, Bolton. At the time Mr A. T. Walton was tenant and paid to the Manor of Bolton a rent of six shillings and six pence and five shillings on St Thomas day to the overseers of Bolton for the use of the poor in respect of John Blaymires Charity . The land sold with the property amounted to 20 acres and 12 perches. David Hodgeson changed the name of the house to Sunny Bank

David Hodgeson died in July 1935 and left the property in trust to his wife Elizabeth Alice to use for her lifetime. On her death or on her leaving farming it was to be put back with the rest of his estate, which was to be sold. The money was to be invested to pay Elizabeth an annual income for her life and after her death a legacy of £25 to be paid to each of his sons Anthony and John. The rest to be divided equally between the beneficiaries. However, after Elizabeth s death in 1938 they applied to hold the property in trust until 21 years after the death of the last one of them. The property passed into the ownership of Alice Hodgson and Jane Bellas, nee Hodgson.

Jane Hodgson was married to Jackson Bellas (who came from Kirkoswald) in August 1935. *The Herald* reported the event to have taken place in real wedding weather. The bride was conducted up the church by her uncle Revd J. W. Hodgson from Matlock and the Revd Foster officiated.

Hay making time at Sunny Bank (Glebe House). Left to right - Jessie Bellas, Jackson Bellas and Kathleen Bellas (Jessie was Jackon s second wife).

41

SOME HOUSES & THEIR INHABITANTS

After the ceremony a reception was held at Sunnybank (Glebe House). The wedding attracted a large number of well wishers including friends and family, as they were well known in the neighbourhood. The happy couple left for a honeymoon in Morecambe. Jane and Jackson had four children, Audrey, Kathleen, Dorothy and David, who all appear to have very happy memories of living at Sunnybank.

Audrey made a few jottings as follows about her time at Sunnybank: *Village children were taught to call friends of their parents (and more often than not the relations of their peers) Auntie and Uncle. We had a number of these. Mum's sister Auntie Alice (No 1 on the photo) never married and lived at Sunnybank all her life. After we, her nieces and nephew came along she was fondly known as Auntie by every one in the village.*

Two little tales of such Aunties - Dad had a small milk round and we were often commandeered to run up and down the paths with the bottles of milk - full cream (there was no pasteurised, semi-skimmed, skimmed or soya) and every bottle had over an inch of cream on top and woe betide us if we if we shook them up too much! Unfortunately for dad when we got to Auntie Evelyn's (the Laycock children's Auntie) we would go no further and dad had to continue on his own and then pick us up on the way back. The reason - a basket full of bits and bobs - beads, buttons, photos, fancy lids and perhaps some sweets. Nothing of importance but for us a treasure store hanging on a beam.

Dad had a small lorry to deliver the milk. This lorry had running boards on which we used to stand, making it easier to hop on and off, but as we approached certain houses we would climb in the back as we knew it was likely a dog would run out and nip our heels.

We had no bathroom for quite a while and like other such households, the tin bath was placed in front of the living room fire for our weekly bath. Imagine the luxury then when Auntie Mabel (No 17 on the wedding photo) who lived at Violet Bank got a modern bathroom fitted and we were all taken by mum for our weekly ablutions in her beautiful, comfortable bath.

Stories at bedtime read by mum or auntie could not compete with those read by Auntie Fanny (mum's bridesmaid on the photo) - she would go down the bed and tickle our feet! We loved her visits.

Children were given rations of rosehip syrup and orange juice and we would take our coupons to Grandma Butterworth to collect theses items. We also received chocolate powder, a gift from America I think. This was supplied to be made into a warm drink, but as it contained sugar, which made it very tasty, we usually licked our fingers and had the powder as a dip - often before it got home.

My Grandma and her sister, Auntie Belle Robinson, used to look after new mothers and their babies during the two weeks or so that the mother was in bed.

Grandma told me that letters, cards and newspapers all had to be aired before being given to the new mother.

On the Sunday School anniversary the chapel would be full to overflowing with about 50 or so children. The children would recite and sing. At the close each child was presented with a book. At harvest festival there would be a large display of fruit, flowers and vegetables. Again the Chapel would be full to over flowing. On the Monday evening after the Sunday service the produce was auctioned. This was great fun as those who had brought it tried to out bid each other to buy it back. This generated quite large sums of money.

The property then passed to Harry and Doris Nancarrow in 1960 and is still referred to as The Nancarrows today by some of the older inhabitants of Bolton. They changed the name of the house to Glebe House. Presumably because of it having belonged to the church. In the deeds to the house they were still subject to the payment of five shillings in respect of John Blaymire s charity.

BOLTON HALL FARM

On June 13th 1839 Dorothy Birket of Etterby Lodge, Carlisle bequeathed to William Halton of Carlisle and George Saul of Brunstock and Lady Grant, wife of Sir James Grant, Bolton Hall and Bolton Low Moor. A note in the margin of the deed reads, the last of old deeds made were two old deeds of settlement 28 May 1766 made on the Marriage of Henry Birkett Esq. There had been some query as to Mrs Birket being the rightful heir to the property.

On the 1st June 1842 probate is granted to George Saul one of the executors but William Halton appears to have declined all interest in the property, possibly because of some doubt as to his eligibility to inherit. On 23 May 1843 it appears that George Saul conveys his share to the Grant family and on 3 May 1844 conveyed to James Robert Grant and Mary Tomlinson widow. Women were not allowed to inherit in their own right and any money or property would have been in her husband s name. Mary Tomlinson appears to have been a Grant prior to her marriage.

On the 31 August 1844 Sir James Robert Grant died leaving Lady Jane Grant with two young children Mary Teuzah born 17 December 1842 and Jamesina Roberta born 8 July 1844. On the 3 September 1855 letters of administration were made to his widow Jane Eleanor Hodgeson, late Grant, the wife of the Revd Joseph Lowther Hodgeson.

On 14 March 1858 the said Jane Eleanor Hodgson formerly Jane Eleanor Grant died. By the 28 November 1862 the letters of administration of the estate of her late husband James Robert Grant had been left unattended and the administration was granted to Charles Bernard Hodgeson one of the guardians of the children.

SOME HOUSES & THEIR INHABITANTS

An indenture was made on 2 December 1862 between Charles Bernard Hodgeson and Mary Tomlinson widow and Thomas Houghton Hodgeson of Houghton House. Money was exchanged for Thomas Hodgeson s interest in the estate.

On 2 December 1863 Mary D. Grant spinster, 19 years, wanted to marry Charles J. Mounsey, a captain in her Majesty s 71st Regiment. Charles Bernard Hodgeson of Harker Grange challenged this and Mary became a ward of court. Because of her intention to marry it was ordered that an enquiry should take place to assess if it was a proper and fit marriage and that the petitioner should be at liberty to lay proposals for a settlement before his honour with consequential directions . The marriage was approved but not before a very detailed investigation into her birth and right to her share of the value of Bolton Hall and Bolton Low Moor. This was made as a settlement on her marriage.

Since the original bequest the number of people involved had grown and they decided to join together and sell the house and the land. Thomas Houghton Hodgeson and James Farday of the first part, George William Mounsey Robert Houghton Mounsey of the second, and Charles James Mounsey and Mary

Back row, left to right - Alice Hodgson, Jack Hodgson, Gertie Jackson later Metcalf, Ada Addison. Middle row - Agnes Blackstock, Nellie Bellas, Mark Bellas, Jean Butterworth, Tom Pape, Annie Pape, Emily Bellas nee Jackson, Alice Hodgson nee Atkinson, Matthew Holmes, Jinny Holmes, Rob Addison, David Hodgson, Mabel Robinson later Sowerby, Nellie Hodgson later Snow, Mary Armstrong nee Butterworth, Fanny Wilson later Tatters, William Jackson Bellas (bridegroom). Front row - Jane Bellas nee Hodgson (bride), John Hodgson, Christopher Butterworth best man, F. Foster local vicar.

Teuzah his wife of the 3rd, Jamesina Roberta Grant of the 4th, and Mary Tomlinson Grant of the 5th, Francis Grant of the 6th, and Grant Tomlinson Grant of 7th and Hugh Gandy of Eden Grove late a captain in Her Majesty s Regiment of Infantry was the 8th part.

Hugh Gandy purchased the whole for £5250. It was rented at the time by Mr Thomas Todd and Mrs Oldcorn. Bolton Low Moor was later sold to Hugh Rigg Esq. Since that time Bolton Hall farm has been owned by Mr William Graham, the Tatters family and latterly by Mike Smith who ran a pig farm. The property has now passed to a private developer Russell Armour and the farm buildings are to be made into houses. Sadly another farm has been lost to the village.

THE HERMITAGE

An interesting house in the village is The Old Hermitage. Sadly there has not been time to research the history thoroughly but it is understood that the old deeds show that it was a monastery in the past.

Many of the sites with the name Hermitage attached were the dwellings of a religious recluse. Because of the nature of the hermit s calling their dwellings were often sited at bridges, fords, ferries and cause-ways that led into inhospitable country. Some of the buildings could be subsidiary houses of monastic foundations and could be quite substantial. They may have had a chapel and accommodation for travellers. Perhaps the hermit in Bolton ran a small farm.

The Old Hermitage

Population

Prior to 1801 there were no accurate figures for the population of England. It was in this year that the government asked that all the people be counted as well as the number of acres of land that were in crop. This was the first official census. Since then a census has been taken every ten years except in 1941 when the country was at war.

However Westmorland had a census taken in 1787. The reasons for the request to gather this information is unknown and it does not appear that the information was ever used. However the information has been preserved for some parishes and it is interesting to see who was living in the village at the time and how they earned their living. In that year the total number of people living in Bolton was 289.

In the 1801 census for Bolton the following information was gathered:

Males 180
Females 184
Total 364
Inhabited houses 65
No. of persons in each house 5 3/8
No. of acres 600
Wheat 79A 2R
Barley 61A 3R
Oats 343 A
Rye 2A 3R
Total 487A
No. Acres per person 1A 1R 14P 24/384

In 1811 the population was counted by the town overseers:
Inhabited houses 65
Occupied by how many families 72
Houses uninhabited 5
Families employed in agriculture 56
Families employed in trades 14
Families not employed in preceding classes 2
Males 167
Females 198
Total 365
19 local militia not included

CHANGING TIMES

The purpose of the census was to provide population statistics and so the census returns from 1801 to 1831 do not provide us with any detail of individuals. From 1841 onwards an increasing amount of information was collected and each census return is available for public inspection after a period of 100 years.

Other sources of information of who was living in Bolton are:

The Protestation Returns 1641-2

The Hearth Tax Records 1662-1689

The Window Tax Records 1697

It is important to emphasise that these lists do not constitute a complete register of all residents of the township of Bolton but do give some idea of the names of people living in the village at the time.

The population figures for Bolton for the years from 1801 to 1851 are as follows:

1801 - 324	1841 - 383
1811 - 365	1851 - 384
1821 - 445	1881 - 404
1831 - 391	1891 - 345

Today the population is approximately 400. However there are more houses and fewer people per dwelling today than there were back in the 1800s, when there were fewer houses but more people per dwelling.

See appendix for the 1787, 1851, 1881 and 1891 census returns.

The Hearth Tax

The hearth money was a tax on the number of hearths in a building. It was levied in the years from 1662 to 1689 at two shillings for each hearth or stove and collected from the occupier in two installments on Lady Day and at Michaelmas. There were some exceptions, those in receipt of poor relief or inhabiting premises worth less than 20 shillings a year and not paying the parish rate. Charitable institutions were also exempt.

In 1663 an act was passed requiring that every one with a hearth had to be included in the returns even if they were exempt and from 1664 all those people with more than two chimneys had to pay. If chimneys were found to be blocked up and they were discovered the tax was doubled.

The returns give us some indication as to the size of homes of the period. The returns for Bolton for 12 March 1674 show the Constable to have been Sam Gibson and the surveyor Reyn Harle.

Name	Hearths	Name	Hearths
1 Gibson Jo	1	27 Allon Jo	2
2 Allon Thomas	1	28 Teabay Wm	1
3 Wilkinson Thomas	1	29 Allon Math	1
4 Allon Wid	1	30 Blamire Tho	1
5 Allon Thomas	1	31 Tompson Rich	1
6 Allon Thomas & Marton An	2	32 Tompson Jo	2
7 Salkeld Jo	1	33 Couper Jo	1
8 Smith Wid	1	34 Richardson Wid	2
9 Atkinson Jane	2	35 Whitfield Wid	3
10 Browne Edw	3	36 Clarke Wid	1
11 Chapalow Jo	1	37 Leaklaand Rob &Hutchinson	1
12 Wilkinson Henry	1	38 Blamire Jo	2
13 Dixon George	1	39 Wilson Lane	1
14 Lickbarrow Thomas	1	40 Houseon Jo	1
15 Newton Henry	2	41 Spedding Wid	2
16 Speding Jo	1	42 Spedding Tho	2
17 Allen Jo	1	43 Dent Jane	1
18 Reeding Wm	1	44 Blaymire Jo	1
19 Bownes Wm	5	45 Blaymire Jo jun	1
20 Bolton Hall		46 Williamson Robert	1
21 Dent Richard & Blaymire Jo	6	47 Fallowfield Rich	2
22 Hall Thomas	1	48 Gibson Sam	1
23 Addison Thomas	1	49 Bewley Castle	
24 Holme Rich	2	50 Nicholson Tho	2
25 Allen Rich	1	51 Burrough Lane	7
26 Williamson Antho	1		

Window Tax

The Window Tax replaced the Hearth Tax in 1697 and every occupant was required to make an annual payment of two shilling with an additional payment of eight shillings if the dwelling had more than ten windows. The assessment could be made without having to go into the dwelling. It was a very unpopular tax and the people complained that it was a duty on fresh air and sunshine.

In 1709 the rates were increased for larger houses. Householders reduced their tax by blocking up windows and as a result the amount of money collected fell gradually. In 1747 new legislation was introduced. The flat rate of two shillings was retained, those people occupying houses with between 10 and 15 windows were charged 6d per window, between 15 and 19 windows 9d per window and those with more than 20 one shilling per window. The revenue did increase but so did the practice of blocking up windows so that the tax had to be increased again and it was doubled in 1784 by Pitt. The tax was abolished in 1851 and replaced by the inhabited House Duty.

Assessors for the window tax for Bolton were John Chappelhow and Richard Bellas. The collectors were Jos Savage and Thomas Chappelhow. Every one

Mansgrove House home to the Forrester family. The blocked window could be a victim of the window tax.

THE WINDOW TAX

listed for Bolton paid three shillings, which does not appear to compare with the decreed charges!   They were:

Chris Parkin	Jos Savage
George Steel	John Horn
Wm. Workman	Thos. Willan
Dan Ion	Will. Savage
Edw. Harrison	James Savage
Sam Oglthorpe	Henry Dent
Richard Bellas	Henry Dent Jr.
Isaac Stephenson	George Ellwood
John Janson	Joh. Tuer
John Dodd	Frances Chappelhow
John Woof	Sam Gibson
Nic Temple	Will Allan
John Lambert	Will Wood
Thomas Earle	John Eggleston
Wm. Gibson	John Spedding
Will Corry	Thomas Lambert
Rich. Addison	James Barbon
Jo Corry	John Chappelhow
Alice Bowlaswell	Mary Earle
Nich. Lunson	Thomas Crosby
John Nicholson	Thomas Wiberge
John Burry	

The Westmorland Protestation Returns

The protestation was a petition by most men against the tyrannical government of King Charles I. It was made in 1641-2, those protestations that survive are preserved in the House of Lords.

The House of Commons organised the petition which was to be publicly supported by all males over the age of 18 years. The Protestation was taken before witnesses and by taking the protestation the men declared their belief in three things:

*The Church of England

*Allegiance to the King

*Support for the rights and privileges of parliament.

The Protestation is often referred to as the Oath of Allegiance. It was read out in church, each man s name was recorded as he answered his allegiance yes or no .   The record provides us with the knowledge of the male population of Bolton for the year 1647.

From the returns for Westmorland for the whole of the east/west wards only a very few men (17 were listed) refused to swear to the petition. Many of the non-supporters, are believed to have been of the Roman Catholic faith and were

The Protestation

afterwards called recusants . They would have found it impossible to declare a belief in the Protestant faith.

William Forrest was curate at the time and may well have organised the event. He would have also been a witness. No one was allowed to hold public office if they refused to take the protestation. As a general rule the most important people in the community would be the first to go forward.

General oaths were common in the 17th century as a means of gaining support for the political issues. How many of the men of the time would really understand what they were agreeing to? Many would have not been able to read or write. The orders were read to the congregation after evening prayer on the 6 March. Those men present took the oath after the service, word would have gone out before hand instructing the men to attend.

There was some distrust for the real motives behind the protestation as some regarded it as a preliminary to some sort of tax assessment or call up for the able bodied for military service. Perhaps this was so in the case of Bolton because oaths were only taken from men aged between 18-60 years, sixty being the usual upper age limit for the military.

The Protestation made by the men of the township of Boulton from eighteen years to three score AD 1641.

John Gibson	John Speddinge	John Westall
John Whitfield	Mathewe Dent	Cudybart Addison
Edward Spedding	Richard Harrison	Peter Cowper
John Blaymyre	Thomas Dent	John Allon
Thomas Hanson	John Gibson	Thomas Holme
John Gibsone	Matthew Allan	Thomas Spedding
Edward Blaymire	Thomas Gibson	William Gibson, church
William Allan	Edward Browne	warden
George Matteson	Thomas Atkinson	Cuthbart Cleark
Jon Blaymire	John Wilkinson	John Blaymire, church
John Matisson	Lancelot Smith	warden
Thomas Allon	John Chappelhowe	William Blaymire
William Spedding	Thomas Lickbarrowe	William Forrest, curate
Richard Richardson	Jeffrey Railton	John Hanson
Alexander Spedding	John Robinson	John Allon
Thomas Ubancke	Christopher Westall	Steven Railton
Thomas Spedding	John Lindall	Thomas Railton
John Speddinge	John Winder	Thomas Keddie
William Allon	Thomas Speddinge	
Francis Richardson	William Calvert	
Lancelot Willan	William Speddinge	

Social Structure

Following the conquest of 1066, England was divided among the followers of William I who in theory was the owner of the kingdom. The smallest holding within these granted estates subsequently became known as the manor. The highest level of tenancy was lordship in fee. Those in this category sometimes let to lesser lords, (*mesne tenants*) who on occasion let to their followers who became *tenants in demesne*.

The lord of the manor could belong to any category but was always the tenant the actual feudal obligation rested upon. The term means land lord and as such did not have to be titled or armigorous. Many held several often widely dispersed manors. The day to day management would be entrusted to an elected officer known as a reeve and the administration of the manor to a steward. When Roy Boff, Eden Fold, became rector of Romaldkirk he became Lord of the Manor according to some old medieval custom. He had his own solicitor to collect the rents and ensure the village green was kept cut.

A manor may encompass a number of townships and farms or it may have been organised around a much larger village. It may have retained the boundaries of an earlier Saxon or Roman estate. It could be a parish or a number of parishes.

The term Manor House is not what it may seem as many acquired the name because of the social aspirations of a previous owner. The term is sometimes wrongly applied to the principal house of an estate or village but it is mainly used to describe a late medieval country house in architectural terms. For example Eden Grove is described in the old directories for Westmorland as a manor house in the Elizabethan style.

Bolton has served many lords through the ages as shown below:

After the death of Robert lord Clifford in 1314 Ralph Baron of Greystock, held Dufton, Bolton, Brampton and Yanwath.

From 1326-27 John de Derwentwater held the Manor of Bolton for the Derwentwaters held the same of the Greystocks as mesne lords, the Greystocks holding immediately of the Cliffords.

Sir Nicholas Radclife of Dilston in the county of Northumberland knight married Margaret, daughter and heir of Sir John de Derwentwater. He later became lord of the manor in 1452.

George Ratcliffe knight then held the manor from William lord Dacre, as the said lord Dacre held the same of Henry Earl of Cumberland (Henry Clifford 2nd Earl of Cumberland).

The Fletchers of Hutton were the next to own the manor purchasing it in 1554. The *demesne* was bought by Thomas Wybergh whose family held it for three generations. It was then bought by the Broughams and in 1779 Sir James Lowther Bt. bought it from the Broughams. In 1809 William the first Earl of Lonsdale purchased it and it became known as Fletcher s manor, sometimes known as Fletcher/Vane manor. It appears that Bolton now had two manors Lowther and Fletcher. Eventually the manor was consolidated and a steward appointed - Mr John Wordsworth, father of the famous poet.

In 1796 Lowther met Vane in the House of Commons. He asked him what right he had to appoint a gamekeeper to the Manor of Bolton. Vane replied he had every right to as he had a tenement there. Lowther told Vane that he was a tyrant and challenged him to a duel. They met in Hyde Park but Vane apologised before the duel took place and the incident ended peacefully. Lowther and Vane had a serious interest in the manor of Bolton because of their political interests - the seat at Appleby was hard fought for between them.

The Manor was governed by a Manor Court in which a meeting of tenants was convened and presided over by the lord of the manor or his steward. The court would consider both judicial and administrative matters such as the transfer of property. All tenants were obliged to attend the manor court and were eligible for election as jurors. If they failed to attend they were fined. When the lordship of the manor changed hands, a special Court of Recognition was held at which the new lord was formally seized of his tenants service and received their renewed oaths of fealty. A Court of Survey was also convened to record all the manorial lands and the customary dues by which they were held. A record of court proceedings was kept by the steward s clerk including disputes and changes of occupancy of holdings.

The Manor remained in the possession of the Lonsdales until the death of William Lonsdale in 1944 when the customary holdings passed to the large landowners in the village i.e. John Dent 180 acres, Rowland Slack 200, Will Oldcorn 100, Thomas Nicholson 109, John Savage 100 and Robert Addison 203.

Prior to the 13th century French and Latin terms defined social class in England and were based on tenure and legal status. After this time they were replaced by terms indicating general social standing or economic function. Some terms were hardly affected by the changes. For example Knight was used more often than the French term Chevalier but the meaning remained unchanged.

By the 15th century local society comprised, in descending order Knights, esquires, gentlemen, yeomen, husbandmen. Only knights and esquires possessed armigorous qualifications. 15th century sumptuary legislation decreed a strict hierarchy and it was determined in 1445 that knights of the shire attending parliament could include notable squires and gentlemen of birth but not those of Yeomen and bynethe (sic).

A yeoman was therefore a freeholder below the status of gentleman but above that of most copyhold tenants and was eligible to serve on juries and to vote in the county elections.

From the Court Rolls for Bolton three types of occupant emerge:

1) Freeholders - these people possessed their property and it was not subject to manorial custom and could be disposed of without restriction.

2) Copyholders who were subject to manorial custom with an obligation to under take certain services for the lord of the manor. Tenants held their land by right of a title entered in the manor court rolls a copy of which was given to them: hence the term copyholder. When the property was transferred to a new occupant the copy had to be surrendered to the lord. The new tenant would then receive it upon payment of a fine . The fines in Bolton were always very high but rents remained low.

3) Tenents of the Dean and Chapter of Carlisle.

In 1200 Adam son of Waldeve de Kirkby thore granted Holm Abby 5 acres of arable land one acre on the cart load from Bothelton. The priory at Wetheral had five tenements in Bolton of the yearly rent in whole of £2-11-8d and at the dissolution of the Abbey of Shap, it appears that the abbey had a rent out of Bolton of 16d a year paid by Sir Cuthbert Ratcliffe Knight.

In 1544 King Henry VIII granted Shap Abbey to Sir Thomas Wharton knight. The particulars of their lands and rents include: At Bolton, a messuage and ten-ement in the possession of John Benson, and a rent of 16d issuing out of the lands of Cuthbert Ratcliffe knight, 8d out of the tenement of Richard Gibson, 8d out of the tenement of John Dent and 3d out of the tenement of Edward Allayne.

The Manor had its set rules and below are a few examples :

Here set by sevrall Juries houlden and keept at sevrall times and estreated (i.e. copied from the Rolls of a court) and colected fourthe of the Court Rooles within Manor of Bolton beeing keept by John Blencow esqr Steward of the same. Begineth Anno Domm 1627.

Imprimis we lay a paine that none shall oversett or put stint (wth Cattell) the fallowes under paine of 6d

Itm that none shall keep his kine in the streate upon the day nor Carrye them into the ox foulde upon the night.

Itm It is laid in paine that none shall Rescuse nor take any Goods from the Baill for the levying of any precept or for some service left undone according to the costomes of the said Manor under the paine of every default 20d. (rescuse = forcible retaking of persons or goods detained by legal authority)

..that none within this Manor shall hinder or stop the water course which is in anuy way prediudiciall to their Neighbours..

noe fforrener without this lordshippe shall tedder any Cattell within the jurisdicssson of this Manor in the summer time .

it is set down by the jury that none shall Cuttaany willeyes in the Lawe Willeyes without the licence of the Baill or the frithmen.

if any ma be warned by the Baill or other officer to be a wittnes betwixt Neighbour and neibougher soe refusing not to come haveinge noe lawfull Cause to the Contrarye shall be andiced (?indicted) for his default.

that any maid or women that is Evesdroppers wch standes under walles or windows by night or day to heare tailes or Carrye them away to others to make striffe and Debate betwene Neighbours under the paine of every default . 3 / 4 d .

It is agreed and sett downe by the Jurye thay evrye acree shall have two sheepe in the fieldes and every oxegaite ffower sheepe and that none shall take any fforeine sheepe for every oxegate.

Itm that none shall Cutt any willeyes beneath Rowland Close without leave of the Baill or the frithmen

Itm that none sshall cut any Whitethorns in the willeyes under the pain of every default, 6/8d

Itm that none shall take any thorns of there hedges unless they lay new ones thereon.

Itm that evrye one shall make there Low More hedges evrye year before the first day of A p r e l l

Itm that we the Jurye doe set downe and say it in paine that evrye auncient householder shall gett but one burthen of grasse a day and to get in the willeyes but on the Saturday to get two and no more under the paine of .

Itm that none graw any fodder to make the hedges within this lordship

Itm it is laide in paine that none within this lordshipe Tenant or Occupier, henceforth Tedder any mares or foales within the fealdes in the summer time or harvest but in the bigg (?barley) landes or the fallowes quarter.

Itm it is sett down by the Jurye that no Brewster within this Towne keepe any Card in his house but betwixxt St Thomas Day and Twelfth Day, but only on Candlemas over and Candlemas night under the paine of every default 6/8d

(This Item Erased)

Itm it is set down by the Jurye that none within this lordshippe (lowse) within the bigg quarter when they sow there bigg .

It is set down by the Jurye that noe man within this lordshippe shall keepe any sheepe in the sommer time in the closes nether Rallowes nor without they will hould ..under the paine.

Itm it is set down and layed in paine by the Jurye that none shall Cut anie willowes in the lowe willowes but with the liscence of the frithmen and the bailiffe and every defaulte to be so distreaneed by the frithmen and the bailiffe for the use of the towene.

The above extracts come from the Lowther papers at Carlisle Record Office and were contributed by Bob Thwaites, Morland.

The people paid their tithes, a tax, which was originally levied to support the clergy and the church. It is a tax of one tenth particularly a tenth of the annual produce of land or labour. There were three types of tithe. One calculated on income from produce, mixed tithes calculated on income from stock and labour combined and that calculated on income derived entirely from labour.

In Bolton where the incumbent of the parish was a perpetual curate the tithes were annexed by an ecclesiastical body. The tithes were apportioned between the Dean and Chapter at Carlisle and the vicar of Morland consequently the living here was very poor. Agriculture dominated life in Bolton as it did through out the rest of the country. Life was very hard and precarious with the staple diet being bread and beer. The harvest was dependent on the weather.

At the mid-day meal meat was eaten as long as the stores in the chimney lasted. A piece of meat would be boiled on Sunday and would be eaten cold the rest of the week. Soup might be made and flavoured with herbs from the pot herbs from the garden and this could also be poured over meal when it would be known as crowdy . If there were any potatoes they would be a welcome addition. Blue milk cheese called wangy and beer was always on the table at which both servants and master sat together. The larger farms used barley to make into malt. The malt mill would stand in the corner of the down house or barn and the malt would then be used to brew the ale which was drunk at every meal.

Clothes were made of a rough grey wool from the native sheep, carded and spun at home and woven into cloth by the village weaver. In 1773 Thomas Idle was weaver in Bolton. He would be able to earn a good wage then but by 1830 the trade was in decline because of competition from the power looms. The cloth was called self grey or duffle and was sometimes dyed blue. Buckskin knee britches were kept for best. Tailors would travel the country calling on farms twice a year to make up the duffle. A finer material called russet was used for the ladies clothes. A tailor could earn ten pence to a shilling a day plus his food and lodging. He may have stayed at the house for up to a fortnight making the wardrobe for the family and servants. Clothes formed part of a servant s wages. The Bland family were tailors for the village for several generations dating back at least to the year 1700.

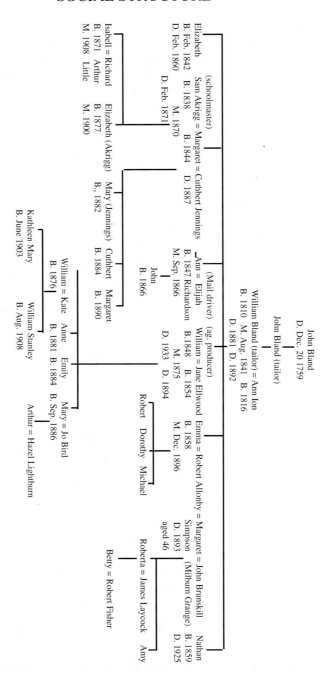

The Bland family tree. Bolton, Westmorland

CHANGING TIMES

Peddlers were very welcome at the out lying cottages and farms not only for their goods but because they brought the news. The only other way to get news was to go to the market or to church. Dates of sales, fairs, notices of lost or strayed animals and all matters of public interest were given out at the church porch or from the top of a tombstone after the service. It was customary in the out lying districts for at least one farmer to attend church and carry the news back to others.

Most people wore clogs made of strong leather with a sole of wood and bound with iron. Leather shoes were kept for Sunday best.

The Black Death in the mid 1300s precipitated a rapid decline in the rural population and there was consequently a reduction in the availability of labour. This reduction in labour resulted in an increase in sheep farming which was less labour intensive and more profitable. A very lucrative woollen trade was soon to be developed exporting wool to the continent and the sheep also provided meat for the diet.

In 1660 the export of wool from Britain was prohibited and this did a great deal of harm to the industry. In order to try to rescue the trade and keep the prices up an act was passed to ensure every one who died was buried in wool. In the church registers we can see evidence of this for example in 1672:

Apr 23rd Stephen Gibson

Oct 25 Margaret daughter of William Spedding at Orton

Mar 1st Thomas Allan junr

All entries for the last two years are from Bp Transcripts and all in woollen according to the Act.

Or *1686 June 1 Elinor Mason an Affidavit taken by Mr John Dalston Esqu that she was buried in woollen only upon the oath of Ann Browne.*

Jan 1st Matthew Allon householder in woollen onely as appeard by the oaths of Mary Tebay and Eliz Allon taken by Mr John Fenwicke Rector of Cliburne.

The Corn Laws first introduced in 1815 were an attempt to maintain the prosperity of British farmers during the Napoleonic Wars. It originally allowed the import of grain from other countries only after the price of home grown wheat had risen above 80 shillings a quarter. It was an attempt to balance the price of grain and the cost of production so the poor could afford to buy it whilst the farmer continued to make a reasonable living. The legislation had the opposite effect and every one suffered. When the Corn Laws were abolished many farmers turned away from corn production and started to produce beef and dairy products for which there was a ready market. Hence people like Squire Graham became well known and respected for developments in this area.

The common lands in Bolton were enclosed by an act dated 1808 and the date of the award was made in 1813 with 410 acres allotted. The principal of the enclosure legislation was that the lord and commoners would each receive an allocation of freehold land for the legal withdrawal of their former right. For example the endowment of the school at Morland came about by an agreement between the Dean and Chapter of Carlisle as lords of the manor and the vicar and tenants. The tenants had certain customary estates in Morland and the inhabitants of four tenements in Bolton claimed the right to cut wood in the woodlands for the repair of their houses, buildings and foot bridges over their becks. The said tenants agreed to relinquish their claim and the Dean and Chapter agreed to give to the vicar of Morland and the tenants and owners in trust 34 acres of land within the manor. Two acres on the north of the vicars allotment for repairing the Chancel . Five parts out of six of the rents remaining 32 acres in trust for the maintenance of the schoolmaster of the school at Morland, on condition that the customary tenants and inhabitants contributed £8 yearly to the schoolmaster. One sixth was to be employed for the repair of foot bridges and gates across the roads in the said manor, in keeping the school in repair and in cultivating and improving the said 32 acres.

Common land was any land subject to the common rights i.e. wastelands or common fields. Common wasteland was almost always owned by the lord of the manor and subject to rights of common exercisable throughout the whole year i.e. rights to pasture and to take profit out of the land such as fern, heath, and gorse. The common fields were open tracts of arable or meadow belonging

Threshing Day.

Frank Richardson and his work force using the steam tractor to split and saw wood in the yard of Greystone House.

to various owners. By 1801 the number of wastelands enclosed in Westmorland were nine, a total of 10,283 acres and an increase in the acres of wheat grown went from nothing to 272 acres. Only four common fields had been enclosed and one of those was in Bolton with twenty-two acres enclosed in 1808.

Once it was determined that the principal land owners agreed to and were committed to the enclosure a surveyor and a valuer were appointed by the parish to assist the commissioners in determining the enclosure awards. The Commissioners for Bolton were Jo Fryer and Thomas Harrison and the survey-or was John Nicholson from the Malt and Shovel Inn, now The Poplars. Following the survey and valuation a public consultation was held and then the land re-allocated in compact holdings which was equivalent to the combined portions of common land held by a particular claimant.

The cost of administrating the system plus the hedging and ditching, the building of walls and the planting of hedgerows fell on the recipients of the enclosure awards. Each person benefiting from an allotment had to pay 20 shillings an acre.

Altogether 562 acres were enclosed mainly along the Village Street. This included Water Ridding, Bolton Moor, Intake and Cowper Close plus the smaller closes of Bolton High Moor, Luzbeck Close and St Johns Close. Some people exchanged small plots for larger ones and vice versa, some sold their rights and others bought several plots. Altogether 17 plots became freehold passing into private hands.

In 1828 John Dixon and John Dent were the largest land owners and the third was Robert Hodgeson from Bewley Castle who rented the freehold from the Dean and Chapter of Carlisle. The smallest land owner was James Atkinson who held four acres.

Many cottagers were dependant on the common land and the enclosure of it caused destitution for many people. The common lands were enclosed and an allotment of 382 acres 3roods and 10 perches were made to the Dean and Chapter. The corn and hay tithes, 35 acres and 3 roods were appropriated to the vicar and 1 acre 3 roods and 20 perches to the perpetual curacy of Bolton.

There was very little technical innovation on the farms before 1850. There was a plentiful supply of cheap labour to be had and this did not help in making any technical advancement. Most of the development in agriculture has taken place since 1880.

It was not until people began to move out of the country into the towns at the time of the industrial revolution and there was a shortage of labour to work on and around the farms that a limited mechanisation was introduced. Threshing by steam was introduced from about 1840 and in 1851 horse drawn reaping machines were introduced followed by reaper binders in the 1870s.

Isabel Cooke, nee Smith, records in a Hired Lass in Westmorland her time at Brigham Bank Farm: *that the steam threshing machine used to come to thresh the corn out of the straw. It was a very busy time for every one in doors and out. The machine was usually brought to the house the day before from another farm and it would be set up ready to begin work the next morning. Three men went with the machine to operate it. At 7 in the morning the engine fire was started and then the men would go in for breakfast. Every body would help each other and a man went from every farm around to help at Brigham Bank. At mid morning tea and eats were taken out to the men and they would all come in at 12 for a big cooked dinner. Mid afternoon tea and food was taken out to them again.*

Isabel loved to hear the hum of the machine and could remember that when she was younger her mother would take clean double bed linen ticks to the farm to have them filled with the chaff: *It was lovely and soft and every year they were emptied the ticks washed and then refilled.*

Audrey Dent, nee Bellas, some fifty years later also recalls threshing day as an exciting event: *It must have been hard work for the women of the house but as children we didn't really think about that. The machine arrived first thing in the morning and started to work on the five or six stacks of corn in the stack-*

Russells Joiners on the site of Russell House home to the Cowan family.

yard. After a full mornings work with a coffee break provided by the farmers wife the men would be summoned by the children (home from school for lunch) to go to the house for a meal. My sister Kath and I always found this exciting. I seem to remember there being up to eight or so men sitting round a large table tucking into a hot pot, shepherds pie or steak pie. This was cooked in the oven of the black leaded fireplace before we had an aga cooker. As children we used to try and guess what was cooking by the smell drifting through the door as we entered the house. Modern ovens dont seem to have the same magic .

Padget Richardson's father had a threshing machine business in the village at Orchard House. He kept the big machines in the great big barn at the side, now converted into two private houses. He would travel from farm to farm with the men he employed to do the threshing. He also used the steam threshing machines to saw wood.

Milking machines were available in 1880 enabling cooled milk to be transported to the towns but the making of butter and cheese was still labour intensive. About this time a number of engineering firms were beginning to produce a variety of lightweight metal cultivators. Pairs of horses drew these and many of these implements were in use until the 1940s.

In a letter to the editor of *The Herald* on 15 January 1989 T. Robinson from London writes of memories of Bolton village smithy and says: *A great uncle of mine Henry Dent of Bolton emigrated to Australia in 1852. He wrote to his father John Dent at Elm House asking him to order two ploughs from Joseph Simpson the blacksmith. His request was for one single plough of the pattern Joseph Simpson has been lately making. It must have a pike sock and two extra mould boards. One double iron plough to run on a plate in the centre and have mould boards to widen or straighten according to the work to be done.*

Henry Dent was very keen for Joseph Simpson to emigrate to Australia as he would soon make a fortune by plough making. If I had his practical knowledge of the trade I would not despair at making a fortune in six or seven years. I should not recommend him to bring many clothes - a good suit for Sundays, a few clothes for working in such as mole-skin trousers, blue flannel slops and two or three pairs of good boots.

The first oil driven tractor was introduced in 1899. Since then the technical developments have increased to a point where for example a 100 acre farm would support two families and perhaps three workers in the 1940s compared with today when one man with perhaps occasional part time help would work that amount of land to support a much smaller family.

The number of farms in the village has decreased steadily since 1851. At that time most of the open field system had been converted into one of small compact farms worked mainly by tenant farmers. Agriculture would have been a major part of the economy of the village. If only a small number of acres were owned the farmer may also have some other occupation.

Occupations noted in the church registers are cabinet maker, carpenter, carpet weaver and clock-dresser. In 1821 John Miller was a dancing master and in 1771 William Longmire is listed as being a fiddler. Mary Airey, nee Nicholson, is a mantu maker. There have also been potters, riddle-makers, glovers and cordwainers (shoe makers).

Tom Howe ploughing in the field just past Bolton Lodge.

CHANGING TIMES

By 1881 the number of farms in the village was 22. Bolton Mill now had 28 acres and the smallest number of acres, just two, were farmed by Mr Brunskill.

In 1891 there were 20 farms with other occupations listed as agricultural producer, gamekeeper, joiner, cycle agent, gardener and school master. Mr Robinson was a mason, builder and grocer. Mr Russell was a joiner, builder and wheel-wright. There was also a blacksmith, carrier, general stores, victualler, cow keeper, shoe maker, tailor and a miller. Mr Ellwood was a grocer, postmaster and farmer while Mr Richardson ran a steam thresher and sawyer s business.

Since then with the improvement in transport people have travelled further afield to work whilst still living in the village. Other occupations have enticed people away from the land for example at British Gypsum at Kirkby Thore and the railway.

Today there are just nine farms left in the village - Bolton Lodge, Eden Fields, Mansgrove, Laithia, Peatgates, Crossrigg, Brigham Bank, The Mill and Street House. When farms have been sold land has been bought by other farmers to make their holdings bigger. In some cases land and farm buildings have been sold on which to build new houses.

New economic development within the village has been in tourism. The mill has a static and touring caravan site. There are several bed and breakfast establishments - The Larches, Eden Grove Farm House, Croft House, Tarka House and Glebe House. There are also several barn conversions let as holiday cottages. There are four other farms not farmed by the owners but the land is let to other farmers in the village.

Farming as a way of life is sadly disappearing and few of the village children will have the memories that Isabel Cooke had or Audrey Dent has. Audrey can still remember the excitement she felt when the hay was brought into the barn:
We were all given the job of trampling it down in order to get as much in as possible. This was very exciting for me until I realised my head was almost touching the roof and somehow I had to get down. Not liking heights, I wondered how on earth I d got there and although dad would put a ladder up, I daren't step on to it. In the end dad would get frustrated and say: just walk about with your eyes shut, you ll soon come down. I always managed some how and was always ready the following year to do the same again.

Times have changed dramatically in the country side within the last fifty years and perhaps the effects of the Foot and Mouth Disease will bring about further major change.

All Saints Church

In the Commonwealth Survey of 1649 Bolton was a chapelry in the parish of Morland and described as belonging to the vicarage of Morland: *with one house for the curate abutting on to the churchyard.* It remained in the parish of Morland until 1868. The chapel and Morland church were attached to the priory at Wetheral near Carlisle. It was probably built in the second half of the 12th century. The parish church and chapel have been the focus for the community s religious and social activities through the ages.

Most of what can be seen of the church today is from the restoration of the church in 1848 during the incumbency of the Revd William Shepherd who was curate from 1834—1880. The chapel was about to be rebuilt in 1829 with £100 from the Society for the Building of New Churches. However there are several interesting Norman features still remaining.

It had no maintenance but the vicar of Morland's duty was to find a reader there and pay him £7 a year out of his tithes and glebe lands. The high turnover of curates reflects the poor living. In 1829 the landowners were patrons to the curacy which was valued at £4-0-0d with £3-0-0d per year being paid by the vicar of Morland and 30/- from the produce of the yard, surplice fees and tithes of garths, chickens, eggs, ducks, hemp and flax. In 1753 this was augmented by £1000 with £800 coming from Queen Anne s bounty in 1754, 1761 and 1785 and £200 given by the Countess Dowager Gower daughter of the third Earl of Granville (successor to Palmerston in the Cabinet). Two estates were purchased with £800 (Glebe House and Bewley Farm) and the remainder laid out in the purchase of the Scarside Estate at Orton.

There was formerly a chantry founded by the Derwentwater family in the

BOLTON ~ PARISH CHURCH OF ALL SAINTS

SCALE OF FEET

12TH CENTURY   14TH CENTURY
LATE 12TH CENTURY   17TH CENTURY
CIRCA 1200   18TH CENTY & MODERN

The Vicarage

church. The Derwentwaters once held the manor of Bolton (see appendix).

The church makes a pretty picture whatever the weather: a small sandstone building with a bell tower set at the end of an avenue of yews. A walk around the church and churchyard can take you on a journey through many centuries noting inhabitants of Bolton as you go.

In the churchyard to the left of the porch is the stone effigy of a lady upright against the wall. Her hands are clasped across her breast and she is dressed in a long cloak. Her dress may be that of a 12th century Norman. Her head appears to be resting on a pillow suggesting that she may once have lain on a tomb perhaps inside the church. Was she a member of the Norman nobility?

Moving further to the left in the south west corner of the church on the face of the buttress is an ancient sun dial scratched onto the stone.   To the right of the porch are some table-top tombs and a sundial, erected by the church wardens in 1747.   Sadly the top was stolen in 1985. The words CHURCH WATCH and the date 1747 with the initials JB — (James Bowness) and RA — (Richard Allen) church wardens, can still be seen. The pillar stands on a stone base probably extracted from Bolton quarry. The church wardens accounts show a charge of 14 shillings for the erection of the sun dial and a further 1/6d for beer for the occasion.

On the north side of the church and built into the wall above a window is a relief in red sandstone measuring 26 by 16 inches of two knights fighting. It appears to commemorate a tournament. The two knights are wearing mail shirts and tall pointed helmets. They are on horseback and carry kite shaped shields and lances of the reign of Henry II (1154-1189).   One is smaller than the other and is inferior in rank because his lance has no banner. He has broken the guard of the other who has thrown up his shield and dropped his lance as the point of the other is thrust into his face in the vulnerable spot under the nasal of his helmet. Beside it is another slab, which appears to be the companion to it. It is built into the wall and at one time measured 21 by 13.5 inches and was inscribed:

+Ds LVRREN DE . WERE
DVN: qS: HoM ES DE . BO
ELTVN: + .11 .OMRS:QV
SeAT IF MV . R. ESNE
LVRLALYV R: OS
+RAT : O N . RAM
DSLVRHEI

Sir Lawrence de Vere gives to the men of Bolton....   This is the only part to be translated up to now and so we may never know what was given to Bolton men.

Vere is an old Norman name. Perhaps the stone effigy of the lady described earlier was Lady de Vere. The inscription is now almost completely worn away by the weather and air pollution. There is a similar relief in Fordington in Dorset dated about 1110.

To the right of the church porch lies the tomb of William Bowness benefactor to the school. His will dated 9 February 1709: Charged a Cholem, Colby

The bells arriving at the church

The effigy of a lady on the south wall of Bolton church. Perhaps she is a Norman lady from the time the church was built.

Field Butler Horn, with an annual rent of 10/- to be distributed upon his tombstone to the poor of Bolton by the church wardens and overseers with the approbation of the heir or chief of his family on the Feast of Saint Thomas the Apostle yearly forever.

Stepping into the church through the porch which was probably added in the 18th century we can see the inner Norman doorway circa late 12th century. The doorway has an attractive pattern of six petalled rosettes, to the left a figure holding a hammer in one hand and to the right a figure with wings. Also to the left resting upon the stone seat is what appears to be the tombstone of James Hanson, parish clerk, who died aged 79 in 1721 and his wife Elizabeth.

The font is not dated but looks to be very old. The oak cover has the initials TG (Thomas Gibson) WH (William Hanson) and the date 1687. On the right of the door is the poor man s box made of oak which used to have two padlocks. It is inscribed 1634 The Poor Mans Box and very faintly the words church warden s seat and their initials I.L. and R.C.

The church wardens, the overseers of the poor and the parish constable were the parish officers and carried out the duties of the parish council. Another important person was the parish clerk. In many parishes the clerk was and still is the person responsible for the completion of the registers for births, marriages and deaths. His pay was often very small and may have been supplemented with provisions in kind such as eggs from the parishioners. In order to be able to do the job he would have had to have been more or less literate. The church warden accounts for 1707-1785 show them to have been: *Scriptured By Me Joharrnie Earl.* Joharrnie Earl was the curate at the time but perhaps he also had the job of church clerk.

The accounts show that in 1771 the clerk received 5/-. Two years later it was increased to 10/- and in 1775 to £1. What had he done to deserve such a huge increase in wages over such a short period? There are several interesting little entries apart from those mentioned in the text:

> *For glazing the windows of the church* - This appears to have been an annual necessity.
>
> *1732   0-2-0d Spent for Gunpowder treason* - An annual event.
>
> *1762 0-2-0d For Crownation day* Presumably this was to celebrate the accession to the throne of George III in 1760.
>
> *0-2-0d To Thomas Longmire for Mending the pulpit.*

Opposite on the north wall is a former Norman doorway now a window. At one time the nave ended on a line with this window on the south side. We stand in the middle of what may have been the west tower. The wall on the far side of the vestry and the staircase to the gallery is apparently four feet six inches thick and has large buttresses. There may have been a large belfry here but now there is an extension of the Norman nave into the tower area and above a gallery and stone arch supporting the bell tower. The roof of this 16th century bell tower was restored in memory of James Bell and a service of thanks giving held for the restoration in August 1985. It was repaired to retain its ancient appearance and the wooden louvered windows and bird guards renewed at the same time. There are two bells cast by W. Scott of Wigan in 1693 (see appendix). They are apparently much as they were when they were installed over 300 years ago. There are interesting references to the bells in the church wardens accounts:

> *May 12th 1694 Disbursed*
> *to Robert Lacklin for carrying the bells —8*
> *to William Cookson touching the bells 1-0*
> *to William Bowness for work and a rope-3-0.*

How would the bells have been brought from Wigan and how long did it take? The total seating in the nave, chancel and gallery is 140. On the supports for the roof beams are carved stone faces. In the vestry there is a framed list of vicars and curates from 1663 (see appendix).

A lady in Norman dress

The tracery in the church so lovingly restored by Jennie Bell

The lovely oak screen of the chancel probably dates from the restoration of the church in 1848. The framed chest is possibly 16th century and may have held the parish records. At the time of the thanksgiving service it made useful storage for the Sunday school materials.

Electric lights were fitted in place of the oil lamps in 1934 and the wiring renewed in 1983. New ladders were provided to the belfry in 1964. The harmonium had an electric blower fitted in 1975 and the churchwarden staves were given in memory of members of the Pinnington family in 1969. Up until 1927 there were five box pews in the chancel. These were converted into choir stalls and two reading desks. The very low window on the south side is a leper window. It perhaps gave lepers standing in the churchyard a view of the priest as he took the service.

At the communion step the windows on the north and south walls are late 12th century but the stained glass in the east window dates only from 1847. There is some very ancient glass in the little round window above the priest s door showing the arms of the Derwentwater and Ratcliffe families in a shield which is upside down. The next window in the south wall shows the Risen Lord and is in memory of Mary Graham of Eden Grove 1908.

The processional cross was made by Harry Jones in1972. He worked at Eden Grove and was helped by some of the boys to make the psalm board. The oak panelling round the sanctuary is a memorial to the Revd. Philip Pinnington and his wife Alice. The brass cross was provided in 1913. The alter was installed in 1846. It is made of oak and has a top of marble. The church has a number of chalices and patens (hallow dish used for bread) made of either pewter or silver (see appendix). The oldest is said to be a silver-plated chalice seven inches tall. It is inscribed with the words: *The Gift of George Harrison of Whitfield Brow To The Inhabitants of Bolton For The Church.* It is not dated but George Harrison lived at Whitfield Brow (now Eden Grove) from 1786-1813.

A framed list of the names of people who have made bequests to the church hangs on the wall and is pictured below. The war dead are also commemorated in the church.

What of James Bell for whose memory the Thanksgiving Service for the restoration of the belfry was being held? James Bell was a joiner by trade and worked for Thwaites at Kirkby Thore and owned the village shop, where the Post Office is today, with his wife Jennie, nee Alison. He spent many hours in the church repairing and restoring it.

He made and erected the notice-board in 1984 and renewed the lamp post half way up the path. The frame for the list of church wardens was made by him as were the bookcase and cupboard for prayer and hymn books below the Poor Man s Box. Jim also fixed the shelf for literature on the pew nearest the font. Jim removed the wainscot from around the walls of the nave and did repairs to the flooring and the joists and he fixed new panelling in the vestry to protect the cassocks and surplices hanging on the walls. The oak screen of decorated tracery in the chancel was covered in paint but Jennie Bell lovingly restored it to the beauty we see to day. Jim converted the box pews. He was obviously a man

Bolton Church

The old sun dial dated 1717

who recognised what a gem of a place Bolton church is and who took time and trouble to preserve what he could.

Today Revd. David Wood is the vicar. David and Di his wife moved to Crosby Ravensworth in June 1995 to become priest in charge of the parishes of Asby, Bolton and Crosby Ravensworth. Before coming here they worked at St Thomas Church in Kendal from 1991. They have three sons - Ben 24 who married in 2001 and hopes to become a teacher, Mark 22 and James 19, who both work in the catering industry.

Prior to going to theological college in 1989 David and Di had spent many years farming in North Lancashire, milking large herds of cattle (180+) but after milking quotas were introduced in the 1980s David was unemployed for a short while. He then started a wholesale green grocery business supplying hotels and restaurants. It was during this time that God called us into ministry and we went to theological college in 1989 .

Roy Boff moved to Eden Fold three years ago with his wife Marie after taking early retirement from ministering in the church. He is firstly a member of the congregation but is also involved with All Saints in a voluntary capacity standing in for David when needed. As a youngster in Leamington Spa he was persuaded to join the choir by a friend and as he could sing a little thought this a good idea for the 1d a week he would receive. It did eventually go up to 2d a week and we would sometimes get 3d for a wedding. If we sang a solo we could get an extra 3d. My friend didn t tell me I would have to attend church three times on Sunday and Monday, Wednesday and Thursday for practice .

It was not until he was in his second year at Oxford that he decided to go into the ministry. He had not really thought about it until then. He was ordained at Southwark Cathedral in 1957 and afterwards started his curacy at Woolwich. Roy's career with the church has spanned 44 years finishing with him being Rural Dean of Richmond, North Yorkshire.

LIST OF THE SEATS IN BOLTON CHAPEL 1741

In the pew in the choir on the north side is:
William Allan one
John Spedding one
William Bowness

John Newton hath two pews which is five seats
The next pew
William Allen one
John Gargatt one (where the pulpit is now AD1923)

The next pew Mr. Birkett s which hath four seats
The seat next to Mr. Birkett s is Mr. Fletcher one
John Spedding one
Thomas Lambart one

Ann Gibson one

The second seat is:
William Bowness one
Johnathan Fallowfield one
Stephen Cowper one
Thomas Gibson one

The third seat is:
Thomas Carleton Esq one
Mr. Christopher Carleton one
John Dixon one
Robert Wilson one

The fourth seat is:
John Newton one
James Bowness one
Joseph Bleamire one
Will Wood one

The congregation in their pews in the church. The ladies would have sat separately from the men.

CHANGING TIMES

The fifth seat is:
John Brougham and John Lambert
John Atkinson two
Thomas Gibson one

Next is John Burry s seat

The seats on the south side in the chair are:
George Smith one
James Bowness one
Thomas Nicholson one
INO Brougham

Bewley Castle now hath four seats

John Brougham pew hath two seats

The next is Mr. Birkett one
John Farrell one
Wm Bowness one

The seats below the reading pews:
Thomas Carleton Esq one
Will Bowness one
Thomas Jackson one

The second seat is:
Thomas Carleton Esq one
Thomas Spedding one J. Lambert
George Smith one
Wm. Allen junior one

The third seat is:
John Spedding
Math. Spedding
John Tailor one
Joseph Bellas one

The fourth seat is:
Mr. Birkett one

Thomas Chappelhow one
Nathan Savage one
John Atkinson one

The fifth seat is:
William Bowness one
Mr. Chris Carleton one
John Stable one
James Bowness one

The womans seat in the south side is:
George Smith one
William Allen one
Mr. Chris Carleton two

The second seat is:
Thomas Jackson one
Will Allen senior one
Ann Gibson one
Jo. Bellces one
The third seat is:
John Brougham one
John ? Trawel one
Nathan Savage one
John Atkinson one

The fourth seat is:
Thomas Carleton Esq. two
Will Wood one
John Stable one

The fifth seat is:
John Spedding one
Will Allen one
John Newon one
Thomas Gilson one

The sixth seat is:
John Hewton one
Jo Bleamine one
James Bowness one
John Brougham one

ALL SAINTS CHURCH

The seventh seat is:
Mr. Fletcher one
Will Bowness one
Matt Spedding one
Thomas Nicholson one

The womans seat on the north side:
John Gargatt two
Will Bowness one
Thom. Gibson one

The second seat is:
Bewley Castle one
George Smith one
Wm. Allen one
Thomas Gibson one

The third seat is:
Mr. Birkett two
John Brougham one
John Dixon one

The fourth seat is:
Jonathan Fallowfield one
Thomas Lambart one
Wm. Bowness one
James Bowness one

The fifth seat is:
Wm. Bowness one
Thos. Spedding one
Wm. Addison junior one
Nathan Savage

The sixth seat is:
Mr. Birkett one
John Taylor one
John Atkinson one
Robert Wilson one

The seventh seat is:
Will Spedding one
John Atkinson one
Robert Wilson one
Will Allen one
The eighth seat is:
Thomas Chapelhow one
Thomas Langham one
John Cowper one

Same list as in 1678 - 34 pews and 125 seats.

Highways and Byways

The village of Bolton was very isolated from the main road as can be seen from Jeffrey's map of 1768. The inhabitants of the village would have had to ford the river to reach the road. It could be forded at the mill where a series of weirs linking two islands allowed foot passage. The river could also be forded at other points along its boundary with the village.

The roads leading to and from the village would be little more than tracks and would not appear to have been kept in a good state of repair. On 23 April 1770 it is recorded in the Appleby Quarter Sessions Indictment book that:-

Presentment that from the time whereof the memory of man is not contrary there was and yet is a certain common and ancient Pack and Prime way leading from the village of Bolton to the village of Great Strickland for all the liege subjects of the King on horseback and on foot, to go and return at their will, and that a certain part of that way beginning at a certain place called Little Lane End and so along that way to the high road on Bolton Moor. Containing in length 333 yards and in breadth one yard was and yet is very ruinous, miry, deep broken in decay for want of due reparation. And that the inhabitants of Bolton ought to repair and amend when and so often as it shall be necessary .

The first act of parliament authorising the construction of turnpikes in Westmorland was passed in 1752. The Fly a stagecoach first started running over Stainmore from London to Glasgow in 1774. Before that date all trade was carried on pack horses along narrow pack horse tracks. Gangs of pack horses led by a bell horse were one of the rural scenes of the time. Inclosure of the common land brought about the making of roads finally displacing the pack horse tracks.

Bolton Bridge

Jeffreys map 1768

Other roads were improved and single horsed carts were brought into use in the more remote parts of the area. They appear to have originated in Cumberland and Westmorland because of the small acreage of farms where only a single horse was required. They were called clog wheeled carts or tumblers .

The acts of Parliament relating to the construction of turnpike roads provided for the appointment of trustees, with the power to erect gates and demand tolls. The money obtained was used for repairing and making the road. The

Bolton's old horse troughs

trustees also had the power to take material without payment for the repair of the roads out of any brook, river or waste or common ground. The trustees also erected milestones. People were still liable for statute work on the roads.

The Highways Surveyors Book for Bolton for 1818 lists the names of those liable to perform statute labour. Every one living in the village had to pay money to be used for the making of the roads and in 1818 this amounted to £19-0 5d. It appears that those who could not pay had to do the labouring to keep the roads in good repair. Some of the entries in the book read as follows:-

> *Paid to Thomas Sewall for making 5 roods of new road at 3/11d per rood 19/7d.*
> *For opening gutters T Sewall 1/6d*
> *To Stephen Longmire for repairs to Coat Syke Bridge 6/6d*
> *To Stephen Longmire for leading stones to near Mr William Corrys house £1/0/6d. For breaking stones one day 10/-*
> *To Stephen Longmire for patching North End 1/5d*
> *To Thomas Sewel repair Sowerby Lane, Issac Hill, Morland Lane near Dents Trees 12/-*
> *To Stephen Longmire - Steps over Luz Beck 0-6-6d.*
> *To Stephen Longmire for widening and repairs from Newtons to near brigge16/0d.*
> *To Lancelot Bellas for repairs near school 0-4-6d.*
> *To Joseph Longmire to patch and splice from Brigham to Temple Gate 4/8d*

At a vestry meeting held in the school house on 24 April 1837:

> *Persuant to regular notes it was resolved that the surveyors should make a rate at 3/- in the pound for the township of Bolton. Signed John Dent Chairman.*
>
> *To John Savage to finding and breaking 2yds and 24 feet of stone and patching with the same upon different parts of the road at 2/9d a yard 8/-*
> *To Will Horn for sacrificing a part of road .with finding and breaking 6yds and 7feet of stone at 2/10d per yard near his own place 17/3d*
> *To David Bowman for altering and erecting a guide post.*

At a vestry meeting held at John Nicholsons: *It was resolved that the surveyors of the high road of the township of Bolton should print or cause to be printed hand bills to the following effect: Any person leading or carting any stone from Bolton quarries to any place not within the said Township or any person quarrying or carting away stones for any purpose but solely for the use of the proprietors of the said Township shall be prosecuted according as the Law Directs and the said surveyors shall cause the said handbills to be properly circulated as witness our hands the overseers.*

Signed Nathan Simpson, John Mitchell, Thomas Steel (churchwarden), John Dixon (churchwarden), John Dent, Thomas Lambert, William Dixon, Sam Ogglethorpe, Thomas Barton, Will Chapelhow, Richard Temple, Thomas Nicholson, Will Thompson, Thomas Atkinson and John Corry.

There was a turnpike on the road at Long Marton and a side gate was installed in 1815 where Bolton Lane joined the turnpike and Bolton was then linked to the important route west over Stainmore. In 1861 Joseph and Anne Peasgood were living in Turnpike House. Hodgesons map of 1838 shows a side gate linking the route to the turnpike at Long Marton and also shows a way through Redland Bank down to the iron bridge.

The earliest reference to the bridge is made in the Appleby Quarter sessions Indictment Book 1808/1807. On 9 August 1807 the Quarter Sessions ordered that the High Constable of the west ward be appointed to superintend the erection of a bridge over the river Eden near to the village of Bolton. It was to be paid for by public subscription and was to be built big enough and strong

The old sign to denote the high way district going out of the village over the bridge on the east side at the end of the railings.

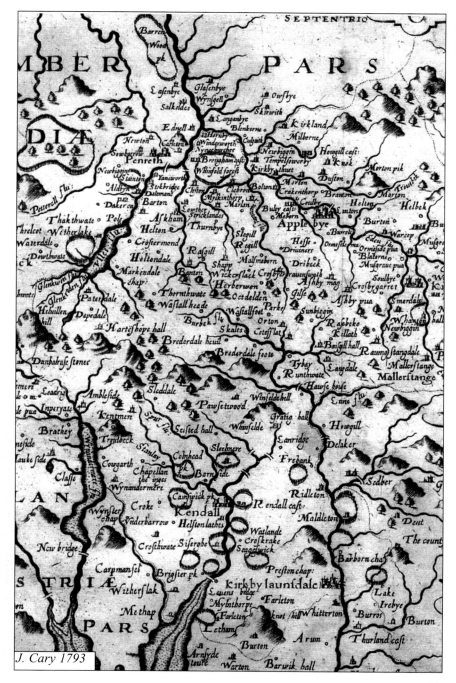

J. Cary 1793

enough for the passage of horses, carts and carriages.

On 9 January it was certified as being substantially built and commodious for public use. Only six years later on 10 January 1815 it was observed as: being so much in decay as to render the taking down of the same expedient. It was ordered that it be rebuilt either on the old site or on any other site convenient to the public but it had to be within 200 yards of the original site. Notices were issued proposing to build a good substantial stone bridge 21 feet wide within the parapets and also for erecting two stone abutments whereon to place an iron bridge of the same width in case a stone bridge should not be adopted.

Messrs Gowling offered to build the stone bridge for £2500 exclusive of the cost of materials of the old bridge or £2400 including such materials. They required £1800 to build the stone abutments on which to place the iron bridge. Mr Smirke submitted a plan for an iron chain bridge and on 3 June this was approved and adopted. It appears that Mr Gowling submitted a revised estimate of £1000. Messrs Douglas tendered for £856 and Messrs Johnstone for £600 for the building of the stone abutments and it looks as if one of these estimates was accepted.

The new bridge was thirty yards in length and was originally supported by stone abutments at either end, but just two months after its completion the iron work started to sag and two more massive pillars had to be raised to support the bridge.

As has been witnessed in recent years the river Eden can rise and fall very

Padget Richardson s grandfather John s caravan

Padget Richardson's grandfather John's steam roller pictured with Sam Ridley

quickly especially after heavy rains on the nearby fells. It becomes a swirling torrent and often covers nearby fields and foot paths. As quickly as it rises it will fall but in the meantime can have caused considerable damage. On the 2 February there was a record flood caused by continuous heavy rain. In Appleby the water flowed over the bridge and was three feet deep in the church and Bridge Street. It entered many of the buildings in the town. This flood caused considerable damage to Bolton bridge and other bridges in the area. It appears that the flood washed away the last two pillars to be built.

On 20 November 1868 the bridge master reported that: *within the last 40 years the bridge at Bolton has been re-timbered in the planking twice. The timber is again so rotten that it is inadvisable to re-use any of it in the necessary repair.*

The following day a committee meeting was held and the members instructed to: make enquiry into the expediency of repairing Bolton Bridge. If it were decided that it was not repairable they were to obtain estimates for the cost of a new iron and stone bridge. Tenders were advertised for the construction of a stone bridge of one arch in July 1869 and on 20 October 1869 the tender from Mr Little of Penrith was accepted for £1570.

With the abolition of the Turnpike Trust in 1882 the toll gates became relics of the past. The roads were then managed by 89 rural bodies, five local boards and two corporations each having a surveyor. When the county council was formed the responsibility for new roads and repairs came within their remit and this responsibility was handed over on 25 March 1889.

On six days in August 1910 the county council took a census of traffic passing by on the principal roads in the county from 8am to 8pm each evening. The amount of traffic was increasing and large quantities of tar and other bituminous material was being used to keep down the dust and prevent the rapid wear and tear caused by fast motor traffic.

Steam rollers were first used in Westmorland in 1886 for repairing the main roads. Padget Richardson's grandfather John Nicholson Richardson had a stone crushing business. He would travel to different quarries in the area taking with him a hut to erect on site so he had some where to stay whilst he worked. The work may have necessitated him staying there a whole year. When the stone was crushed it would be used to make and repair the county s roads. John Richardson made and repaired the road over Kirkstone Pass using one of his steam rollers.

The early steamrollers weighed ten tons; later smaller ones were used on the minor roads and in 1903 larger ones with scarifier attachments were introduced. Thelma Jackson s father John Frederick Nicholson worked on the village roads. He had a length which was his responsibility to keep in good repair. A length could be several miles long. Mr Nicholson was expected to repair the road surface, clean the gutters, cut over hanging trees and trim the hedges. Every man with a length of road to look after took great pride in their work and

Frank and Mary Richardson in their Lagonda car outside Orchard House. Arthur Bird says his father used to say when the car was started up in Bolton he could hear it at Birdby.

would strive to make their length the best.

Thelma remembers the steamroller coming into the village and the excitement it gave to the children, who would all climb into the cab for a ride. The driver would entertain them by turning the big steering wheel back and forth as they travelled slowly along the road. He would share the baccy he was chewing with the children who would copy him by also chewing it but spitting it out quickly at the horrid taste. He also shared his snuff with them and it made them sneeze and sneeze.

Thelma said: It is the one and only time I can remember my father giving me a good hiding after a ride in the steamroller because I got tar on my dress. He must have been in a bad mood as I m sure I did many more much naughtier things than get tar on my dress, and he never smacked me.

Today the county council have the responsibility for keeping the roads in good repair, but much of the work is put out to tender to private companies.

Bolton s Poor

Vagrancy was a continuing problem throughout the medieval period. In the latter part of the 15th century a labourer was prevented from leaving the parish without a testimonial from the local justice. Any beggar unable to work and provide for himself and family could be returned to his place of birth.

In 1391 the Statute of Mortmain stated that in parishes where an ecclesiastical or monastic foundation held the tithes a proportion of that income was to be reserved for the relief of the poor. In the 15th century whipping or hanging was used to punish able bodied vagrants and later on those who were unable to work had to obtain a begging licence from a magistrate.

After the dissolution of the monasteries, responsibility for the care of the poor passed to the parish. In order to discourage vagrancy able bodied vagrants were required to work and it was an offence to give private alms to the poor. In 1547 a vagrant who refused to work could be branded with a V and given servitude for two years. If he absconded during this time he was judged to be a slave for life and was branded with an S on his cheek.

The poor law of 1563 required at least two able people to be appointed to collect charitable alms of all the people living in the parish. In 1800 the Church wardens for Bolton assessed the Poor Rate for the parish as follows:

Assessment of 9/- per ox gang towards the relief of the poor within the Constablewick at Bolton April 25th 1800

Wm Swainson	4—13—5d	Thomas Chappelhow	2—6—8d
Thomas Chapellhow	0—3—7$^1/_2$	Mr Jackson	0—8—11
Wm Kilner	0—12— 3$^1/_2$	Ino Bowness	1— 0— 6d
		J Lambert	1—9— 0$^1/_2$
William Allen	0—18—1d	Elizabeth Beasley	0—5—7$^1/_2$
Wm Swainson	0—6—11d		
Samual Longmire	0—19-10	Sam Gibson	0—12—0$^1/_2$
Sam Ogglethorpe (junior)	0— 4— 3$^1/_2$	Earl of Lonsdale	1—3—3d
		Wm Gibson	0—6—3$^1/_2$
Ino Spedding	0—7—4$^1/_2$	Isa Garner	0— 1-0
Joseph Bellas	0—17— 2d	Ino Crosby	1—5—9d
Jane Samson	0—9—5d	Christopher Bird	0—10—0d
George Ellwood	0— 3— 0$^1/_2$	Nicholas Lunson	2—7—0$^1/_2$
Samual Ogglethorpe	0—4—5$^1/_2$	Robert Semple	0— 8—10d
Thomas Barton	0— 6—8d	Ino Nicholson	0—2—11d
Isa Stephenson	2—1—9d	Hr Semple	0—0—2d
Mrs Jackson	0— 7-11d	George Harrison Esq	3—19—10$^1/_2$

Robert Atkinson	0—5—5$^1/_2$	William Corry	0—5—11$^1/_2$
Wm Longmire	0—3—0	Joseph Savage	0—11—2$^1/_2$
Betty Bellas	0—7—11d	Matthew Mattinson	0—3—2d
Josh Corry	0—13—10$^1/_2$	Samual Savage	0—11—2$^1/_2$
William Savage	0—0—3$^1/_2$	Richard Metcalf	0—0—3$^1/_2$
Nat Simpson	0—1—5d	Thomas Allen	0—3—11$^1/_2$
Ino M Carlton	1—15—3d	Joseph Horn	0—2—11$^1/_2$
William Lee	0—3—11d	John Horn	0—2—4d
Henry Dent	3—4—7	John Atkinson	0—2—1d
Ino Chappelhow	1—13—8d	*Thomas Heelis Esq	0—16—8d
Samual Richardson	0—13—10$^1/_2$	George Atkinson Esq	1—8—4$^1/_2$
Thomas Robinson	0—8—11d	Matthew Atkinson Esq	0—3—7$^1/_2$
Mrs Jackson	0—6—8d	Lady Suffolk	0—1—0
Thomas Lambert	0—16—6d	Joseph Jackson	0—0—9d
Christopher Gibson	0—2—6d	Jho Workman	0—1—4d
Peggy Franklin	0—8—11	Sythe ?Barn J Ives	0—9—0$^1/_2$
George Relph	0—1—8d	Sythe Hay H Dent	0—8—2d
Ino Monkhouse	1—4—6d	Do Chris Bowness	0—8—2d
Joseph Lambert	0—1—5d	Do Chris Bird	0—1—6d
Robert Wilson	0—17—10	Signed	
Isa Dixon	0—1—5d	George Harrison, Henry Dent	
Bow Harrison	0—1—0d		

* *Thomas Heelis was agent to Lord Thanet at Appleby Castle. He was the great-great-grandfather of Willie Heelis husband of Beatrix Potter.*

Any stranger could be removed from the parish if they were unable to find work within forty days or who did not rent a property worth £10 per annum.

In the Appleby Quarter Sessions for 1741 a remand case is recorded for the 12th of January asking for counsel s opinion about Edmund Ellwood, wife Elizabeth and children Daniel 13, Lydia 11, and Ann 6 removed from Dufton to Bolton. Bolton appealed against the removal. Thomas Cowper of Dufton gave evidence that Ellwood had absconded at Michaelmas but had not been seen since. Ellwood had been an apprentice of William Bowness of Bolton when the last Rebellion was. Bowness refused to give evidence. Cowper said that in 1726 Ellwood had bought a house in Dufton and sold it in 1737. Doubts arose about the value of the evidence and it was counsel s opinion that Ellwood s settlement was in Bolton. A long dispute followed about payment from Dufton to Bolton for Ellwood s parish relief.

Registers of those receiving poor relief were kept and paupers were required to wear a large letter P on their clothing with the initials of their parish. The Settlement Act allowed this just as it allowed strangers to settle in a new parish if they first obtained a certificate from their own parish agreeing to take them back if they fell on Parish Relief.

The Speenhamland system of 1795 encouraged employers to reduce wages because they knew the parish would make up the difference and claims for poor relief went up considerably.

In 1828 Edward Jackson curate wrote: *The following will show a few instances of the number of acres in each persons occupation and the amount of the poor rate per acre assessed thereon for the year 1828.*

No of Acres	Occupiers name	Rate Per Acre	x by no of rates per year
300	John Dixon, Lodge	$3^3/_4$	$1-1^1/_2$
206	Robert Hodgeson Bewly Castle	$5^1/_4$	$1-6d$
28	Matt Atkinson Esq	$3^3/_4$	$1-0^1/_2d$
82	Jon Lancaster	$5^1/_2$	$1-6^1/_2d$
4	James Atkinson	$8^1/_4$	$2-5d$
35	John Stephenson (vicars)	$3^3/_4$	$1-1^1/_2d$
70	Thomas Todd	$6^3/_4$	$2-0d$
110	Thomas Barton	4	$1-2d$
120	Richard Heslop	$2^3/_4$	$0-9^1/_2d$
102	Thomas Steel	6	$1-9d$
13	Curate of Bolton	$8^1/_4$	$2-5d$
153	John Dent	$5^3/_4$	$1-0d$
17	Sam Gibson	$9^3/_4$	$2-10d$
12	Johnathan Gibson	$8^1/_2$	$2-5^3/_4d$
41	Thomas Nicholson	9	$2-7^1/_2d$
73	James Savage	$9^1/_2$	$2-9^1/_4d$
69	Mr Moses	$3^1/_2$	$1-0^1/_4d$
81	William Slack	$6^1/_2$	$1-10d$
66	Richard Tinkler Esq	$6^3/_4$	$1-11^1/_2d$
31	Robert Temple	$5^1/_4$	$1-6d$

NB - In the year 1800 the poor rate was rated by ox gang and amounted to £50-16-0d. The township and tithes raised £46-3-5d and Bewley Castle £4-13-5d. Since that time the rates have been raised by valuation and amount to £56-12-10d. The township and tithes raise £51-11-1d and Bewley Castle manor £5-1-9d. Signed Edw. Jackson.

CHANGING TIMES

Did the method of collecting the poor rate have to be changed in order to bring in more revenue to meet an increased demand in Bolton?

The Poor Law Amendment Act of 1834 greatly reduced the provision of relief and the work houses were made so unpleasant that they were seen as a last resort. Many old people today fear going into a care home as it is reminiscent of the old work house.

The Overseers account book for Bolton for the years 1787-1910 survives in the County Record Office and gives details of regular payments to the poor of Bolton and occasional payments to others. Payment stopped when people found work. Relief could also be given in the form of food or clothing. Some extracts from the Overseers book are as follows:

1797 to Dr Bushby for delivering Jane Nixon 10/6d cash paid for Do laying in 10/6d. Doctor John Bushby was surgeon to Appleby Gaol. His wife died in April 1807 aged 35 and is buried in Bolton Churchyard.

1798 Expenses Journey to Carlisle 2 days 3/-.

1799 Cash paid for repairing the work house.*
* Here is evidence of Bolton s work house, but where was it? Some inhabitants think it may have been in the field at the cross roads bounded by the Pinfold on one side, and Elm Close on the other. There certainly appears to have been some sort of building there by the very uneven ground and boulders that can be seen.

May 26th Ino Robinson for straw £1-4 -0d
28th Nicholas Dent 18/-
To Thomas Barney - 1100 Flacks 1/10d. Cutting Wattling

The field to the west of the crossroads where the workhouse may have been.

To thatching 5 yds at 11/- a yard
To mending Thatch 17/7d
31st to Robert Marfan for a window 0-5-0d
June 1st To Ino Longmire for Leading Straw 0-3-0d
June 6th To Ester Nixon for leading ? 0-4-0d
Ditto for leading wattling 0-1-0d
June 15th to N Dent for repairing the door 0-2-0d
March 25th to Ino Nicholson for wattling and lime 0-14-0d

Dereck Longmire says that perhaps the work house was not only being repaired but extended at this time as the account book itemises the cost of straw and distinguishes between repairing thatching and thatching.

Monies paid out regularly to Susan and Ester Nixon, James White, Isaac Wilkinson, Eliza Miller, John Stephenson
1805 Paid to William Hutchinson for the wife and child of James Shaw a substitute in the militia for John Spedding from 12th march to 10th June14 weeks at 2/8d per week.

December 2nd Paid for 2 stamps at 1/6d (crossed out) each 3/7$^{1}/_{2}$d.
Someone couldn t do his sums!
January 1st Paid to William Corry to keeping a poor man 5/-
To Nathan Simpson's daughter for watching on Isabel Addison before let to board 6/-
Paid to Nathan Simpson for Isobel Addison's board £1-14-0d
Paid to Issac Wilkinson Mill Island Land Rent 7/9$^{1}/_{2}$. Expenses during the

measurement of the land and a boy for assistance £2- 6- 0d
March 15th To Ester Nixon for Isobel Addison 4/-
17th Paid to Nathan Simpson for Isobel Addison £1- 12- 0d
Paid to William Allen For Isobel Addison s clock £1 —14-0d
21st paid to Ester Nixon for Isobel 4/0d
28th
April 4th
October 3rd 1809 Paid to making a shift for Isobel 6d

It would appear that there was money to be made out of the poor law if an individual was prepared to act as foster parent or carer.

May 10th 1808 a memorandum at the vestry meeting held at the church:
We the undersigned being a majority do agree that the master of the Grammar school shall keep in a regular manor the books and accounts belonging to the township of Bolton and that he shall be allowed for his trouble 20 shillings annually at least for the first year.   Signed: Edward Jackson curate, Will Swainson, Sam Ogglethorpe, John Abram, John Nicholson, Will Allan, Thomas Lambert, Thomas Barton, Will Nicholson

CHANGING TIMES

Memo - Thomas Crosby was public let to board to William Longmire for one year beginning June 8th 1812 at 4/6d a week

Meeting of 17th March 1808 - Following resolution it was agreed to alteration made by a majority of the people present whose names are unto subscribed 1st that Issac Wilkinson shall only receive 1 shilling per week.

The following particulars were agreed upon at the vestry meeting held at Bolton Church this 15 day of April 1809:

Isaac Wilkinson 2/-d
James Parkin 1/-
Elizabeth Corry 1/-
John Bowlerwell 3/-
Elizabeth Miller 2/-
John Stephenson 2/-
Mary Idle 1/-
Ester Nixon 1/6d
Thomas Yare 6/-
Sent to Isobel farmer 1-1-0d

Witnessed Ed Jackson, Will Swainson, Wm Allen, Chris Gibson, John Lambert, Will Longmire, Thomas Barton, John Nicholson

26th November 1821 overseers shall shake the whole truth out of Stephen Longmire — they are puzzled what to do as he has disowned his wife — the doctor to advise - stone of meal awarded.

To Richard Bellas new coat waistcoat and britches to establish him as school master.

Sarah Mason ill relief as act of Mercy

Will Graham and Will Murry passage to America.

H. Bird taken before the magistrate 31st March 1828 refusal to pay poor rate

27th May 1824 Richard Metcalf brought his wife and three children — not theirs and it was ordered that his goods should be fetched and he have a room in the poor house.

Dinah Lunson Baptised 4th March 1790 daughter of Jane Lunson.

1st January 1798 To Nicholas Lunson for Dinah 0-12-6d

2nd March 1798	*0-12-6d*
7th October 1799	*£1-5-0d*
1st June 1800	*12-6d*

December 1805 To Stephen Longmire for Dinah

2nd June 1805 to board with John Horn at 2-5d per week until the 6th March. He is to carry her to Dr Taylor as often as the Dr requires within that time.

Paid to Dr. 9 Weeks £1-1-9d

6th March 1805 Dinah entered with Stephen Longmire for 3-3d per week

3rd June 1808 Bought of Robert for Dinah

1 Hanky 2-2d

A Petticoat 3-3d

A Shift 3-9d

Clogs and cokering 4-0d

7th June 1805   Making Dinah a petticoat and shift 0-1-2d

10th June1805 to Stephen Longmire 1 week 3 days 4-11d

Dinah entered to board at Coupland Beck for 2-0d a week for a year

4th January 1806 Paid to Matt Mattinson and Thomas Teasdale $1^1/_2$

years Dinah

15th February 1806 Bought from Robert Atkinson for Dinah

3yds of Duffle 7-6d

$2^1/_2$ yds for shift 2-$0^1/_2$ d

1 Handkerchief 1-10d

$1^1/_2$ yds for Apron 1-0d

6 yds Calico 6-0d

Lining 0-11d

25th April paid Mary Nicholson for mending Dinah's gown 0-1-0d

31 May 1806 Matt Mattinson and Thomas Teasdale 28 weeks 2-6d, yarn 1-0d

15th November 1806 Grace Carr a petticoat for Dinah 6-0d

Mary Nicholson mending 0-3d

1st January 1807 half year board £2 12-0d

5th April 1807 Close as ye bill £1-8-10 1/2d

1st May 1807 Dinah board 20 weeks at 2-10d £2-0-0d

19th September Dinah new shift, for Thread and making 9/-

1st January 1808 New Clogs 4-3d

2nd October 1808 2 pairs of clogs caulking 1-0d

New shoes and mending1-6d

New clasp and hat nib 9d

6 Dec 1808 Board 25 weeks at 2-6d, £3- 2-6d

New bed gown and linen 8-8d

To an every day hand ? 1-6d

10 Dec 1808 To one weeks board 2-0d

17 Dec 1808 A pair new shoes 10-6d

23 Dec 1808 2 pairs stockings 5d

12 March 1808 New petticoat $3^1/_2$ yds 8-6d

8 April 1808 A new Gown 7-0d

20 May 1808 Making and lining a new gown 2-8d

Will Swainson for board £1-16-0d

The treatment of people in times gone by always appeared to be very harsh

H.B.

Dinah Lunson

but the above account of poor relief given to the care of little Dinah does appear to have been very kind. Derek Longmire says of his observation of the Court Rolls at the time that Brougham held the manor that the poor were treated with kindness. Dinah s visits to Doctor Taylor in 1805 may have been because of an illness but perhaps because of the care given to her she may have been delicate in some way. Dinah was the illegitimate daughter of Jane Lunson who died March 20th 1797 aged about 30 when Dinah was seven years old. From the list of clothes one can imagine Dinah s transition from childhood to young adult hood. Much of the money for her care was paid to male members of the community. It was a very patriarchal society. However it would have been the female members of the families she was boarded with who would have done the caring. Dinah died in March 1817 aged 27 years, nine years after the last entry in the overseers book. What happened to her in the intervening years? Would she have lived so long if she had not received the care? Why did n t her extended family care for her? She had a grandfather, aunts and uncles in the village. Their own lives appear to have been poor so perhaps they were unable to carry the additional burden.

It is assumed that Elizabeth, Agnes and Isobel are Nicholas Lunson s offspring. No baptism entries are entered in the parish registers for any of the girls or marriages for Elizabeth, Agnes or Nicholas himself.

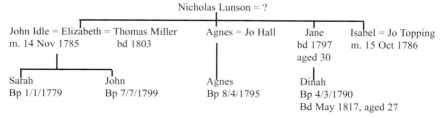

Nicholas Lunson = ?

John Idle = Elizabeth = Thomas Miller	Agnes = Jo Hall	Jane	Isobel = Jo Topping
m. 14 Nov 1785 bd 1803		bd 1797	m. 15 Oct 1786
		aged 30	

Sarah	John	Agnes	Dinah
Bp 1/1/1779	Bp 7/7/1799	Bp 8/4/1795	Bp 4/3/1790
			Bd May 1817, aged 27

BOLTON'S POOR

The poor in Bolton appear from the records to have been treated with some humanity but there is no comparison with today s system of social welfare.

There is evidence to show that the care did not stop when a youngster reached the age to be able to work as shown by an apprentice indenture dated 5th May 1787: *Richard Bellas and Isaac Stephenson Chapel warden of the chapelry of Bolton and James Savage overseer of the poor of the said parish. Put and placed Mary Addison a poor child of the said parish to Matthew Hanson of Brampton Stone Mason To dwell and serve from this day until the full age of seventeen years. To be instructed in the best manner in the art of Housewifery.*

It is further agreed the officers to give Matthew Hanson the sum of £1 13/- towards clothing the apprentice and the said Matthew Hanson is to give her two suits of clothing at the end of the term one for the working day and the other for holidays.

Bolton Charities

The trustees of charities do not have the right to use the funds in their jurisdiction just as they choose. They must always keep to the instructions as laid down by the charity even if that charity was formed many years ago. There are many influences that affect the discharge of the duties of the charities. For example the change in the value of money, the change in the standards of living, the founding of the Health and Social Services.

The charities for Bolton are :-

Number 237904	Harrison s Charity	Income £12-80p (today's value)
240978	Charity of John Blaymire	Income £0-25p
237903	General George & William Bowness	Income £4-0p
240933	Poor Stock	Income £2-0p

The correspondent for all the above charities is the vicar of Bolton

Mary Clarkson undertook a review of the charities on behalf of Westmorland County Council between 1967-1973. Copies can be seen in the reference section of Penrith Library. The above charities are also mentioned in the chapter on the church.

Another source of income for relief of the poor was the money from the Willows. The Willows land is today still in trust for the village people and the money gained from letting the land is distributed equally between the inhabitants of the village. The land is managed by the trustees: Christopher Butterworth, Frank Baxter, Harold Forester, Dennis Dent and George Ellwood.

Edward Jackson was curate for Bolton from 1799-1834. He was always interested in the life and history of the village and often made representations to the vestry meetings about matters that concerned him. The following is a letter to the members of the vestry meeting from Edward about the Willows Land:

From upwards of 30 years observation by me Edward Jackson, the oldest and most authentic account respective of a parcel of ground called the Willows from it being formerly overgrown with Willow bushes now about 10 or 20 acres is from the oldest people living in Bolton and an old book of accounts is as follows. Originally it contained a number of horse baits which belonged to the land owners of Bolton who baited their horses occasionally but find that some got more advantage than others — an agreement was entered into to sell it to form and appropriate rents to relief of the poor or to take it for any other necessary public use accordingly it was let to Joseph Corry by a jury appointed for that purpose for £4 per annum. The letting either annually for a term of years by a jury or overseer and inhabitants being present has continued ever since the rent increasing till it now amounts to £30 per annum. Out of the rent hath been saved £10 church stock which was payed out together with £200 Queens Bounty in the purchase of the estate in the Orton Parish for which the curate pays annually 1/11d part of the rent, half to the church warden and half to the overseers. Out of the rent the mole catchers wages, the church rate, water leasing and draining, the said ground have been taken against the remaining rent. Bewley Castle and the Tithes have invariably been rated when nothing has been taken, then they have been rated against the whole the rate was formerly by ox gang but since 1806 has been by value. There was formerly an Estate in Bolton consisting of a Dwelling house and upwards of 4 acres of land 12½ Grasses in the Low Moor and 4 Horse Baitings in the Willows, belonging to a family named Brougham from an old writing it appears that this Estate had been valued previous to sale — the value is £35- 15- 6d

12½ Grasses 4 each £2 — 10 — 0d

4 Horse Baitings in the Willows Assumed no value at the time of valuation

The above Estate was sold in parcels and the dwelling House and upwards of 20 acres of land was purchased with the Queens Bounty to the Chapel at Bolton to which at present it belongs. What became of the 4 horse baitings whether they are mentioned in the deeds at the Bounty Office I have not had the opportunity of ascertaining but this I know that for the space of upwards of 30 years I have received a certain portion of the rent of the Willows annually in the years 1804 I received 8/11d if it was not for the four baitings I can not tell what it was for - Bewley Castle which has no right upon the commission when divided and the tithes previous to commutation were always excluded from any benefits arising from the lands and were rated against the rent. Two exceptions only can I remember in the course of 34 years — which was immediately rectified by a regular adjustment signed by the magistrates. There has been with the new farmers both of Bewley castle and the Tithes a little scruple about paying against the Willows they not understanding the nature of it. But the late Henry Dent father of the present John Dent who had a very good estate in the Township for many years and who was lessee of half the Hay Tithes always reaped benefit for his own estate and of the Willows rent but never refused pay his portion for the tithes against it. I believe it is the option of the inhabitants of Bolton appropriate the Willows rent to what ever purpose they may think proper without regards to the owners and farmers of Bewley Castle and the Tithes

Edward Jackson Curate of Bolton.

Health and Social Care

Several people living in the village work within the health and social care services and the following cameos will give some comparison of delivery of health and social care between that of 1800 and the year 2000.

Anne Graham lives at The Larches at North End. In 1983 she attended Preston Polytechnic College to study for a diploma in social work and then went to work as a social worker for Cumbria County Council. She works from the office in Friargate. Penrith and her speciality is elderly care. She visits elderly people in their own homes, hospitals and care homes and her work involves assessing people to enable them to live in their own home, advising about entitlement to benefits and arranging crisis care. She has responsibility for a huge area travelling from Penrith to Kirkby Stephen, Shap, and the Yorkshire border including villages in-between. Bolton also falls within this area. The work has become increasingly difficult since Anne started as a social worker, with a larger case load, little time to do the counselling for which she was trained and fewer resources with which to do the job.

Prior to be coming a social worker Anne was a qualified driver of heavy goods vehicles. She taught her husband Mike to drive an articulated vehicle. Mike and Anne moved to Bolton from Little Salkeld in 1983. Anne originates from Embleton and Mike from Warcop.

When **Ann Shepherd** first left school she cycled to Bolton from Kings Meaburn to work in the plastics factory, on the site of Mr and Mrs Coward's house. She worked there for three months trimming plastic toys after they came out of the mould and then painting them.

When she left there she went to Carlisle as a nanny for a year. From there she moved to Brougham Castle to work for Mr and Mrs Slack. When she married Ken she moved to Bolton and worked for a time in the school canteen until her children Claire and Timothy were born.

About 18 years ago Ann started work as a home carer with Cumbria County Council just as the title and the role were changing over from home help to home carer. The work involved lighting fires, preparing meals, washing and ironing. In the course of her work she covered many miles, Penrith to Glenridding to Brough and all the villages down the fell side including Bolton. Ann was successful in obtaining a certificate in care from City and Guilds to qualify her for the job. The job has changed over the years with the focus becoming increasingly more on the caring aspect. For example bathing, showers, toileting, dressing, getting people up and putting them to bed. It is important for her to communicate with social workers, nurses, doctors and members of the family.

HEALTH & SOCIAL CARE

Ten years ago she became a patch worker with the added responsibility of organising work rotas for other members of the team. Ann now worked along side the social worker and her area stretched from Shap, Tebay and along the Fellside. Reorganisation came and Ann decided to relinquish her role as patch worker to develop her caring role. The service is now managed by a private company Cumbria Care to which Social Services contracts out. As with other areas in health and social services the service is suffering from lack of money for training and resources.

Hazel Mullen works at Eden Grove School as a school nurse. She was born at Great Asby and after her education in Appleby went to Edinburgh for nurse training. She became an Enrolled Nurse (a training that is not available now) and returned to Cumbria to marry and have a family. Once the children were old enough she returned to nursing taking a post at Kirkby Stephen within the district nursing team. She was there for four years but had always nurtured an ambition to become a Registered General Nurse. However it was not until she left Kirkby Stephen and went to work at Eden Grove that she was able to begin the further training required to do this.

Hazel s role at Eden Grove is to over see the general health and welfare of the boys there. When they first arrive she carries out an assessment and registers them with the Appleby doctors. She cares for them if they are ill and is a listening ear if the boys need to talk about any problems they may have. She also has responsibility for the different medicines the boys may have to take. This area of her work is increasing as more of the conditions the boys suffer from can be treated or kept under control with drugs. She has a responsibility to liaise with the parents.

Health care is forever changing and Hazel has a personal responsibility to keep her knowledge up to date by attending refresher and new courses. A record of courses attended has to be kept and written up to be presented to the UKCC if required prior to renewal of her registration every three years.

Margaret Jones, nee Sowerby, (a long established Westmorland family) came from Morland to live in the village 15 years ago. At first she lived in the headmaster s bungalow at Eden Grove where her husband Andy works, moving three years ago to Whinfell View. Margaret started her training at the Cumberland Infirmary, Carlisle in 1965 and after qualifying as a State Registered Nurse worked in the general theatre assisting with surgical operations.

She left nursing to get married and bring up a family before returning to work part time as a district nurse at Appleby in 1983. In 1987 she was successful in completing a district nursing course. In the course of her work she travels to nurse people in their homes within a five mile radius of Appleby. Prior to 1983 her role was task orientated, doing such things as bathing patients and getting them up and perhaps putting them to bed at night. She now cares for people who would previously have gone into hospital for treatment. For example newly diagnosed diabetics would have gone into hospital to be stabilised on insulin. This is now carried out in the patient s own home. Patients with terminal illnesses are also nursed in the comfort of their own home. Margaret also has the responsibility of managing a small team of nurses. She needs good communication skills to liaise with other professionals, other team members, patients and relatives and she is responsible for keeping her professional knowledge up to date in the same way as Hazel.

Barbara Cotton moved to live in the village with her husband Derick in 1992 on Derick's early retirement from the RAF. Barbara completed her nurse training with the United Sheffield Hospitals (The Royal Infirmary, The Jessop Hospital for Women and the Sheffield Childrens Hospital) in 1964. After qualifying she worked for a short time in general theatre before moving to become a staff nurse on a male surgical ward at Doncaster Royal Infirmary.

Marriage and bringing up a young family, plus the many inevitable moves with the RAF meant a career break of several years. After midwifery training at Mill Road Maternity Unit in 1975/6, followed by health visitor training at Stevenage she spent five years working as a health visitor in and around Peterborough. The hours were not really compatible with bringing up a still comparatively young family and when an opportunity arose to teach health-related subjects at Peterborough Regional College she took it. Working in education gave her the opportunity to gain a teaching qualification and a degree in Health Science from Leicester University.

After moving to Bolton she spent about four years teaching first at Kendal College and then at Carlisle. The past four and a half years have been spent as a health visitor working from Shap and Temple Sowerby surgeries. The role is that of public health nurse, supporting and educating people to maintain good health, the priority being families with children under five. Liaison with colleagues, other professionals, clients and relatives are very much part of the role. A wide knowledge of health and social care, good communication skills, counselling and facilitating skills are required. Health visitors are registered on the nurse register with the UKCC (Registered General Nurse is a requirement for health visitor training). Barbara is also required to keep her professional knowledge up to date in the same way as Hazel and Margaret.

Dr Tim Young lives in the village with his wife Fiona and children Kirsty, Katrina and Iona. Kirsty attended the village school before going to Appleby Grammar School. Katriona and Iona are still at the village school.

Doctor Tim MB ChB qualified in Edinburgh in 1982. He worked in hospitals in Edinburgh and West Lothian during his pre-registration year and then went on to complete three years GP training. After this training he looked for a post in general practice and whilst he was looking spent a year working in opthalmics. When Dr Donald Ainscough retired Dr Tim joined Dr Gavin Young at the Temple Sowerby surgery. Before moving to Bolton in 1988, Tim and Fiona lived in Temple Sowerby for a year.

Doctor Tim has seen many changes in medical practice since he qualified but perhaps two of the most significant changes have been the introduction of CuDoc (the out of hours call system) and computerisation. Medical advances have also brought about change. Patients no longer have to put up with their ailments because of new discoveries. Patients are more informed because of information to be found in the media, newspapers, magazines, radio, television and more recently the internet. All the above plus the introduction of the Patients Charter have raised peoples expectations and as a consequence the work-load has increased not only for the doctor but also for all medical personnel.

Fiona met Tim at Edinburgh University where she was studying maths. After graduating she went to work in a stockbrokers for six and a half years. When she and Tim moved to Cumbria she worked with a stockbroker in Carlisle before she was made redundant after the big bang of 1987. Fiona then spent a short period of time working in the Midland Bank in Appleby before going to work at the Cumberland Infirmary, Carlisle in the personnel department.

Kirsty was six months old when Fiona went back to work, this time to the surgery to help with the computerisation. She then became computer manager and was also very involved at home with the running of the practice. Out of hours she was the first point of contact for patients and she had to take all the messages and relay them to Doctor Tim if it was his turn to be on call. On call duty came around often prior to the introduction of CuDoc.

Whilst Fiona was still working at the surgery she began a teacher training course with the Open University and qualified as a teacher in 1999. Since then she has taught numeracy at Bolton School and maths at Ullswater School. Supporting Tim with his work, raising a family and looking after a home and studying in order to develop her own career has meant a very busy and full life for Fiona.

Linda Prance came to live in the village in 1988 with her husband John and two children Adam and Joanna. They moved from Watford into the house Mary Sowerby had owned which was then known as East View but is now called Apple Garth. John was instrumental in getting the guide hut rebuilt in Appleby, was a member of the Village Hall committee and in 1992 directed the village concert The Bolton Barnstormers. Prior to moving to Bolton John and Linda s main hobby had been amateur dramatics.

Linda had always been in a job where she met people and she very much prefers the face to face interaction. In September 2000 she applied for and was successful in being accepted for a post in the surgery at Temple Sowerby working with Dr Tim and Dr Gavin as a receptionist. She is the first point of contact with the patients when they need help from a doctor.

Today many more people are employed in the health and social services than 200 years ago and it is organised in a more formal and structured way. In 1800 the doctor would have been a lone worker with perhaps some help from one of the village women at the birth of a child, or to sit with some one if they were very ill. His housekeeper or wife would have taken any messages that would be delivered on foot. The doctor would have made up his own lotions and potions in his dispensary and the efficacy of them would have been very suspect. In fact today we would find them laughable. In the Kendal archives there are several prescriptions for medicines for different individuals and a commonly occurring direction is to sleep on a shilling for variable lengths of time, presumably depending on the complaint. Our medicines are much more sophisticated and we know they work.

Health care is free at the point of delivery. Two hundred years ago it would have been a major expense for a family. However today some items do have to be paid for by those who are able to afford them for example eye tests or a contribution to social care. A variety of social security benefits are available to help those in need.

The distances travelled today are much greater than in 1800 but then the motor car makes it possible. A pony and trap would not allow the health or social care professional to travel very quickly in order to attend an emergency.

People live to a much greater age today and consequently suffer more diseases associated with age such as arthritis, heart disease and cancer. In 1800 people would not expect to live much beyond 50. Dr Bushby's wife died at 35 years of age and this would be considered very young to day.

The contraceptive pill has meant that women do not have a child every year so gone are the days when big families were the norm. It is very unusual for a woman or child to die in childbirth. Children are better nourished and are protected by vaccination against infectious diseases, which killed so many of them years ago.

The doctor would have had to rely on previous experience and a training more unsophisticated than today to make a diagnosis. There were no aids such as x-rays or scans. Many illnesses and discomforts had to be tolerated, as there were no treatments the doctor could use to cure them. Our quality of life today is so much improved that perhaps we take it all for granted.

Bolton School

It is known from the church records that at least two of the curates of Bolton were licensed to teach school. Nathanial Beck in 1663 and John Breeks in 1693 and Robert Nelson taught school in the years 1673, 1675 1678,1671-1673, 1675-1678. William Martin was licensed in 1674. He perhaps came from Warcop and was the son of the vicar there. William Parkin taught from 1680-81. He was formerly schoolmaster at Orton and Warcop. He was curate of Asby and ordained a priest in 1687.

There may have been a separate school but it is more likely that the classes were held in the in the curate s house which abutted the church yard. In smaller endowed schools and chapelry schools it was frequently the curates who were in charge and not all were well educated men. Good schoolmasters and clever scholars could move to the better endowed establishments.

The key to the growth of education in the area appears to be in the five major grammar schools acquiring close relationships with Cambridge and Oxford for the establishment of scholarships and exhibitions. Some of those Westmorland people who became successful in their chosen field would then take an interest in their old school and county.

There is evidence that a free endowed school has existed in Bolton since 1731. It may have stood in the track leading on to Mr Ewbank's land between

Glynn House used to be the home for the head teacher of the old school.

Bolton School at the turn of the 20th century. Today the school is a private residence and is the home of Mr. and Mrs. Neilson who run a bed and breakfast business in the house.

The Poplars and the new houses at Hill Crest. The school was built by subscription and endowed with several benefactions to pay for its costs. James Hanson, curate of Bolton, left 40/- to the school in his will dated 1st July 1721 and his widow gave a further 10/- *for teaching four or more of the poorest children of the inhabitants of Bolton.* A verse from Hanson's epitaph reads —

> *In memory of James Hanson*
> *Who to this town poor out of his store,*
> *His last will makes relation;*
> *Ten pounds he gave and forty more*
> *For children s education*

This money was initially used to buy land which later sold for 100/-. Joseph Railton, a successful London merchant, endowed 40/- *for the poorest children in the township.* William Bowness gave 50/- in 1762, *the income to come once in every seven years. The singing master to teach the inhabitants to sing Psalms in chapel, otherwise for the instruction of poor children.* William s son George was educated at Bolton School and Appleby Grammar School and became a Major General in the British Army. Dr Michael Richardson a clergyman in Berkshire gave 50/- in 1765. Nicholas Dent gave 50/- in 1782 and 21/- by bequest of John Fallowfield in 1802: *for the education of two of the poorest children.*

BOLTON SCHOOL

The school was rebuilt on the old site (where Tarka House is today) in 1856 at a cost of upwards of £500 paid for by Mr Richard Tinkler of Eden Grove. There was no accommodation for the master but later Glynn House became available for the head teacher.

In 1865 the school was described as - a mixed elementary village school. There was one master receiving 13/- a year from endowment and 32/- from fees and other sources. Between 30 and 40 boys and girls attended the school and most were described as being very young. Thirteen paid a reduced fee of 1/- a quarter on account of the endowment.

The school was not connected to any religious denomination but prayers were said before and after school and a Sunday school was held. The village green was the playground. The school was open for 46 weeks of the year and the children spent 5 hrs 45 min a day in school and had two breaks for recreation. The subjects taught were English, writing and mathematics. One of the benefactors had also recommended that Latin be taught.

The school was governed by the master and three yeomen of Bolton. Any vacancies that occurred were filled by persons voted in by the remaining governors. In 1867 the Trustees were — Rev W. Shepherd, Colonel Rigg, J Dent, yeoman, M Savage, yeoman, T . Simpson, yeoman and the master was W. Jennings.

The schools in the area were inspected just as our schools are today and there follows an account of school inspector Mr. D. C. Richmond s report in the late 1860s: *On account of the 13/- a year arising from the endowment, 13 children are instructed at a reduced charge of 1/- a quarter. Instruction in Latin is prescribed by one of the benefactors, but it is not now taught, nor does the master profess to be able to teach it. A new building was erected by private munificence*

The new school in autumn 1963.

CHANGING TIMES

Bolton School c 1920. Pictured left to right, back row - Earny Arnsion, Maggy Clark, Frank Morland, Jenny Hodgson, John Graham, Annie Walton, Jeremy Graham.
Row 2 - Annie Bellas, Alan Robinson, Mary Graham, Sissy Walton, Mona Bell, John Simpson.
Row 3 - Spiers Jackson, Mable Simpson, Sid Smaile, Margaret Graham, Billy Jackson, Mary Jackson, Charlie Walton.
Front row - James Oliver, Florence Jackson, Isabel Graham, Jim Bell, Francis Bird, Muriel Walton, Edna Arnison and Billy Howe.

in 1856, which contains besides the school room a library and reading room for the use of the township. There is fair accommodation for the 30 to 40 children belonging to the school most of them being very young. Only 20 were present on this occasion, and only one had reached 12 yrs of age the average even in the highest class was but 10 yrs. Their attainments were of a very modest kind: in arithmetic three only had advanced so far as the reduction of money, the rest being either too young to have begun the subject, or at the best practising the simple rules. The spelling of a few boys was comparatively good, and pains had been taken with them to inculcate some principles of English grammar but geography and English history are not attempted. The girls on the whole are more backward than the boys, and their attempts to write a very easy passage from dictation betrayed in several cases almost complete ignorance.

The master has been at the school two years, and is still a very young, man.

105

BOLTON SCHOOL

*It is found very difficult to secure the services of a practiced or a highly quali-
fied teacher on so small a remuneration as is here offered, but it would seem to
require neither long experience, nor superior attainments to raise the average
proficiency of these children.*

Mrs Maisie Parkin was head teacher at Bolton school for 27 years. Prior to
coming to Bolton she was a teacher at Appleby for six and a half years. It was
whilst she was at Appleby that she met her husband Allan who had left the RAF
after National Service and was gaining some experience of teaching before
going for teacher training at Kirby College, Liverpool. When their first child
came along Mrs Parkin took a short career break to care for her. She returned
to full time teaching at Bolton in 1957. The first six years of her appointment
as head was in the old school with an assistant Mrs Waiting who had a gift for
teaching children to read.

Space in the old school was at a premium and many former pupils will
remember having to walk to the old corrugated church hall for school dinners.
The school plays also had to be performed there.

During Mrs Parkin's time at the school she collected many photographs and
memories of the children she taught there. One of her memories is of Thomas
Savage in one of the school plays. He had the part of a grandfather clock. When
it was time for the clock to strike he was supposed to say Tic Toc very slowly.
At the moment he was supposed to say his words no sound could be heard and
he couldn t be seen inside his costume. A teacher had to creep round and give
him a little poke. The clock started to tic away very fast indeed.

Mrs Parkin can remember another play when the young lady who was to play
the Queen of the Fairies was away and it appeared that she may not be back in
time for the play and so she gave the part to Margaret Fleming who made a
lovely fairy. The original leading lady returned two days before the play and
was so cross she had been replaced she took one of the queen s dresses and hid
it!

Mrs Parkin often thinks of children who were in her care. She remembers
with affection Dennis Fleming who was so mischievous and such a practical
joker. Adrian Hewitt another lively youngster and full of fun; sadly Adrian was
killed on his motor bike on the Keswick Road.

Mrs Parkin remembers the Harrison children and Judith Metcalf as being very
helpful and polite. She feels privileged to have taught Jean Robinson who
achieved her ambition to become a doctor. She remembers the Shatz children
with their good looks and many, many more. She identified all the children on
two school photographs and she had a story to tell about each one most of them
happy but some of them sad. The afternoon passed all too quickly with this dedicated teacher who retired in 1984.

Bolton School circa 1950. Pictured, left to right, back row - Mrs. Waiting, Michael Allinson, Adrian Fleming, Brian Nicholson, James Bell, Joe Harrison, Mrs. Parkins.
Row 1 - Margaret Harrison, Jean Tatters, George Hall, Jeffrey Wills, Margaret Fleming, ?, Thomas Savage, Richard Birkbeck, Judith Metcalf, Ann Thompson.
Row 2 - Anne Ellwood, Gwenny Bell, Margaret Ellwood, Allan Fleming, Annette Trueman, ?, Rosemary Dent, Neil Richardson, Linda Park, Sandra Carrick, Mary Harrison.
Front row - ?, Kathleen Stubbs, Dennis Flemming, Paul Schatz, Derek Murray, Peter Hutchinson, Richard Hall, Robert Harrison, Susan Birkbeck, Janice Schatz.

The school today stands on a new site and was opened in the 1960s by the chairman of the North Westmorland Rural Council, Mr J. W. Millray. It was built at a cost of £17,000 and was designed by the county architect Mr W. R. Wark to the latest specifications of the time.T he three main rooms could be made into one by a removable partition.

In 2000 the school had 38 pupils - 14 boys and 23 girls - and ages ranging from four to eleven. Vanessa Richards appointed in 1994 is the head teacher and there are two teachers. The school has infant and junior playgrounds and a sports field. A varied curriculum offers a range of extra curricular activities including a computer club, netball and football clubs, guitar, recorder, clarinet and flute tuition, school productions and residential visits. The school has strong links with the local community and supports a variety of charities.

The approach to discipline is one of high expectations of behaviour with consideration and respect for one another. Christian values underpin the values of the school. The school rule is *be safe , be considerate.* The school uniform is a green sweatshirt with the school logo. It is optional but most children do wear it.

The OFSTED inspection of October 1997 described the school as being a very good school with excellent features. The head teacher and staff and governors work in partnership with the community to provide a good quality of education to high standards. The progress made by almost all the pupils under five and in years 1 and 2 is either satisfactory or good. Pupils behave very well, they are courteous and friendly and almost all have an excellent attitude to work. Teaching is almost always satisfactory or good and sometimes very good at Key Stage 1. At Key Stage 2 there is a high proportion of very good teaching. Overall there are no serious weaknesses and many strengths. Links with parents and the community are particular strengths of the school. Spiritual and moral dimensions underpin the whole ethos of the school. Children go to Appleby Grammar School at eleven years of age for their secondary education.

The History of Eden Grove

The very early history of Eden Grove is a mystery. It is described in the directories of Westmorland as *a modern mansion in the Elizabethan style.* We know from the church records that it was called Whitfield Brow in the late 1700s when it was the home of Mr. Harrison. The name may have come from a family called Whitfield who lived in Bolton in the mid-1600s. The date of the original building is not known but it is obvious there have been considerable extensions over the years.

In 1824 the owner was Richard Tinkler. He is mentioned as a beneficiary in his uncle s will: *The last will and testament of Francis Tinkler of Street House, in the parish of Warcop, 29 November 1824.*
To Margaret, my wife, household furniture
To my two nieces Mary and Margaret Simpson, a freehold field and enclosed, Kirkby Thore Low Moor, equal shares.
The residue to my nephews Richard Tinkler of Eden Grove and Edward Lamb of Sandford. Witnessed by Richard Tinkler of Bolton, senior; Elizabeth Jackson, Bolton; Edward Jackson, curate of Bolton.

Richard Tinkler died in 1831 aged 71 years. His last will and testament leaves the following property: *To my sisters Margaret Gill, widow and Mary Robinson, widow and Sarah wife of William Simpson, £20 each*
To my niece Sarah Coates, wife of Jo Coates, £30 for her sole and separate use not to be anywise subject to the control debts or engagements of her present or any future husband
To my niece Jayne Robinson, £100
To five sisters, the daughters of my sister Mary Robinson, £30 each
And to Mary Gill s five daughters, £30 each
To the two daughters of Sarah Simpson, £30 each
To my niece Anne Taylor, £30
To my nephews William Gill, Thomas Gill and William Harrison, the sum of £30 each.
To my nephews John Harrison and Tom Harrison £5 each with respect to my nephew Richard Harrison, I leave it entirely to the discretion of my son Richard to do what he thinks best.
An annuity for life to my sister Anne Harrison, yearly the sum of £20, two and a half yearly payments all after one year of death. If anyone should die before the year is up the legacy to pass to any children the executors feel most advantageous. The rest to my son Richard Tinkler.
2nd February 1830, witnessed by William Nicholson, Thomas Nicholson and Edward Jackson.

THE HISTORY OF EDEN GROVE

Richard Tinkler junior is listed in the 1851 census as living at Eden Grove. He was then unmarried, aged 53 years and was a magistrate and landed proprietor born in Middlesex. He died in 1859 aged 61 years.

The house was bought by William Graham on 8 January 1888 in a conveyance between: *Thomas Davis Burney Rawlins of Wimbourne Minster and Maud his wife and William Thompson of Mardale Hall, Lambrigg, and Robert Thompson of Inglewood Bank, Penrith, and of the second part Amelia Isobel Thompson of 15 Sinclair Road, West Kensington, spinster, of the third part Elizabeth Thompson of Mardale Hall, spinster and the fourth part William Graham of Eden Grove, near Appleby.*

Squire Graham

Mr. Graham was born in London and lived at The Lodge, Highbury. He was educated in London and Trinity College, Cambridge, where he studied law. His family originated from Cumbria - he was descended from the Grahams of The Nunnery, Kirkoswald, and his grandparents owned Stone House, Hayton, near Carlisle. After he left Cambridge he moved north and bought Eden Grove where he started farming and stock breeding. The estate was 100 acres but Mr. Graham gradually bought more until it amounted to 1000 acres, much of it pasture land beside the River Eden.

He started breeding shorthorn cattle in 1877 and built up a herd based on good characteristics of the breed rather than any special bloodline. He also bred Clydesdales and in 1888 bought several mares from the dispersal sale of Sir Robert Loder s Clydesdale stud. Shorthorns and Clydesdales were his main interests but he also helped improve the breed of black-faced sheep.

Mr. Graham was a familiar face in public life. At the age of 25 he was made a magistrate and was elected as one of the first aldermen of the county council. He was very interested in local politics but as his agricultural interests increased he found it increasingly difficult to be involved and retired as alderman after 14 years.

In 1890 he served as High Sheriff for Westmorland. He was also chairman of the Penrith Farmers Club, vice-chairman of the Cumberland & Westmorland

Eden Grove

Chamber of Agriculture and a member of the Clydesdale Horse Society. In addition he served for three years as president of the Wensleydale Sheep Breeders Association.

Mr. Graham travelled to Canada and the North West provinces of the United States in 1881 and in 1884 he toured India, New Zealand and Australia. In 1901 he was invited to go to South Africa to attend the inter-colonial show at Bloemfontein to act as referee judge for English horses, cattle and sheep. Sadly he was unable to go as the event was cancelled because of the outbreak of the Boer War.

Mr. Graham enjoyed fishing, shooting and hunting. His hobby was horticulture and he grew cactus dahlias, carnations and sweet peas. The Eden Grove estate extended from Bolton to Appleby and included Redlands Bank farm, Bridge End at Kirkby Thore, Bolton Hall, Mid Town and Pennine View. He married late in life to a Miss Thompson, Kirkby Stephen, and through this marriage took possession of more estates in the Ravenstonedale area.

Although a wealthy man, Mr. Graham was also a gambler and spent his money freely. In 1913 he was indebted to General Palmer of Buckinghamshire for the sum of £24,140. In order to pay the debt he mortgaged Eden Grove to General Palmer as security for £15,000 and Redlands Bank for £8000. On 8 June preparations were being made to transfer the estate to General Palmer s son, Captain Palmer. William Graham was suggesting ways of General Palmer allowing him to continue to live in the house and to enable him to be discharged from bankruptcy.

Robert Davidson was tenant of Redlands Bank and he must have been aware of the trouble brewing and surrendered the tenancy of Redlands Bank and Westley Bank Cottages. As a result of Mr. Graham being declared bankrupt, his property had to be sold and was put up for auction on 22 July 1913. On 23 July the Cumberland Evening News reported the sale as follows:

Sale of Mr. William Grahams Estate at the George Hotel, Penrith, due to bankruptcy - well known shorthorn and Clydesdale breeder. Eden Grove including the mansion and 172 acres - only bid £8,000. For the Bridge End Farm £5,500 bid. Redlands Bank and 251 acres offered in two lots £5,500. The prices offered for these properties did not reach the reserve. All Eden Grove, Redlands Bank and Bridge End were offered together. Having been bid in lots to £18,950 a start offer was made and by bids of £1000, the amount was carried to £30,000. After consultation with the solicitors and the trustees that the vendors needed £40,000 and this had not been covered, so the offer was withdrawn. Lot 2 which was let to Mr. N. Simpson was withdrawn at £275.

Lots 3 & 4, 17 acres withdrawn at £3,400

Lots 4 & 5 Bolton Hall and 108 acres, was bid to £2,800, withdrawn

Lot 6, two freehold fields, eight acres, withdrawn at £275

The first lot to be sold was a three acre meadow at Bolton to Mr. Ellwood from the Post Office £125.

Lot 8, house and land, part of Mid Town farm, and 4 acres withdrawn at £360.

Lot 9 4 acres of old pasture, Mid Town farm started at £50 and was sold at £140 to Mr. Robinson, Bolton

Lot 10 part of Mid Town farm 43 acres, withdrawn at £1,050

Lot 11 A cottage and two acres was sold to Mr. Crowther, Manchester, for £140

Lot 12, Pennine View and 2 acres started at £200 and sold to Mr. Sisson, Appleby

The Lodge Eden Grove

above the market price for £400
Lot 13 pasture, 3 fields, £3,275 to Mr Chapelhow, Bewley Castle
Lot 14 29 acres went to C. Stephenson for £1,200
Lot 15 meadow and pasture 14 acres withdrawn at £300
A cottage used as a reading room was withdrawn at £50 and another let to Mr. T.
Robinson was withdrawn at £90

General Palmer was furious about the outcome of the sale and in a letter to Mr. Graham accuses him of interfering with it. Mr. Graham was a much respected and well liked person in the area and it does seem that the locals may have closed ranks.

It is known that Palmer was in residence at Eden Grove in 1917 because he hosted the ladies of Bolton s fund raising event for the Red Cross in the grounds that year. In 1918 North End farm on the estate was struck by lightening causing £255 of damage. It appears at this time that William Graham was renting Redlands Bank from General Palmer and was trying to persuade the General to sell it to him.

Once he lost his estate, Mr. Graham s health began to fail and he went to live at Culgaith. He died in a nursing home in Cambridge in July 1934 aged 79. His name does not now appear on the official list of High Sheriffs of Westmorland, probably because of his bankruptcy.

Some time in the 1920s Mr. Fred Tatters took over the estate which had been empty for a few years. Fred was married and had seven children - Henry, Jonathan, Charlie, Doris, Emily, Fred and Arthur. There are descendants of this family still living in the village.

During the Second World War Eden Grove was used for evacuees for a short time. It was later rented to Birmingham Wagon Repairs so they could carry on their work away from the bombing in Birmingham. Mr. Tatters kept the land to carry on his farming interests. He was active in village affairs as chairman of the Memorial Hall and for many years he served as a county councillor.

George Ellwood s grandfather, Sam Richardson, was farm manager at Eden Grove when it was owned by Mr. Graham. Tom and Robert Richardson worked on the farm. George can remember coming from his home in Milburn,with his brother to spend his holidays in Bolton. They would race round and round the box hedges. His brother always got a ten yard start and Mr. Graham gave him the penny while George would get a halfpenny.

There is a legend that a ghost haunts the house. It has reportedly been seen by several people and is described as a man, smartly dressed in a sports coat and flannels. It is accompanied by the sweet smell of carnations and cigarette or cigar smoke.

After the Birmingham Wagon Repairs company moved, Eden Grove became a county council property and was used for a short time for educational activities before it became Eden Grove School.

Eden Grove School

Eden Grove School was opened in 1952 after the building was bought by the Cole brothers Tom and Cyril. Tom had worked with children described then, as educationally subnormal (ESN). Cyril had been a classics teacher. They decided to open a school together for ESN children.

Their sister Ada was married to Harry Jones and they were living in Devon. Harry was a teacher at Ladysmith Road School in Exeter teaching woodwork and other handicrafts. They were very happy there and had many friends. Harry enjoyed his teaching and had developed a hobby renovating old properties. Tom and Cyril begged Harry and Ada to come to Bolton so Harry could teach in the school and in the end they relented. They moved into the vicarage in Appleby whilst Staveley was built. Harry and Ada s daughter Margaret still lives there. It is a wooden clad house, a model known as Devon Lady. Harry had seen the show houses at Honiton and had it erected here in Bolton. It is the last house on the Colby road towards Colby on the right. Mr and Mrs Shaw s house is on the same side of the road and is an identical one.

Harry taught woodwork at school and Ada worked locally. Minnie another sister taught the intake class, and when Minnie became ill Ada took over. They were all musical. Their father had been organist at Liverpool Cathedral, and Ada and Minnie played the organ at Bolton Church for many years. Tom wrote and directed the pantomimes for the school.

Tom had three children who went to boarding school and when Harry and Ada came to work at the school Margaret went too, she says this came as a bit of a shock, being the only child and having had all her parents attention. Cyril and his wife Honourine lived opposite Staveley at Windy Ridge. Cyril died in 1966 and Honourine stayed on as school secretary, until she retired. She then moved to Carlisle to be near her son Peter a consultant surgeon. Tom s wife Elizabeth had been the school matron, she died in 1999.

It was very much a family business. Ted, Tom s son took over as principal when his father died. His sister Maggie returned after nurse training as school matron. She later opened the Pines Nursing Home in Appleby. When this was sold she bought Haybergill House at Warcop and opened it as a conference centre. Ann her sister trained as a teacher.

Margaret Jones is herself a teacher and has worked in several schools in the area including Eden Grove. She remembers many happy times spent at the school and is rightly proud of her father s woodwork. He had a flower motive as his trademark, which he carved into the items he made. The boys used to make items under his instructions for an annual sale of woodwork. This was held in Appleby and proceeds enabled Uncle Tom to take disabled adults to Pontins or Butlins for a holiday.

An Eden Grove pantomime production

The first boy to attend the school was an Italian boy admitted on 20 September 1955. Margaret remembers many of the boys and still gets calls and cards from some of them. She is always interested to hear how they are getting on. She also has fond memories of the staff. Brian Lamont who lives in the village did sporting activities with the boys, and helped with supervision. Although Brian is now retired he still takes a keen interest in the school.

Major Rose a retired army major who lived at Dufton came to do the supervision. Ken Eggleston who was a teacher married a local girl who became a teacher and then college lecturer. He was a very good swimmer and taught the boys and Margaret to swim in the river Eden. Annie Kirkup, who still lives in the village, was cook from when the school first opened when there were only eight boys and Annie earned two shilling an hour. Sam and Doris High lived in the Lodge and Sam was the maintenance man. Annie Miller, Ida Gildhart and Nancy Hudson were the linen room staff. Tommy Rutherford the vicar and his wife Sally played a big part in the day to day activities of the school.

Margaret remembers Peter the school pony living happy days in the field, where Eden Fold is today. Every year the boys went to Ullswater to camp. One of Margaret s happiest memories is the New Year and first footing. They would be up all night visiting every house in the village. She was very sad when this tradition died out.

In 1995 the school passed to Priory Health Care and in January 2000 was bought by Westminster Health Care but has retained the Priory name. The school is registered for 96 pupils 12 of whom could be aged over 16. They come from all over the country, the biggest referring county being Lancashire.

The school has always catered for children with special needs; however, today the children who attend the school have far more complex problems than ever before. They come with complex syndromes and mental health problems attached to physical problems.

In 2000 a new class room block was built and a residential block making space for 25 extra beds. The main building is listed and so the new building has had to blend in well with it.

There have been school trips to Swansea and to Oasis. Other activities have included fund raising for Animal Rescue, serving teas at the Day Centre in Appleby; the Christmas Concert supported by the village people. Some of the village children attended the Christmas party and were delighted to see Father Christmas was there.

During the year some of the pupils have been involved in work experience. Approximately fourteen organisations offer places for example Richardson s in Appleby, Warcop Army Base, Tony s Sports in Appleby, Graham Middleton in Appleby, several local farmers and the Computer Shop in Penrith. At the end of the summer term prize giving day is held. Prizes are awarded for academic achievement, personal achievement and sports. Every one gets a prize.

The school provides employment for local people. There are 94 members of staff several of whom live in the village. One of those people is Andy Jones (husband of district nurse Margaret Jones). Andy was an instructor in the Army Cadets in Penrith and came to Eden Grove on detachment. Prior to this he had been in the Scots Guards with the Army Youth team. He was asked if he would go and work at Eden Grove and help set up a cadet group, which he did in 1984. He has been there eighteen years and is now a senior care officer.

In 1999 the school received an excellent report from the annual care inspection carried out by the Cumbria School Services Inspection Team. The team spent two full days and an evening at the school. They reported that a marked feature of the school and a significant strength is the relaxed and friendly atmosphere which staff and young people identify as a vital part of the service the school provides and there is a wide range of abilities and behaviours in the school. There were numerous occasions observed when pupils referred to other pupils with particular disabilities in a caring and respectful manner. The team noted the action packed activity programme for the summer months. The schools cadets were to spend time at the national Army Cadet Force training camp. Several other camping trips had been planned and the schools 7 — a side soccer team had a successful tournament season. People from the village sit on the advisory board. Presently they are Alan Kingston and David Ridehaugh.

Crossrigg Hall

Crossrigg Hall is on the road leading from Bolton to Cliburn. It is a Grade II listed building dating from about 1850. The building we see today and refer to as Crossrigg Hall is not the original house. The original house is thought to have been where the stables and dovecote are.

The known history of the Hall goes back to the early 1700s when Nicholas Temple a wine and brandy merchant of Fleet Street owned it. He is listed in the 1787 Westmorland census as husbandman living with his wife Elizabeth, nee Woof, and two children Robert and John. Nicholas may have been born at Crossrigg Hall and his father Nathan may have owned it before that, Nicholas inheriting it from him.

However in an abstract of 3 May 1834 in preparation for the sale of the hall it is recorded that: *The admittance of Nathan and Nicholas Temple herein mentioned do not appear in the title deeds.* The abstract goes on to record the land that Nathan Temple was admitted to as tenant. Nicholas inherited 50 acres from Nathan Temple in 1810 and a further 50 acres from Jo Wells of Fleet Market, whom he described as being utterly useless.

In 1823 a Mr Robert Temple a victualler of Clerkenwell Street was admitted to the estate for £800. It would appear that Nicholas was bankrupt by this time. Perhaps Robert was able to rescue his inheritance by buying the hall. In his last will and testament, Nicholas left an annuity to his wife Elizabeth, of £200 yearly and one of his best Meld cows which she could choose for herself. He requested that his executors maintain the cow for her. He left her all his household goods and furniture and the exclusive use of three rooms in the hall, the parlour, the forehouse and the parlour loft. Did Robert allow her, her inheritance? He was her youngest son so perhaps he looked on her kindly.

Just prior to this in 1820 an indenture of mortgage is drawn up between Robert Temple and Thomas Lowis of Brampton. There is a note in the deeds questioning whether this was ever activated. Thomas Lowis died and the will is never proved. Recorded in the Court Rolls for 1824 — Belonged to Nicholas Temple a bankrupt received by this morning s coach the Deeds. 15 May 1824. There is some confusion now as to who owns the Hall because it appears to pass to a Margaret Robinson and her daughter from Culgaith on 14 November 1827.

Details prepared for the sale for 3 April 1834 - *For sale in two lots to be held at the house of Thomas Nicholson, inn keeper (Malt and Shovel)*

Lot 1 *Messuage and Estate Known as Crossrigg Hall in the Township of Bolton in the parish of Morland. Consisting of a commodious and well built dwelling. Has barn, byre, stable and all necessary out buildings in good repair* with land 31 acres 1rood 3perches.

10 acres plus Dwelling House are freehold, the rest is held by the Earl of Lonsdale. Except a small field called Peatmire held by the Earl of Thanet 6d rent as a customary state of inheritance. Several parcels of land inclosing upon which there is a good barn and byre set in Morland. Hathwaite, Low Holme, Stone Rickles, Burtree bank, High Holme, Woodland amounting to 26 acres Hathwaite and Low Holme are freehold and rest with the Dean and Chapter of Carlisle at 5/9d rent and 9d Mill Rent.

Lot 2 all the messuage tenement and estate called Low Whitber situate within the Kings Meaburn. Dwelling, Barn, Byre, Stable and other out buildings with several closes amounting to 50 acres.

10 acres are freehold and the remainder customary held under the Earl of Thanet as parcel of his Lordship of Kings Meaburn paid rent of 12/6d and other dues and services.

Lots 1 and 2 were sold to Robert Addison of London who bid £3,200. In 1834 Robert Addison of Great Russell Street, Bloomsbury, owner of the Jasinga Estate in Jarva paid: £3,538—7—0d to others for those and other premises. In the 1851 census he was listed as head of the Hall, unmarried, aged 75 and farming 203 acres. He employed 12 labourers. Robert was born in October 1775, the son of Christopher Addison of Wickersfield, Kings Meaburn and Elizabeth, nee Graham, of Dufton Wood. He died a bachelor in 1862.

In 1871 Hugh Rigg a great nephew of Robert s inherited the estate. He was the son of the Revd Hugh Rigg from Yorkshire and Maria of Crosby

Crossrigg Hall, photograph courtesy of Mrs. Anita Wood

Ravensworth, a niece of Robert Addison. He served in the 21st Madras Native Infantry as a Lieutenant Colonel until he resigned his commission in 1862 on inheriting the Crossrigg estate. He became High Sheriff of the county in 1867. He replaced the old Crossrigg Hall with a new building built of stone from Barwise Hall Quarry. A timber raising ceremony took place in September 1863 for the new hall. The *Penrith Observer* reported that Mr Monkhouse of the Grey Goat Inn, Penrith, had supplied the dinner for the celebration on the Colonel s behalf.

Mr Ockley was the architect and Mr Grisenthwaite of Penrith the builder. The Hall was built to a Jacobean design by Anthony Salvin. A celebration of timber raising when a new house was built appears to have been a custom in the area and peculiar to the north. Mr Monkhouse appears to have been well known in the area for his hospitality, and hosted other timber celebrations in the Grey Goat.

Colonel and Mrs Hugh Rigg had seven sons and two daughters. His third son Robert Addison Rigg was educated in Cheltenham and then went to the Woolwich Academy gaining a commission in the Royal Field Artillery. He served in Ireland and Gibraltar as well as various places in England. In 1884 he was seconded to Canada by the British Government to become professor of artillery and mathematics at the Royal Military College in Kingston. Robert married in 1885 in Nova Scotia, Miss Paddison Picton. He served for five years in Ceylon and on returning to England received the rank of Lieutenant Colonel. For three years he commanded the artillery garrison at Sheerness and then went to command the British Artillery in Halifax, Canada. He became a full Colonel in 1904. After his retirement he became president of the Kendal Ivy Leaf Club for ex-service men.

Herbert William Rigg was Hugh Rigg s youngest son, who after a period of time in Canada and America, emigrated to Victoria, Australia. He married and lived there with his family for over 40 years before his death. He had five sons and two daughters. Hugh Rigg died in1881 and his eldest son Hugh Carthend Rigg who remained a bachelor succeeded him.

Hugh Carthend Rigg was the eldest son, for whom the house near to Bolton Lane Ends may have been built by his father. Hugh is said to have served his apprenticeship here before inheriting the estate.

In the early part of the 20th century Isabella Smith was a servant at Brigham Bank Farm. The farmer would fatten and kill two pigs for the yearly supply of meat. There were no facilities at the farm to cure some for bacon and so some of the meat was sent up to Crossrigg Hall for the purpose. One evening Isabella was sent to collect the cured meat from the hall. She cycled from Brigham look-ing forward to her visit as she knew the housekeeper Mrs Wilkinson very well and enjoyed her company. Mrs Wilkinson cooked and cleaned for Major Hugh Rigg.

When it was time for Isabella to leave the hall she tucked the bacon under her arm and set off for home. It was very dark but she was not afraid. She went through the gate half way down the drive and started to cycle towards Brigham when she thought she heard someone walking behind her. She could hear this pad, pad, pad. She was so afraid she peddled faster and faster until she reached the farm only to find that her mistress had locked the door and she had to find her key to get in with. After this incident, she never went for any more bacon - the men had to fetch it.

The brow of the hill near to Crossrigg Hall is called Kate s Brow and is said to be haunted, some say by a young girl who was murdered near there and others by a big black dog.

Hugh Carthend Rigg never married and died in 1913 when Joseph Torbock bought the hall. Joseph Torbock made his money from steel and shipbuilding. He married Florence Hoste Henley who was the heiress of the original owners of the Sandringham Estate. Many of the portraits adorning the walls of Crossrigg apparently came from there. Joseph Torbock became High Sheriff for Westmorland in 1903.

Mr and Mrs Torbock had two sons, Richard Henley and Henry Cornish. In 1915 the Torbocks extensively enlarged the hall but since that time it had remained untouched until the time of the sale recently.

Henry, known as Cornish, was educated at Eton and New College, Oxford. Cornish spent all his life at Crossrigg apart for a time in Edinburgh as a chartered accountant and service in the Second World War as a captain with the Royal Artillery. He played an active part in local events especially in those connected with the art world. He was the representative of the National Arts Collection Fund and a trustee of Abbot Hall Museum Kendal.

Cornish was instrumental in refurbishing Rose Castle the home of the Bishop of Carlisle. He toured the antique shops seeking suitable antiques with the help of many of his friends in the trade. He was a senior layman in the Church of England and played a major part in diocesan affairs, being vice-chairman of the Board of Finance and a founder member of the Glebe Committee. He started collecting watercolours as a young man and did so to the end of his life. When he died he bequeathed many of his watercolours to various galleries and his Lake District collection to Abbot Hall Museum.

His brother Richard Torbock attended Osbourne House College on the Isle of White and was then commissioned into the Royal Navy. He served on the battleship HMS Valiant and saw action in the British victory at Cape Matapan. He was a magistrate in the west ward sitting at Shap and Appleby and was chairman of the bench for about ten years. His mother had also been a magistrate at Shap. Commander Torbock supported Morland Church being treasurer and a churchwarden for many years. He became High Sheriff of Westmorland in 1953. Both brothers were interested in shooting and had their own grouse moors, one in North Yorkshire and the other near Alston.

Local rumour has it that the Torbocks used to be more closely involved with the village of Bolton but Mrs Torbock fell out with the inhabitants when a stranger was allowed to sit in her seat in the church. Harry Bell remembers her giving the curtains for the Memorial Hall. He feels it was a very good gift: *as they are still up.*

Although the house was sold after the deaths of the Torbocks the 1500 acre estate is still managed by the Henleys who inherited the house and estate. A smaller house was built close to the hall for them to occupy.

Mr and Mrs David Wood are the new owners. They moved there from Northumberland but are both Lancastrians from Blackburn. David is a retired-chartered engineer who worked for British Gas for 28 years. Anita Wood used to teach art, design and pottery and her expertise in this area came in very useful when refurbishing the Hall. She decided to take a career change and has more recently worked in residential care and this led to her commissioning a purpose built care home in Newcastle. Mr and Mrs wood were granted planning permission to convert the hall into a hotel. However to date the hall is still very much a family home.

Prior to Mr and Mrs Wood s buying the house the Torbocks had lived there since the early 1900s. When Commander Richard Torbock died on 14 November just a few months after his brother Cornish who died on 17 June 1993, the house was put up for sale. Inhabitants of Bolton who attended the preview of the sale will remember seeing the interior of the house as if in a time warp transporting them back to the early 1900s, the last time it had been altered by the Torbocks when they first bought it.

The fixtures and fittings have been sympathetically brought up to date and as much of the original as possible refurbished. For example wallpaper was taken from seven of the bedrooms to repair that in others. The plumbing and wiring have been brought up to date. The wiring was the original from 1919 with a 110-volt system and generator. There was a good deal of old asbestos, all of which had to be removed.

Although the Hall has not been opened to date as a hotel it is licensed for weddings and used for fund raising events for local charities. In 2000 fund raising events for the NSPCC and the RNLI were held and Morland garden party was held there to raise money for the church.

Bewley Castle

South of the village of Bolton are the ruins of Bewley Castle, situated on a tributary of the river Eden known as Sweetmilk Sike. Travelling from Bolton to Colby one would not know it was there, as it lies down a long track unseen in a green hollow to the left of Sweetmilk Sike Bridge. When Harry Bell was farming he used to take the cattle there to graze over the summer and, he said: They would always come back in real good shape.

The survey of historical monuments in1937 describes it as being formerly three storeys high and the walls of rubble and ashlar. What remains of the castle seems to date largely from the 14th century. It was originally known as Fithnenin but became known as Beaulieu in the 13th century.

The castle at Fithnenin the river-side pasture was granted by Ucthred de Botelton in 1170 to the church at Carlisle. In 1186 after the death of the second bishop Bernard the diocese remained vacant for 32 years. During this time the canons appointed their own bishop and swore allegiance to the Scots king. This annoyed Henry II and he consulted the Pope, who gave orders for the canons to be expelled and Hugh, Abbot of Beaulieu in the New Forest was appointed as Bishop of Carlisle. The castle was given to Hugh, who gave it the name Beaulieu after his previous home in the New Forest. The name is a French form of the Latin *bellus locus* meaning beautiful place.

On the site of the castle the present building was built in 1325 and in 1402

BEWLEY CASTLE BOLTON WESTMORLAND N°12

New Bewley

Bishop Strickland restored the house, including the chapel and lords chamber. Today Bewley is the home of Val and Dan Bromley who moved there from Lancashire about twelve years ago. Val originates from the other Bolton in that county. Since buying the castle and the house Val and Dan have been very interested in the history and Dan has kept a catalogue of the history known to date. With his permission it is reproduced below with some additions:

1130-1150 The early medieval name of the manor was Fithnennin (Icelandic name Fit-vunnin cultivated meadow near water).

1186 Bernard 2nd Bishop died. The See (the Carlisle Bishopric) was left vacant for 32 years. During this time mayhem reigned at Bewley. The Bewley monks publicly denounce all papal authority and in defiance of the Pope and other religious leaders continue to perform their own divine service. They swore allegiance to the King of the Scots, a monarch also opposed to the Pope. This professed loyalty was probably wise in helping to protect the establishment from frequent raids. They also appointed one of their clerks (who had been excommunicated by the pope) as their Bishop. At the same time they seized the revenue of the Bishopric.

This angered King Henry II and he applied personally to Pope Humorious III with the result that the Bewley canons were expelled and Hugh 3rd Bishop of Carlisle was installed. He had been the abbot of the Bellus Locus Regis religious establishment, known today as Beaulieu, in the New Forest. The name was long ago shortened by the Westmorland people to Bewley.

Bellus Locus Regis was a name much favoured by the Benedictine French order for a prime site and also used later by the Cistercians and the Augustinians. It was given to several of their religious establishments. It appears that the castle was built at the time of Hugh. Parts of the present castle building dates from this time. One of the windows, the glass long gone, has been dated to the first half of the 13th century.

1256 Walter Feadwell was vicar (of All Saints Appleby) as appears by an instrument that year by Thomas Vipont bishop of Carlisle executed at Bewley, on a reference to his   (unreadable on document).

Confirmation of the churches of Shap and Bampton to the said Abbey (Shap) by Thomas de Veteripont bishop of Carlisle, Dated at Buley, on Sunday before the Nativity of the blessed virgin Mary, 1256 with a very fine oval seal two inches broad, with a bishop in his mitre and robes, the right hand erect with a finger pointed up, and the left hand holding a crosier, circumscribed with these words : Sigillum Thomas Dei gracia Karleoleolrnsis Episcopi

1266 Robert Chause, 7th Bishop of Carlisle at Bewley releases the guardian ship of the cell at Wetheral. When Bishop Osbaldistan came to the see he bullied Bishop Fleming s executors out of £200 which the said Bishop Fleming had allowed to his lesses of Buley Castle in Westmorland for his interest in the wood fold there, and for damages and springing it again.

1290 Edward I conceded to Ralph De Isetan, 8th Bishop of Carlisle the right to free warren.

1291 John de Halation, 9th Bishop of Carlisle was granted free warren but all

Bewley Castle Farm House home to Dan and Val Bromley

other privileges were disallowed.

1325 The present building was built, however it appears that several subsequent alterations have been undertaken. A Bishop Sylvester is mentioned in two deeds of 1350.

1402 Bishop William Strickland restores the building including the Chapel and Lords Chamber.

1598 Legend of the Robbers. Manor owned by Sir Richard Musgrave. Manor sold to Robert Braithwaite by the Parliamentary Commissioners for £321-10-0d. The estate is repossessed at the restoration of the monarchy. King Charles II restored to the throne.

1678-1781 In the 18th century Bishop Douglas received £381 from the timber sold from the lands of Bewley to the cost of repairs to Rose Castle. The estate is owned by the Machels until the 19th century. By 1774 the castle is a ruin. Old leases are in the office of the ecclesiastical commissioners to whom the estates of the Bishop of Carlisle became vested in 1856.

1807 June 6th To be let. Occupied by William Swainson. Owned by the Musgraves of Edenhall in 18th century. 1851 occupied by Rowland Slack and Margaret his sister. Rowland farms 200 acres with four farm labourers to help him.

1857 Manor and 219 acres sold to Mr William Brougham by the Ecclesiastical Commission. 1858 Conveyed to the Tufton Trustees.

1881 Occupied by George Hewetson, farmer his wife Jane, son William, and daughter Margaret. Also living there is William, George s brother, a gentleman. Thomas Sewell, Nathan Routledge servants and farm labourers. Elizabeth Witter and Violet Nicholson, domestic servants.

1882 Owned by R. Burra, 32 Chester Terrace, London 22nd September, reading of The Episcopal Residence of the Bishop of Carlisle by R.S. Ferguso, F.S.A. at Appleby. 1883 Owned by Mrs Burra of Sedbergh, Yorks.

1891 occupied by Thomas Johnstone, his wife Sarah and six children. 1954 legal charge between Andrew Park (farmer), Elizabeth Park (wife) Margaret, Sarah Park, Mary Lillian Park, Thomas Frizzal and Emma Frizzal, Neal House, near Carlisle for £3000. 1973 Legal charge between Annie Foulder Pattison, High Garth, Great Corby, Carlisle and Margaret Park. For £2500.

1988 June 17th new trustees appointed - Mary Lillian Park and Linda Murphy. Purchased by Daniel and Valerie Bromley together with approximately 120 acres of land.

In 1982 it was recorded that a 19th century watercolour of Bewley existed and was in the possession of Canon Markham.

The legend of the Robbers of Bewley is well known in Westmorland. A brief account follows. It was on a rough evening in October 1598 that Margaret Dawe, known as Marget, the old house keeper at Bewley, carefully bolted the big oak door leading into the courtyard of the castle. She then returned to the kitchen to sit in the huge chimney near to the roaring fire. She was alone as the rest of the family was in Kings Meaburn visiting friends. Marget was a character in the village and well known for being fearless and out spoken.

Bundles of peeled rushes gathered from the local marshes were strewn around the floor and Marget was using them to make rush lights. Over the fire hung a large iron pot filled with boiling fat to dip the lights in when she had finished plaiting them.

A knock came at the door and on answering it she saw a stranger who she thought to be a woman. Marget led the stranger into the kitchen and bid her sit by the fire and partake of some home brewed ale. The fire was warm and the ale was strong and the stranger was soon asleep by the fire.

The woman s clothes intrigued Marget, for women hereabouts did not wear such garments. She moved to take a closer look, pulling the stranger s skirt aside as she did so. She was amazed to see under the skirt a strong pair of boot tops adorned with large steel spurs. Observing that the stranger s mouth had dropped open in sleep. Marget quickly took a large ladle down, dipped it into the hot fat and poured it down the stranger s open mouth. The stranger emitted a loud yell and rolled about on the floor in agony. There was a low whistle outside and on hearing this Marget ran to the tower at the north end of the castle and rang the alarm furiously.

Her summons was soon answered by a number of pistol shots and a party of men including Sir Robert Musgrave and his son entered the house carrying the bodies of two well known troopers who had been killed in the short fight outside. In the kitchen Marget showed them the body of stranger who was now dead. It proved to be Belted Will Scott, one of the most notorious raiders of the Borders.

There is some evidence that the Bewley estate may have been one of those bought by the church with money from the Queen s Bounty for the living at All Saints, however this would require more research.

At the turn of the century 1780-1800 it appears the occupants of the estate were reluctant to pay their tithes and Edward Jackson, curate at the time, writes to the vestry meeting as follows: *Where as time and other circumstance may and has apparently rendered unequal what might at first be nearly so, with respect to the value of the Township.*

The following proposal is therefore made for the sake of quietness and good neighbourhood, and that all our public burdens may be made proportionally equal as they well can be viz that Richard Tinkler Esq., John Dent, Thomas Lambert, Nich Allen, Josiah Corry and Thomas Steel do meet and take into consideration the inequality of value of the Low Moor, the Common Land, which has not proved so productive as was expected and Bewley Castle 20 acres (which if one eleventh part was formerly, which probably was the case) though its proportionate past with the Township when the commission was unenclosed cannot now be so when upwards of 500 acres of cultivated common is added to the Township. It may therefore be proper to take it into consideration and that they do compare all with the value of the ancient enclosed ground in the Township. I propose also that such a recompense be made them for their trouble as may be thought proper and agreed to at the meeting

Another request shall make, viz, that all the old books of accounts, constable, surveyor and overseers books not at present in use be taken proper care of and be deposited in the church or iron chest as they may be at some future time, of more value to the Township, than we are at present aware of.

Another request is that the last rate upon Bewley Castle and the tithes against the Willows? carefully, to ascertain whether every deduction has been made, that ought to be made, of money taken from the Willows Rent for other purposes than the poor, as they generally apply to have the rate made out the moment they want to collect it, so that no time is allowed to consider of its curacy when this is done, I have no doubt but that every thing will be settled amicably and friendly.   Edw Jackson

The poor man appears to be having a really bad time of things and trying to be so diplomatic.

New Bewley is another building that can be found on the road side up the track from Bewley Castle. Little is known about the dwelling other than that it was built from stone from the castle. Over one of the doors on a sandstone lintel is a coat of arms of the Clifford s impaling Vipont. It is perhaps of note that the St Anne s Hospital almshouses were founded in Appleby in 1652. Entering the quadrangle of the hospital, the west front has an arch way above which is an inscribed panel and two coats of arms, one of Clifford impaling Vipont. There are a number of shields set in panels in the wall faces; one shows the Vipont Arms impaling Bewley. Perhaps this could be a starting point for some further research.

New Bewley is not listed in the 1851 census; perhaps it was empty. In 1881 Thomas Johnson was in residence with wife Sarah, daughter Annie and son Robert. John Parkin was a farm servant there and Elizabeth Longmire a domestic servant John farms 28 acres. Ten years later William Nicholson was living there with his wife and children Joseph, Francis, Richard, John, Jonathan and Frederick. Litany Gowling was visiting, she was 10 years old, probably a friend of Francis who was also 10 years of age. She was from Kirkby Thore and perhaps on holiday. New Bewley now also has a cottage where William Thompson his wife Margaret and daughter May are living. New Bewley is now the home of Peter and Sally Kuzbit and children.

Bolton Memorial Hall

It would appear from records that after the war of 1914-18 a committee was set up to build a memorial hall in Bolton to commemorate the war dead. There is no mention of who the committee members were but we know from correspondence that the late Miss Dent of Elm House was the secretary.

Several fund raising events took place and one of particular note was a fete, sale of work and concert held on 17 June 1920 at Eden Grove. Tickets for admission to the ground at Eden Grove ceased to be sold at 5pm when the sports began in an adjoining field. At 7pm there was a concert arranged by the ladies committee and dancing began at 9 o clock. This was arranged by the young men s committee who provided a marquee with a boarded floor for dancing. The profit made amounted to £112-4-4d, a large sum in those days. Any one attending that fete could hardly have imagined that 80 years on, on 7 July 2000 Bolton inhabitants would enjoy a similar event in the hall and field that that huge profit had gone towards providing.

When the building of the hall was first decided a member of the committee, who also agreed to carry out the building, estimated the cost of the building to be £700. Unfortunately this member died and a new builder had to be found. The estimate was £2300 and so the committee decided *to postpone the project until prices were easier*. The committee continued to fund raise.

At about this time the Mid Town property — two cottages, farm buildings and

The Memorial Hall 1920s

Bolton Field Day 1956

a field came onto the market. The sale was held at the Crown Hotel, Penrith, on Tuesday 1 October 1912 and was described as :- Mid Town Farm occupied by Mrs Wills as tenant and a cottage adjoining the dwelling house in the occupation of Mr Bellas. The land comprised: The Croft Luzbeck, Sleetriggs, Little Strip and Thornber Ends Lane Level Field, Big Thornber, Hill Top Field Back Hill, Top Field. Low Thornber. High Thornber, Back Thornber, Part of OS no 507 is of customary Tenure held as a parcel of land of the manor and forest of Oglebird by payment of the customary rent of 3/6d. Part of OS No 508 is of customary tenure part being held as a parcel of the manor of Bolton by payment of the customary rent of 1d. What would the tenants think of today s rents?

The committee decided to buy the farm house and Bellases cottage with the idea of converting the buildings into Parish Rooms — reading room, recreation room, and public hall and to use the field as a recreation ground.

A cottage assessment had already been given as a subscription to the committee for the memorial by deed of gift from the Dent family, possibly Garth View. This probably meant that any monies made from letting this property would go towards the cost of the hall. The Charity Commission now added the newly purchased properties to the Trust Deed.

The Trust Deed states: *the committee shall hold the said herediments upon trust to permit the same to be used in perpetuity as a non sectarian and non political place of recreation and social intercourse under the name of Bolton Memorial Hall for the advantage or benefit of the inhabitants of Bolton.*

In July 1922 the Trustees applied to the charity commission to sell part of the property as a contribution towards the cost of the hall and eventually Midtown

House Bellas cottage was sold to a Mr Richardson. With the money accrued from fund raising, rent from the cottage, rent from the field in March and September, sale of the cottages, letting of the rooms and a donation from the county council building could begin.

Mr Knewstubb was the architect and surveyor from Penrith, John Russell building contractor, Joseph Atkinson, mason and builder, from Stainton and Frederick Potts, slater, plasterer, concreter and tiler, from Appleby were engaged to build and finish the hall. The hall was built where it is today adjoining the barn kept from the purchase of the Mid Town property.

In 1924 the charity commission sent a draft scheme for the regulation of the hall and this was deposited at the home of Mr Dent Elm House for 15 days for public inspection.

The first elected members of the committee were Mr Nathan Simpson, Joseph Thwaites, Alfred Walton, Joseph Simpson, Mrs Alice Clark, Mrs Sarah Bell, Mrs Elizabeth Thwaites and Mrs Jessie Russell.

After the 1939-45 it was decided to dedicate the playing field as a memorial to the dead of that war. There is some confusion in the records as to whether the field had been sold by the committee back in 1922 and then had to be re-purchased. Fund raising began again and organisations approached for donations. Birmingham Wagon Repairs who had occupied Eden Grove during the war years were only too pleased to be able to help *in recognition of their special affinity with the people of Bolton.* Sheep dog trials were a popular means to raise funds and these were held on the Eden Grove field by the bridge.

The playing field showing the gates which are a memorial to those who died in World War Two.

Jo and John Harrison at the Field Day, 1950s

The AA were approached to carry out traffic control because of the dangerous bend in the road. This request was refused. It was felt that a responsible member of the committee could control the traffic and organise the car parking. In a letter to the committee the AA state: we are no longer able to provide patrols for parking duties or traffic control because as many patrols as possible should be on the roads to give practical help and advice to the greatest majority of members. How many people can remember the AA patrolman on his motor bike saluting as he met you the motorist on the road?

Field Day c. 1975

BOLTON MEMORIAL HALL

And here they come - Prince Philip and Her Majesty the Queen (alias Richard Birkbeck and Sue Birkbeck (now Mounsey) on the occasion of the coronation.

And here come Prince Charles and Lady Diana (alias Philip Hayton and Deborah Mullen) on the occasion of the Royal Wedding.

The field was purchased and in 1947 the war department agreed to level the field. The work was to be carried out as a training project by Polish Troops stationed at Warcop. The project was designated as technical assistance — local welfare for which there would be no charge. A Galleon Autograder would be used to do the work. George Ellwood remembers clearing the field of stones and seeding it afterwards. That same year on 17 June 1947 the hall was used for the distribution of ration books.

The residents of Bolton and the surrounding area have continued to use and enjoy the field and hall since their inauguration. Dances, whist drives, film shows, bingo, bowls, discos, domino drives and country dancing are some of the events held in the hall. The field has been used

132

CHANGING TIMES

Stalwarts waiting to see the real Queen pass by on the A66, 1952/3

for the annual field day when the rose Queen is crowned and for football competitions, junior football, and the bonfire on Bonfire Night. The Bolton Players staged their first productions in the hall.   In 1967 new toilets and a cloakroom were built and in 1984 the W.I. took over the youth club for their exclusive use. The playgroup are also based in the hall.

On 4 April 1973 the hall s golden jubilee was celebrated the same day as the official opening in 1923 when Mrs Weston from Kendal performed the opening and her husband Colonel Weston MP unveiled the tablet to the Bolton men who served in the war. Mr Tatters gave a brief history of the hall from its opening followed by a buffet supper. Dancing followed the supper and entertainment was provided by members from the Bolton Youth Club. Apparently Mr Allan Bainbridge gave a very lively performance as the galloping gourmet assisted by Mr Ken Shepherd.

The hall is still governed by the Charity Commission and is funded by grants, money from the Willows, letting of the field, letting the hall for functions, rents from playgroup and the bowls club.   In the year 2000 the hall was the venue for a number of celebration events including a domino drive and a ceilidh. For the field day a marquee with a wooden floor for dancing was hired. This was also used for crowning the millennium Rose Queen and a large barbecue.

The following day a service was held in the marquee and Revd. Dent officiated. Mr. and Mrs. David Hayton donated the new Memorial Hall clock. The

BOLTON MEMORIAL HALL

Former Bolton Rose Queens

Memorial Hall committee in conjunction with Eden District Council and the Parish Council had a new playground constructed behind the hall.

The committee for the year 2000 were: Allan Bainbridge, chairman; Christine Taylor, secretary; Ken Shepherd, treasurer; Christine Birkbeck, booking secretary; Edith Stockdale, Jo Bennett, Clare Hudson, Allan Fleming, Charlotte Wills, Allan Barker, Barbara Kingston and Richard Birkbeck. The trustees for 2000 were Frank Baxter, Bruce Robinson, David Hayton and George Ellwood.

Bolton Rose Queens

1956 Dorothy Bellas (Laurie)
1957 Mary Jackson (Sowerby)
1958 Mary Ellwood (Allison)
1959 Christine Bell (McNally)
1960 Jillian Roe (Robinson)
1961 Pamela Metcalf
1962 Jean Robinson
1963 Joy Howe (Hullock)
1964 Mary Harrison (Greenhalgh)
1965 Susan Birkbeck (Mounsey)
1966 Dorothy Fothergill (Kirkbride)
1967 Marolyn Iveson (Noble)
1968 Sheila Greenhow (Robinson)
1969 Yvonne Trueman (Keene)
1970 Jane Fothergill (Mumford)
1971 Janice Taylor
1972 Margaret Charlton
1973 Joan Ellwood (McKay)
1974 Mary Howe (Graham)
1975 Pauline Charlton (White)
1976 Sheila Tatters (Brown)
1977 Valarie Jackson
1978 Judith Tatters (Barker)

1979 Yvonne Thompson
1980 Louise Smith (Foster)
1981 Claire Shepherd (Hudson)
1982 Helen Thompson
1983 Lisa Bennett
1984 Vicky Dewis
1985 Julie Bone
1986 Joanne Massicks
1987 Wendy Smith
1988 Claire Hatfield
1989 Debbie Hewitt
1990 Deborah Mullen
1991 Philipa Hatfield
1992 Julie Proud
1993 Joanne Coward
1994 Lisal McVeity
1995 Tracy Wilson
1996 Joanna Prance
1997 Helen Fleming
1998 Rose Blanchard
1999 Jo-anne Dinsdale
2000 Laura Brown

The first Rose Queen, Dorothy Bellas, 1956

The Methodist Chapel

The Methodist Chapel is situated on the road leading to Cliburn. It is one of the oldest Methodist Chapels in Westmorland. On 10 June 1820 an indenture was made between William Dent of Bolton, yeoman of the one part and John Dent of Bolton and many others of the second part: *Witnesses that in consideration of 10/- the said William Dent has conveyed to those of the second part, all that parcel of ground in the village of Bolton upon which a newly erected building used as a Chapel and Meeting House of the Wesleyan Methodists, now stands on north east back from the town street, 44 feet on the south-west, 47 feet on the south east, 37 feet and on the north west - 36 feet. Together with the said Chapel to hold services there, etc., Ref Close Roll 9953 pl 6c.*

There had been a Methodist Chapel at Kirkby Thore since 1798, but it was not until 1803 that Methodism was introduced into Bolton, and by December of that year Bolton was listed in the Circuit Records as: *one of the fifteen societies and as having paid a quarterage of 4/6d.*

The Dent family had always had close links with the parish church. Henry Dent was a churchwarden three times by 1800 and again in 1812. The family lived in the middle of the village at Gilflosh (meaning Valley Swamp) now called Elm House. Henry Dent was head of the household and he had six children — William being the eldest and John the youngest. The Dent family gave

The Methodist Chapel, Bolton

Bolton Band of Hope at the parade in Appleby.

the Methodists a warm welcome and Henry opened his house to the Methodist preachers. Gilflosh continued to be used for preaching until 1818, by this time the Brough Wesleyan Methodist Circuit stretched from Renwick to Kirkby Stephen and from Hilton to Orton. Every Sunday a Service was held in Bolton at 7pm.

It was through the effort and commitment of John Dent and other members of his family that Bolton had its own chapel in 1818. John s brother William gave the site (the garden of Gilflosh) as described above and £30 towards the cost of building.

No doubt a frequent visitor to the new chapel was Hodgson Casson a Weslyan Minister born in Workington. In 1819 he came to serve in the newly amalgamated Brough and Penrith Circuit. He married Mary Dent, John s sister who he described in his autobiography as: an amiable female, of decided piety. Sadly the marriage was short lived as Mary died in 1823. Casson had a two year ministry in the area including a camp meeting that was held in a large field near Bolton. A long cart served as the platform with Casson as the principal speaker.

In 1833 a Sunday School was started in Bolton Chapel with John Dent as superintendent. In 1861 the average attendance in the morning was 45 and in the afternoon 53. Band of Hope meetings were also held in the chapel.

Methodism in Bolton was much affected by national events. On the death of John Wesley the Methodist conference of 100 Methodist Ministers assumed his great power, but it was felt that the conference never allowed the voice of the laymen to be heard. In 1827 a decision of a district meeting was overturned by

The Methodist Chapel, Bolton and Elm House a century ago.

conference and many members left the Wesleyan Church. There was more discontent voiced when conference proposed a training school for ministers with Jabez Bunting as principal.

Reform was demanded when over a hundred delegates gathered in Sheffield in July 1835. They all had some grievance against the conference party of the Wesleyan Church. John Dent went to represent those demanding reform in the Appleby Circuit. The conference refused to receive the delegates. The delegates were determined to continue with their association and broke away from the parent body, calling themselves the Wesleyan Methodist Association. They held their first annual assembly in Manchester in August 1836. Wesleyan Association circuits were formed and a new branch of Methodists came into being. All the Methodists at Bolton withdrew from the Wesleyan Church.

However, a grave difficulty now arose because Bolton s Methodist Chapel belonged to the Wesleyan s and the new Methodists were not allowed to use it for their services. Gilflosh had to be opened up for services once again. For four years the chapel was unused because the Wesleyan s stood firm in their refusal to allow the new Methodists to use the chapel. This must have been infuriating to the Dent family, as they had provided the land and monies to enable the chapel to be built in the first place.

It was only in 1840 when the chapel was deteriorating that the Wesleyan s accepted the offer of a payment of the cost of the building beyond the original subscriptions. Methodism progressed from then on in the village.

CHANGING TIMES

In 1926 a major renovation took place, the building was heightened and the interior redesigned and refurbished. Thomas Bert Irving of Morland did the stonework and Joseph Dent of Warcop, the woodwork. The stained glass window was fitted at this time and the chapel was reopened by Mrs G J Williamson, the mayoress of Appleby.

Revd Joy Rulton is the current Minister at the Methodist Chapel, Bolton. She was sent here by the Methodist Church in 1999 to complete two years probation before being ordained in June 2001. An Essex girl born and bred she certainly found it a culture shock when she arrived here with husband Bryan. She has two sons, Simon (who is at Bradford University studying archeological science) and Chris and a daughter Katherine. Danielle, Simon's fianc e also moved with them. Before being called to the ministry Joy worked in a primary school for ten years helping to teach children with special needs.

Despite the culture shock she says: It has been a wonderful experience for myself and family to live and work among the people here. The Chapel at Bolton is very much alive, meeting each week. We may not be large in number, but I pray that we are growing in faith as we meet together to worship and to pray for this village of which we are all a part.

Adapted by kind permission of Rev. Tony Dent
from Bolton s Other Little Stone Edifice.

Bolton Post Office

In medieval times Royal messengers carried government documents to their destinations. By the beginning of the 16th century the term post was used to describe men with horses stationed at certain points along main roads leading out of London. They were responsible for carrying the mail to the next relay station.

The job of postmaster of England began in the early 17th century with the responsibility of collecting and conveying all parcels and letters. From 1609 all post destined for the UK had to be carried by the Royal Mail. In 1644 Edward Pridoux established the first weekly delivery of post to different parts of the country. In 1656 an Act of Parliament created the position of Post Master General for England. A private penny post had operated in London for some time, as had other private organisations. These were all incorporated into the General Post Office in 1710. The number of mail coach services gradually increased and was extended throughout the country. Each coach was painted with the words Royal Mail and at first carried an armed guard.

In 1786 the first mail coach in the county passed through Kendal to Edinburgh and by 1809 a second started to travel from Bowes over Stainmore, through Brough and Appleby to Eamont Bridge. With the coming of the railways the mail was first carried by rail from Liverpool to Manchester in 1830.

In rural areas like Westmorland in the late 19th century the service was the only main means of communication and the postman s job was seen as respectable and secure. Great pride was taken in wearing the uniform but the discipline was very strict, the hours long and the pay low.

The building where the Post Office is today before it became the general store. The photograph is from before 1899 and Matthew Savage is the man in the top hat holding the horse.

Greenside where Mr. Ellwood had the general stores and Post Office

Bolton General Stores where the Post Office is today. Pictured left to right - Margaret Savage (married Christopher Butterworth 1874-1949), Agnes Savage 1835-1931, Elizabeth Graham (nee Savage 1870-1965) and Robert John Savage 1879-1931.

Annie Kirkup s home where the Post Office used to be when her mother-in-law ran it.

In 1858 the letters for Bolton came via Kirkby Thore by foot post and Robert Lamb received them for delivery in the village. In the 1851 census Robert is described as a gardener aged 41 years and living in Bolton with his wife Elizabeth, son Fergus and daughter Jane.

In 1897 Mr. Thomas Ellwood owned the village stores and Post Office which was situated where Greenside is today. People could buy postal orders there and letters came via Penrith arriving at 8.30am and being collected at 5.30pm. There were other shops in the village, for instance in 1829 Samuel Gibson had a butcher s shop, John Ion was a grocer and draper and Thomas Nicholson also operated a grocery business.

In the early 1900s Bolton Post Office was situated where Annie Kirkup lives today near the Memorial Hall. There was a post box built into the wall and a telephone box. In the early 1940s Annie s mother-in-law was looking for a job and decided to open a Post Office in her home. At that time the Bells ran the General Stores, which is the Post Office today. Mrs. Bell bought the premises from her older half brother, Henry Savage, who was then living in Australia. Mrs. Bell was assisted by her daughter-in-law Mrs. Jenny Bell who took over the business around 1950. When Mrs. Kirkup stopped being post mistress in the late 1950s, Mrs. Jenny Bell took over the post office and incorporated it into the general stores.

Stone Croft, adjoining the post office was a barn prior to 1938. Mrs. Bell senior used to buy large quantities of flour from the mill and with a weighing machine hung from a rafter in the roof of the barn would bag up smaller quantities to sell in the shop. Travelling salesmen from Carlisle, companies Pattinson & Winters, Ridley & Dickenson and Kirkby Stephen based Simpson's, would call to take orders for items to be sold in the shop.

In 1982 the business was taken over by Kath and Jimmy Ludgate from Darlington. Kath s parents, Pat and Michael Mac MacNulty moved to Eamont Bridge and Pat would come from there on the bus to help in the shop when Kath s children were young. Pat enjoyed getting to know everyone in the village and Mac took a job as a handyman at Eden Grove. They moved to live in a bungalow in Stephenson s Croft in the village. Pat was a keen member of the WI and Mothers Union while Mac joined the Bowls Club. Sadly he died suddenly in 1995.

In 1993 Kath and Jimmy moved on to other work and John and Judith Cotter became the new owners. John had been looking for a post office to take over on retirement from the Royal Navy. He had served for 34 years as an accountant which would stand him in good stead for his work in a post office. The couple moved to the Post Office on 29 September 1993. The shop sells a wide variety of goods and the mail arrives in the morning and is collected twice a day. In December 2000, Wendy , the new computer system (as christened by John), arrived to help him run the Post Office. There has been much speculation about the future of rural post offices, following the government s decision to change the way pensions and benefits are paid to customers in 2003. Hopefully when you are reading this book in years to come, the village will still have a shop and a Post Office.

The Post Office today. The post master is John Cotter.

On the Banks of the River Eden

by Brian Lamont

Walking along the banks of the river Eden with my dogs I have observed a proliferation of wild flowers and plants of all descriptions. The best time to see these is from late May to November. From Bolton Bridge to the little wood at Kirkby Thore can be seen butter burrs which can just about take over the bank making access to the river very difficult. The plant got its name because people long ago wrapped the butter they had made up in the large leaves of the plant. As there was no water supply in the village, the butter would have been churned by the river.

In amongst the butter burr grow plants like red campion, dames violet, meadowsweet, meadow cranesbill and various types of wild parsley and grasses. Most of these plants have their seasons with the red campion holding out for most of the summer. Walking by the river early morning or late evening after some rain the scent of the sweet rocket can be quiet alluring. If the wild garlic is crushed under foot its pungent smell is released. Many of the plants growing by the river would have been used by the villagers as herbs for medicinal purposes and for cooking, for example wild garlic and chicory.

Grasses such as meadowsweet would be used as air fresheners in the houses. Other plants such as ox-eye daisy grow in patches according to the suitability of the climate. Some years they are there in profusion and others very few. The Indian balsam flower has become a riverside and lake-side pest in recent years growing in profusion to the exclusion of the more indigenous plants. It has become such a nuisance that serious attempts have been made to clear it from such places as the shores of Lake Ullswater.

The road side edges have not been cut over the last few years because of council budget restraints and a great profusion of wild plants spring to life each summer, making it a joy to walk along the many roads around the village; in particular the long stretch of the Colby Road down to Bewley Castle, scented with meadowsweet and honeysuckle in mid summer. Earlier this spring there was even a wonderful show of the previously quite rare cowslip.

The bird and wild life of the Bolton countryside is many and varied through out the year. During the winter months from October onwards a group of some forty whooper swans fly in from Iceland and Greenland to spend the winter feeding on young grasses or winter barley. These large birds with very big feet rarely go near the river leaving the water to the occasional pair of mute swans. On their long travels up to their breeding grounds in the near Arctic there are casualties but each October/November successful breeding pairs return with their dark grey gangly young. These young will not be ready for breeding for some five or six years. Eventually towards the end of March the swans will migrate back to remote areas of Iceland and Greenland to start their breeding cycle again. Through out the winter months mute swans patrol the river usually feeding down the river from south of Bolton Mill to the shallower waters nearer Kirkby Thore. They can be seen occasionally winging their way back to start feeding down the river again.

The luck of the mute swans in breeding varies a great deal according to the vagaries of the river floods. In recent years resident pairs have had their nests washed away at critical times but in spite of all this there seems to be a healthy population of our natural swan between Appleby and Kirkby Thore.

A less popular visitor at least from the fisherman s point of view is the occasional marauding cormorant along with the goosanders. Although interesting and attractive birds from a wildlife point of view they are not really welcome on the fishing protected sections of the river. These sawbills are very adept fishermen. Just occasionally it is possible to see the rather delightful waistcoated dipper; this bird can be seen hopping from rock to rock in the fast flowing sections of the river occasionally disappearing under the water to hunt for larva and water crustaceans. It will face the fast current head on with a special depression on its back for the water flow to keep it down but mobile on the riverbed.

Locals and fishermen have reported seeing kingfishers along this stretch of river but I have not been so lucky. Each spring a familiar piping sound announces the arrival of a pair of sandpipers. This migratory bird from Africa will breed and spend all summer along our stretch of river. Very protective of its nest area it will tease and harass walking dogs along the river banking.

Over the last two or three years with my car parked by the river a very regular grey wagtail has chosen to argue with itself in my wing mirror. Pied wagtails are quiet common by the bridge, as are the many different more common finches along the whole stretch of the river.

Each February a convention of oyster catchers arrive from their Morecambe Bay winter quarters and spend up to a month entering into argumentative performances and breeding displays which can be quite comical to the passing observer. Eventually by the end of March/April all are dispersed to their various breeding areas in the district. It is noticeable that the same breeding areas in fields or near farms are used each year.

Each winter a large flock of some six hundred lapwings spend some months in the marshy area by Kirkby Thore dispersing in the spring to breeding areas which now include moor land and the fells rather than the traditional farm land as they used to. Curlews join the oyster catchers in good numbers each spring and their evocative calls can be heard up to the middle of summer all round the village. This area carries several breeding buzzards their general survival and success rate depending largely on the local rabbit population.

Herons can be seen regularly by the river edge but I have not seen a heronry in the area for some years. Two breeds of seagull are residents of the Eden Valley, the larger quite handsome common gull and the more diminutive black headed gull. The black is a misnomer as the head is actually a nice chocolate brown colour and the bird only carries this colour during the summer months. During the winter the colour recedes to a black spot behind the eye. As many as fifty thousand gulls can roost on local lakes such as Ullswater, Haweswater and Bassenthwaite spreading out over the valley to feed each day. Mature birds leave each March/April to breeding grounds and two out of three can travel as far as Scandinavia and Eastern Europe.

Sand martins are the first of the swallow family to arrive by the river each spring. House martins and swallows soon follow to build nests in and around the village. By late May the swifts are in our skies but are the first to leave for Africa, in some years by early August. The village has a swift population of two dozen birds most summers and their screaming flight is a welcome sound through out our summer evenings. One fact that is difficult to grasp about the swift is that the male birds from the moment of hatching spend their entire lives on the wing never landing on any point at any time, feeding, sleeping and even mating on the wing.

One afternoon in July did I hear a corncrake in a barley field along the Colby Road, a unique sound? What else could it have been?

Large flocks of starlings fly in from Eastern Europe and Scandinavia each autumn and spend their noisy winter with us in this valley. They say that a flock of 10,000 starlings can lift up to one ton of leather jackets and other farm crop pests in a day. A true farmer s friend but usually cursed and abused. There are several rookeries around the village but other commuting rooks, jackdaws. etc pass through the area from the north and west of the valley to feed in areas some miles away even as far as North Yorkshire. Birds like the gulls and the crows find a daily journey of up to 40 miles to get to feeding area of little problem.

It is encouraging to see a return to the area of the song thrush. Although numbers have been down over recent years there has been some recovery. Its larger cousin the mistle thrush or the country man s storm cock is present in good numbers in old park land by the river. The name country man s storm cock originated from the bird s habit of singing from a tall tree on the wildest of days, probably in the teeth of the Helm wind.

There are plenty of blackbirds about; in fact this lovely songbird is more numerous than ever. For some reason the song thrush loss has been their gain. In July the colourful goldfinch is a regular visitor to gardens and when the thistle sheds its seeds the goldfinch is at its busiest. There is no shortage of our regular garden visitors such as the chaffinch, the robin, blue and great tit and even these days the occasional great spotted woodpecker can be seen in and around the gardens especially in the winter. One rather sad note in this apparent success of the local bird life is the mysterious fall in numbers in our sparrow population. Perhaps this can be explained by the disappearance of our village farm stack yards. Very much a farm yard bird its environment has changed dramatically over the last 30 years. The rather mournful and monotonous call of the coloured dove was certainly not heard in this area fifty years ago. This bird irrupted out of the Middle East area to spread over Europe is a phenomenon not yet explained and our village has a small population of these seed eating birds. Wood pigeons and stock doves are fairly plentiful in our countryside.

The wild life of our area includes many species of shy and retiring mammals. Badgers, foxes, roe and fallow deer roam in woods and fields all around although not easily seen. It is said that otters are returning to the riverbanks in small numbers. That is encouraging, as they will help to keep the very predatory mink away from our riverbank. Determined efforts are made to keep the mink numbers in check preferably absent all together.

Our lovely part of the Eden Valley is richly endowed with wild life. Changing farming methods over the years have inevitably affected the survival rate of some species but generally speaking it as wild life healthy an area as any in the country.

The Privvy

by Audrey Dent

I remember as a child our small house at the bottom of the garden. It was a purpose built affair, about six by four feet, and the toilet ran along the full length of an outside wall. There were no fancy furnishings; it was simply a brick built compartment with a wooden seat. The wood was bleached and scrubbed white. I guess whoever designed it had just read the story of the three bears because there were three round holes, a choice of medium or large for the adults and a small one for the children. Each hole had a wooden lid. It was quite high but there was a little step for the children to climb on. The floor was covered with stone flags and it was jolly cold in winter. There was never any heating and there were no water pipes to freeze - personal comfort was obviously not considered a necessity.

As children, if we were desperate and found an adult in occupation , we were allowed in to sit with them - a cosy family relationship in those days. The brick walls were whitewashed and there was usually a pile of newspapers so the men would sneak in for a quiet read. Newspapers were also used as toilet paper and were torn or cut up into squares, threaded on a string and then hung on a nail. This was a job for the children.

Audrey Dent s privvy

On the outside wall was a metal sheet which lifted up and about once a month, or even longer, a man came to empty the contents. It must have been an awful job, but he couldn t have objected too much because ours was only one of many that he attended to. One would have thought the smell, especially in summer, would have been horrendous and that it would have been a maternity unit for breeding flies, but I can honestly say I don t remember this being so. Perhaps the fact that the ash from the previous day s coal fire was thrown down each morning had something to do with it. I don t know whether this neutralised or purified it to some extent but it certainly served some useful purpose. I

Edith Stockdale s privvy

understand from an older friend that each cart load of waste would be taken and spread on fields in the village. This was not as revolting as it may sound as my friend told me that the hot ash would have burnt the newspaper and would also have dried up the waste to a great extent and this, together with the ash itself, made very good fertiliser.

Earth closets were always built a long way from the house, a distance of around 30 yards in our case. I suppose this was for health reasons. It was therefore a major event in the middle of the night if a toilet call was necessary. I can remember lying awake, dreading the thought of getting out of my nice warm bed on a cold, dark, winter s night to face the elements. It must have been a funny sight, had anybody been watching, seeing two little nightdress clad, torch bearing, children walking hand in hand to the little house (my sister and I always woke each other up for company). There was no light switch and if the torch failed it was more than a bit scary. This is probably why my sister and I went with each other willingly. There were all kinds of night noises, but we got used to these.

I can remember as older children, we were very cautious about visiting the privvy when it was time for Tom (known fondly to the village as Tomer-Romer), with his horse and cart to come and do his dirty work. We were frightened he would open the door at the back and have a peep-show. This was also the case at school, so we used look-outs there.

The thing I find most odd now about the design of the privy is the fact that there was no law saying there must be a wash basin, or at least a tap, for hand washing purposes, and as far as I know, none of them had. I m sure as children, if we were playing outside, we would not have had the time or the inclination to go into the house to do this necessary chore.

Even the luxury of a new flush toilet was marred by the fact that it was installed in a building outside the house, thus necessitating the aforesaid open air trek; not as far perhaps, but just as chilly in winter and still scary.

A little story I ve just remembered! My sister had to take some medicine,

149

THE PRIVVY

milk of magnesia, which she hated. After having it spooned into her she decided it was so distasteful she would have to get rid of it. Her common sense didn t tell her a quick swallow was the easiest way. Oh no! It was so unpalatable she had to find some other means of disposing of it and the only way she could think of, without Mum seeing her, was to hold it in her mouth till she got to the private place at the bottom of the garden. By this time her mouth was truly coated with the furry stuff she objected to so much and although she may still have had a pain in her tummy, the exercise did teach her a lesson in taking medicine!

THE POOR LITTLE HAS-BEEN
I m a privy at the bottom of the garden
All purpose built and private as can be
An intruder when I m occupied must ask for pardon
Although there s room enough in here for three

I think I m something special, though I wouldn t say I m smart
My walls are painted white and rather bare
I m just an ordinary little building from others set apart
But when you re desperate and you need me I am there

Should you be sitting comfortable and cosy
And you hear a noise behind which makes you quake
Don t worry it s not someone being nosey
It s old Tom whose come to clean me with his rake

Old Tom s the man who, monthly, calls to take away my load
With his job well done, I couldn t feel much cleaner
Oh! It s good to hear his cart wheels on the road
And the fields around are definitely greener!

I ve a secret that perhaps I shouldn t tell you
But I will because, you see, it boosts my pride
If the menfolk through the day get tired, as they do
I m the quiet little haven where they hide

One day a week my mistress goes quite crazy
She attacks me like the waves upon a beach
When she s finished I am whiter than a daisy
Through her scrubbing and her scouring with the bleach

Today I heard a very tragic story
I do believe we re going to get the push
Yes, we at last are giving up our glory
To a new sophisticated toilet that will flush

But, when the plumbing s all gone wrong
Or the summer drought if long
And the water isn t flushing as it should
Ah! then you ll all be wishing that we hadn t gone for good.

Audrey Dent, November 1996

People of Bolton

GEORGE BOWNESS 1762-1837

George Bowness is cited as being one of the eminent men of North Westmorland. He was born at Little Scales near Bolton, the son of William and Bridget Bowness. He was baptised in Bolton Church on 12 January 1762 and educated at Bolton and Appleby schools.

When he was able he joined the British Army becoming a Lieutenant Colonel in 1804 and Colonel in 1813. He was a member of the East India Company and married Harriet Robinson, a London architect s daughter in India. They had six sons and five daughters. They returned to England in 1817 and George became Major General George Bowness in 1819.

He died in Chippenham, Wiltshire, in 1833 after a long army career which is apparently documented in the United Service Journal of October 1833.

John Bowness, George s son also joined the army, the 80th Regiment of foot or Staffordshire Volunteers. He held the rank of ensign 26 August 1815, a rank in the regiment. He became a Lieutenant on 7 April 1825 and a Captain on 11 June 1830. He was placed on half pay 8 July1836 and the last entry on the army list for him was in 1846 when he was still on half pay. General George and William Bowness his father were benefactors of one of Boltons Charities for the poor.

A record in *Bygone Cumberland and Westmorland* by D. Scott and brought to my attention by Bob Thwaites of Morland reads: Penance in connection with illegitimacy was not uncommon; therefore the following entry which occurs in the Kirkby Thore register dated 27 June 1779, after the baptism of an illegitimate child, must be taken only as an example: William Bowness, of Bolton Bachelor, Francis Spooner Widow of this Parish, the parents under went a public penance in this church.

MARGARET JENNINGS 1889—1970

Margaret Jennings was born November 1889 to Margaret Akrigg, nee Bland. At the time of her birth her mother was 46 years old. It appears that she kept the pregnancy a secret because Cuthbert Jennings had died two years before. If the whereabouts of the father was ever mentioned Margaret would burst into tears.

The labour was long and the delivery difficult and mother and child were not expected to survive. In attendance at the time of the birth were Miss Mary Anne Edmonson, possibly a friend of Margaret s, Dr Spencer and the village midwife. Revd. Suttie who was summoned to baptise the child before she died joined them shortly after the birth. Baby Margaret was baptised in the presence of Mary Anne, who assumed the role of the child s godmother whilst the doctor and midwife attended her mother.

A few anxious days passed as the mother regained her strength and the baby struggled to survive but survive she did. There is some mystery surrounding the baby s birth. She is recorded in the church registers as Margaret Jennings with blank spaces where the father s name and occupation should be. Her mother is stated as Margaret a widow.

Margaret senior had married Sam Akrigg a schoolmaster in 1870. He was much older than Margaret and died the following year when their first and apparently only child Isabella was born. A second child was born to Margaret called Elizabeth and baptised in July 1877 and although Margaret s husband Sam had been dead for six years she was given the name Akrigg in the register. No father s name is given and Margaret is listed as a widow.

Margaret met Cuthbert Jennings sometime prior to 1882 as Mary their first child was born that year, followed by Cuthbert in 1884 and Margaret Alice in1889. There is no marriage recorded for Margaret and Cuthbert in the church records and it appears likely that they were not married. No baptism is record-ed for either Cuthbert or Mary but we know they are Margaret s children as they are listed in the 1891 census.

After Cuthbert died Margaret and her family had to live in much reduced cir-cumstances and life was very hard for them. The Blands were a well to do and a respected family in the village and Margaret s apparent fecklessness will have been viewed with disdain. She certainly appears to have been disinherited and ostracised by some members of her family.

They could not afford to live in the family home and were forced to move. Mr Dent of Prospect House came to their rescue and made good his little cottage for them. The cottage was too small for all their furniture and he allowed Margaret to store what would not fit into the little house in his barn. Sadly Margaret never again had room for it and it slowly rotted away. They lived in Dent s cottage until they moved to Appleby some years later.

Baby Margaret s godmother was the daughter of Joseph and Margaret Edmondson. Joseph was a miller possibly at Bolton Mill c1827. Her brother Michael became a farmer at Old Bewley. Miss Edmondson took her duty as godmother very seriously and watched over and supported Margaret throughout her life. Margaret spent many happy hours at Old Bewley and at Mary Anne s home. They were very close and Mary Anne was instrumental in helping Margaret to fulfil her ambition to become a nurse.

Isabella does not appear to have been ostracised by her maternal grandmoth-er. She was living with her, her uncle Nathan, who was a tailor and draper and

Aunt Emma at Prospect Cottage Farm in 1891. She attended the Misses Thompson s school in Long Marton, which appears to have been a fee-paying school. Perhaps the Blands accepted her because she had had a respectable birth. Uncle William lived across the road at Pennine View rented from Colonel Graham of Eden Grove. He had an egg collecting and packing business. When Margaret was older uncle William gave her a job packing eggs but much of the money she earned had to go to her mother to help with providing for the family.

Alice Jennings Darrow

Elizabeth, Mary, Cuthbert and Margaret attended the village school where Margaret certainly suffered humiliation over the circumstances of her birth. The hurt inflicted appears to have stayed with her throughout her life. She describes herself as reckless and started to escape from home at a very early age only to be found hours later at one of her favourite haunts usually Simpson's the blacksmith or playing in the fields by Luz Beck. Once she was very lucky not to drown when she fell into the river Eden and was rescued by one of the villagers working near by.

She had two cats as pets and she adored them. She attended the Sunday school class taught by Miss Dent of Prospect House and was often a member of the congregation in the chapel. Her grandmother had a lodger Joseph Cannon and he and Margaret became very good friends. When he became blind Margaret would happily take him to his friends and to the chapel. He was a religious man and often discussed his faith with her.

When aunt Emma married Robert Allonby a farmer Margaret loved to visit them at Sockridge House, Sockridge. She would feed the hens and ride the ponies. The family also experienced kindness from uncle Henry and aunt Ester who lived in Sale, Cheshire.

One Christmas Cuthbert got a book as a present *Where Glory Calls*. It was a history of the Crimean War and one of the illustrations was of Florence Nightingale carrying a lamp and walking down the middle of a room. On either side were beds with soldiers in them. From that time on Margaret vowed she would be a nurse - a war nurse.

The chances of her achieving her ambition were slight. Her mother could not

Alices step cousins Amy and Roberta Brunskill. Alice formed a life long friendship with Roberta and regularly corresponded with her over the years. Roberta is the mother of Betty Fisher from Crosby Ravensworth who now lives in Cliburn.

afford the training and she needed Margaret to work nearer home to help her and to work to contribute to the family finances.

When her sister Elizabeth married she emigrated to America in search of a new life and in her letters home she told Margaret she could begin nurse training much earlier there and she would not have to pay but would receive a reasonable wage. Margaret was so determined to go she saved as much of the money as she was allowed to keep for herself. Her godmother helped her with the paper work and also provided her with the money for her passage.

Margaret began her nurse training in America in a New York hospital but there was some delay in her receiving her certificate because she had had typhoid and had to have several months away from her studies whilst she recovered. She qualified just as the First World War started and sailed home to begin her work as a war nurse with the Red Cross.

She was sent to the front to work in a Belgian hospital and after the war apparently received five distinguished service medals from three different countries for valour under fire. After the war she returned to America and worked for many years as a field nurse with the Department of Public Health. She worked with the Indians travelling many miles on foot, horseback and by car through Dakota, Colorado and Montana. Her aim was to improve their general health by teaching them basic hygiene and nutrition and setting up mothers clubs. In gratitude for this work she was honoured by being adopted by the Indians into the Sioux-Assinaboine tribe of Indians, of the Fort Peck Reservation. She was given the name Wi-Cha-goi-Wa-Sta Princess Bright Star. Margaret established a grant for education out of her own limited income for the education of the most promising Indian student.

CHANGING TIMES

Margaret was married twice and twice widowed, her second husband being killed in the Second World War. She was active in the Civil Rights Campaign in Cambridge, Maryland and was instrumental in establishing one of the first eye banks in the United States. She campaigned tirelessly to improve the conditions of animals used in laboratory experiments.

She wrote and had published a book *Hold High the Lamp* by Alice Jennings Darrow. It is based on her life from birth up to and including the First World War and gives the impression that her childhood experiences influenced the focus of her work in later life. Some of it is fiction but the majority of it is fact. She preferred to be called Alice, her middle name and the name that family members knew her by.

Alice was very friendly with one of aunt Emma's step-children Roberta (a step cousin.) Uncle Robert had been married before to Margaret Brunskill, nee Simpson. From Margaret s first marriage Roberta and Amy had been born. Margaret can only have been married to Robert for a short period before she died in 1893 at the age of 46.

Roberta married Jim Laycock. She was housekeeper for Nathan Bland prior to her marriage and Roberta and Alice appear to have shared a life long friendship. In 1942 Alice sent to Roberta a little anthology of poems she had had printed called *Threads in the Weave* as a Christmas greeting. The first poem is printed below:

Then and Now
In their great wisdom philosopher and sage
Look not behind upon the past when turned its page;
Its dead and done, we live today, prepare for the tomorrow
For what it brings, and bring it will, both joy and sorrow.

But what of you and me, who have more yesterdays
To count, than we can have tomorrows or todays;
The Meridian has been passed, our fires are burning low,
Flickering, uncertain, in an anguished world at war.

Today when in some stern uncompromising duty,
Be grateful for the past, its memories, its beauty;
We can envision mountains, and the hills of home,
As we perform each war time task which must be done.

I think of England s children, their little faces grim,
Leaving their beds, and marching forth amid the awful din
Of bursting bombs, yet proudly know that some where in the sky,
The RAF will do its best, prepared to do or die.

My childhood seems another age, where neither time nor space
Could dim one scene or change the contour of its line of grace;

PEOPLE OF BOLTON

The Pennine Range of mountains and the Northland weather,
The lightning flashing on the hills and on the purple heather.

Old Crossfell, Knock, and Dufton Pike, and down below the Fells,
Where Nathan s sheep were grazing among the Scotch blue-bells;
Old Tweed the faithful collie, at night would bring them in,
The sheep and lambs accounted for, sent bleating to their pen.

The little island near the mill, I knew its secret bowers,
I waded through each Spring to pick the first wild flowers;
The little Spring white violet, is ever found, such fragrance
Which can be stored in memories chest and so the past enhance.

To church each Sunday morning, and as the last bell rings,
The Sabbath service has begun, the congregation sings
 COME THOU ALMIGHTY KING and outside in the ivyed wall
A lowly bird bursts into song,   Let not the sparrows fall.

My mind is on the tuneful bird, it should be on the service,
The Rector s voice is soothing, soon I'm lost in drowsiness;
 LET YOUR LIGHT SO SHINE ? I wake up, startled, drop my book
My collection money rolls away, I crouch below to look.

The Warden waits; at last it s found, and planted on the plate
A jingling penny to help some heathen through the Pearly Gate;
The benediction then is said, the last Amen intoned,
We leave the hallowed portals with its Holy Writ enthroned.

Through the old churchyard, our friends and neighbours idly saunter,
They talk of next day s auction Mart and other friendly banter;
Walking behind with step uncertain, his vision growing dim,
Is Joseph the village saint, we children worshiped him.

Such were the days so long ago, another world it seems
Where through the woods and lanes, I roamed in youthful dreams;
How blessed that we can not peer behind the future s veil
God grant well always Carry On ; let not our courage fail.

God guard our children of today wipe from their hearts all fears;
Blot out the memory of war, wipe from their eyes the tears;
Oh may tomorrow compensate them for the days that are,
When by the might of all free men, is slain the Monster, War.

Alice Jennings Darrow, 1942

A truly remarkable lady and one whom there is so much more to write about but
time did not allow for the research required.

CHANGING TIMES

ADA ADDISON

Ada Addison was born Ada Savage on 13 August 1903 which was a very wet summer. She was the middle of seven children, two girls and five boys. Their parents were John Wharton Savage and Mary Savage, nee Frith, from Kirkby Thore.

Ada was about fourteen when she moved to Hanging Bank, now known as Eden Bank, from Birkshead, Bleatarn,Warcop. The family were moved there by horse and cart lent by Jack Chappelhow. The cart was flat and much bigger than most so it was easy to load with furniture. Neighbours and relatives all helped to load the cart the day before and that night they all slept on mattresses ready for an early start the following day. Fortunately the day was fine and dry for the journey to Hanging Bank was fourteen miles distant and took many hours. Some one had gone on ahead in pony and trap to take all the food and all the animals were walked to their new home several days before the move. Their new neighbours were the Davidsons at Peatgate, the Wills at Mansgrove and the Thelkelds at Laitha.

Work on the farm was very hard with no machinery, as there is today and little help from horses. The farmers worked from dawn to dusk and every one helped from the youngest upwards. Holidays were non-existent and the only days away from the farm were to go to the local shows. Children might go away to relatives in a near by village for a holiday.

Ada s mother had a poultry enterprise and would sell newly hatched chicks

Ada Addison, nee Savage, pictured left with John William Savage and baby David Nattrass on his knee and Cathy Nattrass, nee Addison.

157

to people living over a wide area. Ada remembers cycling to Ousby to Mrs Chappelhow with chicks in a card board box strapped to the carrier of her cycle. She cycled many miles to deliver new chicks.

William Cherry and his two sisters were grandad's cousins and William had a cycle shop in Bolton. Ada got her first bike from there. It was a Sit up and Beg and she would cycle from Hanging Bank into Bolton coming via the lane on the right, down the track at North End, now, very over grown and impassable.

Ada s mother would take butter to Long Marton station and put it on the train to Valley Road, Shipley. Aunt Alice would weigh it out and sell it to others in her street. Another memory Ada has is of Mrs Torbock from Crossrigg Hall opening the Memorial Hall. Part of the celebrations was a fancy dress parade judged by Mrs Finch Dawson from Burwain Hall and her daughter s Georgina, Felicia and Rhoda.

Her worst memory was of when she was taking an empty cart back to the hay field through a gateway when the cart caught the side of the gate stoop that frightened Teddy the horse. Teddy bolted and Ada was thrown out of the cart. Her screams brought Jack Craig who was working in a near by field running. He picked her up but she was battered and sore for many days. Jack was the hired lad from Milburn.

Robert John Addison the landlord travelled to the farm in his pony and trap twice yearly to collect the rent. He was a distinguished man with a snowy beard and smart clothes. Little did Ada think she would marry his eldest son Robert in years to come.

William Crosby from Powis House, Long Marton used to go to Hanging Bank after the clipping. Ada remembers him very well and can visualise him sitting outside the house. He was a very down to earth man who had many sayings about people who had gone up in the world. Ada s favourite and one she has often used herself was, They forgot the midden on which they grew and think themselves lord knows who.

The house had no mains water. Drinking water was fetched in a bucket from a spring down the cow pasture and the well in the yard provided the water for everything else. The first car the family had was a Ford. Bill, Ada s brother was the driver and now instead of going to Appleby market in the pony and trap and having to stable the horse at the Grapes and leave the trap on the Sands they went in the car. Regular customers would go to the market in Appleby to buy butter, eggs, cream and chickens from them. They would also sell fruit from the orchard.

One day Robert Addison visited the farm at Hanging Bank, their friendship developed and they were married in 1927. They farmed at Greystone House,

Kings Meaburn, for 32 years and their children Mary, Cathy and Steel were born there. Robert and Ada retired in 1959 and moved to Lyvennet House and Steel took over the farm. Robert died on 1 September 1963 aged 70 years.

Lizzie, Ada s sister married Charles Graves (brother of Frank) and went to live at Yew Tree Farm, Kings Meaburn. John, Fred and Tom married and moved to other farms. John to Kings Meaburn Mill, Fred to High Whitber and Tom to Laitha, where Tom's son farms today.

Joe and Bill remained single and retired to Prospect House, Bolton with their father when their mother died aged 68 years. Ada s father died in 1956 aged 87. Her mother, father and four brothers are all buried in Bolton churchyard.

Today Ada still lives independently in her own home in Kings Meaburn and farms from the sitting room window. She taught herself to crochet many years ago. She still does this and tapestry work as hobbies to a very high standard indeed. Two years ago she wrote and had published, just for the family, a little book about her life. It is with her permission that extracts are published here and I thank her for allowing me to spend a very interesting afternoon with her.

BILLY HOWE

Billy Howe who is now 88 years of age, has lived in Bolton longer than any other resident. He was born in Morland and moved to Peatgates when he was two or three years old. He was born in 1913 and started Bolton School at the age of five, leaving when he was fourteen.

When he left school he went to work in Lowthian s drapery shop in Appleby. He has lived all his life at School View except for a short time when he went to live at Guardhouse, Threlkeld, to work as a joiner in the barytes mine at Mungrisedale. He served in the army during the 2nd World War and went to India with the Royal Army Medical Corps, working in the cook house. In September 1935 he married Margaret Jane Baxter and they had three daughters - Ruth, Joy and Mary.

Billy Howe aged five.

Billy Howe and Margaret Peggy Jane Baxter on their wedding day in 1935.

After the war he came back to Bolton and went to work on the railway in Appleby as a joiner, a job he continued for 27 years, travelling by push bike at first and later by car. He learned his joinery skills at the firm of Russells who were based at the west end of Chapel Street in the village.

Billy and his wife Margaret, known as Peggy, fostered many children during their life together. The children came to them as tiny babies and stayed until they could be adopted.

Peggy loved making dressing up clothes not only for her own children, but for children in the village to dress up for the Field Day and other local shows. In the autumn village people would collect rose hips and take them to Peggy to be weighed and packaged ready to be sent to a factory for processing into Vitamin C syrup for children. People were given 3d a stone for their work.

Billy has been a widower for the last thirteen years. He enjoys attending the day care centre in Appleby twice a week and goes to Edenside another day. He has regular visitors from his family and friends.

HARRY BELL

Harry Bell moved to Street House farm with his parents and brothers and sisters when he was about ten years old. He was born at Waterhouses between Soulby and Great Asby on 19 March 1921. The farm had been left in trust to William and John Dent but William was not interested in farming and went to work as a signal man on the railway and John had his interests in Elm House, so the farm was sold to the Bells. Harry worked the farm with his brother Jim. Jim lived at the farm and Harry lived in Chapel Street in the village.

Harry married Minnie Raine in 1943. They were the last couple to be married in Great Asby Church and went on honeymoon to Morecambe with George and Rita Ellwood. They had three children - Christine, Gwen and Robert. Sadly

Harry s wife died 20 years ago. She will be remembered in the village as being a staunch W.I. member being secretary for many years.

Harry enjoyed his farm life especially the cows. They had a milking herd of 97 and Harry viewed them as his friends. He discovered that he had a skill with divining rods and using brass stair rods he was able to detect watercourses on the farm. One day his brother and a friend had spent all morning looking for a drain on the farm and had returned very dirty to the house for their dinner. While they were eating Harry took the divining rods up to the field where the two men had been working and within seconds he had found the drain. He has been asked to detect for other things, for example rock beds. He would hold a piece of rock in one hand whilst using the rods and it never failed.

Many years ago Mrs High who lived at Eden Grove Lodge lost her gold watch but Harry did not think he would be able to find it. He decided to use the same technique as he did when needing to locate rock only this time he held a gold brooch in his hand. The rods swung him round and lead him across the road and there was the watch lying on the grass verge next to where Mrs High s car had been parked in the road earlier.

Another very vivid memory Harry has is of his father Robert who was in the byre at Street House. It was July 1934 and his father was getting ready to take the bull out when it suddenly attacked him. Robert junior, Harry s brother and a farm hand, ran to the rescue and tried to drive the bull away with sticks and pitch forks. Their efforts were useless and Robert and the farm hand ran to the house for more help, the bull continuing to gore Robert senior. The commotion

A ploughing competition at Winderwath when Harry Bell got stuck in the mud and had to be pulled out by Jeff Tatters.

alerted Laddie, Robert senior s dog, who ran up and started snapping at the bull s heels. This distracted the bull long enough for Robert to get to his feet and go up to the house. He received some painful injuries and was very severely shocked but after treatment from the Appleby doctor he made a recovery. Harry feels the incident may have shortened his father s life as he only lived two years after the incident but if it had not been for the dog Robert would almost certainly have been killed that day.

Harry has always enjoyed ploughing ever since he went to help a neighbour. The neighbour was very behind with his ploughing and if he did not get it done he would not get the grant he so badly needed. Harry made such a good job of it that his neighbour said he was going to enter him in the Cliburn ploughing match. Harry really did not want to do this as it made him feel very nervous but the neighbour insisted saying he could use his plough. He did later buy his own, as it was unloaded for the auction. In the first match he entered he came 3rd and the second time he won. His best match being when he beat the world champion at Temple Sowerby.

Harry has been a long-standing member of the parish council taking a term as chairman and a member of the Memorial Hall committee. During the war years he was in the Home Guard. He remembers two German officer prisoners of war escaping from Shap Wells. They looked all night for them in Strickland and Crosby Ravensworth and then they saw them just standing there in front of them. Harry had five rounds of ammunition but was not allowed to use them unless he was fired on. A rule he often thinks about and finds very amusing.

Another memory was of a Spitfire being dive bombed over the wood near the river Eden at Appleby. It caught the tree tops and came down with bullets flying everywhere. The engine was found on the footpath at the top of the wood and the pilot s body was picked up in bits.

Street House was sold using modern technology via the internet. Amongst the interested parties were Posh and Becks and Harry enjoyed showing them around and found them to be very pleasant company. The farm was eventually sold to Malcolm and Tina Strong. They moved to Street House from Sleagill where Malcolm farmed with his brother and late father. Malcolm and Tina have two children George and Daisy.

Harry still visits the farm and helps where he can and pursues his hobby of making weather vanes. He made one recently for Dan and Val Bromley for Old Bewley. Harry has donated a black oak pegged parsons seat to the Methodist Chapel, in memory of his wife s grandfather who made the seat and was himself a staunch Methodist.

ARTHUR BIRD

Mr. and Mrs. Arthur Bird live at Birdby farm on the Bolton to Penrith road. The house is a Grade II listed building and has been owned by the Bird family since the 14th century when it was first built. The Bird family were at one time the largest land owners in the area.

Hazel Bird trained as a school teacher teaching music and singing part-time at local schools, including Bolton School. She sang professionally and was for many years principal soprano with the Penrith Savoyards. Care of her family was always her main priority and she was kept busy on the family farm.

Hazel s husband, William Arthur Bird, is commemorated in the church along with his brother Joseph, as having served in the RAF during the 2nd World War. While serving in the RAF he was known as Dickie. He learned to fly with the Civil Air Guard in Carlisle at five shillings an hour, travelling there every week by car with a few friends. At the age of eighteen, after only four months tuition, he obtained his pilot s licence and joined the Volunteer Reserve. With the threat of war he piloted a Tiger Moth from the Preliminary Flying School in Liverpool via Sywell in Northamptonshire to St. Leonards, near Hastings. He was not there long before he was selected for commissioning and sent to Cranwell for officer training in 1940.

After commissioning he was posted to Aston Down to 23 Squadron the Red Eagles which was Douglas Bader s old squadron. The squadron members were flying their early intruder operations in Bristol Blenheims. In 1941 he flew his first Havoc Mark I and describes his assignments as having to fly at night to seek and destroy enemy air-craft over their own bases on the continent. They carried a 1000lb bomb load on these missions and in addition had four machine guns in the front and one in the back. Their flying range was very limited.

From 23 Squadron, Dickie was posted to 14/51 flight, flying Havocs fitted with a Turbinlite search light in the nose. The idea was that they would use their radar to search out

Arthur Dickie Bird. The photograph was taken at Manston in 1941 by a Canadian who was a rear gunner and who was killed in action the following day.

the enemy aircraft, pick it out with the search light and shoot it down. This was not very successful.

Dickie spent some time as an instructor at the Operation Training unit, Central Flying School, Cranfield, before being posted to 605 Squadron in 1943 to fly with the Warwick Mosquitoes. Dickie thought the Mosquito was a great aeroplane with good armaments and range and should have been commissioned much earlier in the war. He also felt he had a very good navigator in his friend Les Hodder. While he was with 605 Squadron he was awarded the Distinguished Flying Cross for his intruder work.

Dickie was a very skilled pilot, flying many different types of planes. His favourites were the Spitfire, the Mosquito and the Lancaster. When he was de-mobbed in 1945 he was with the Transport Command at Pershore, instructing pilots to fly Beauforts, and also flying aircraft all round the world, including the Middle and Far East and Africa. By 1945 he felt it was time to return to Cumbria as by then he had given his Guardian Angel a good run.

DAVID DENT

David is the eldest son of the late John and Dorothy Dent of Elm House, Bolton and the brother of Dennis, farmer in the village, the Revd Tony, Marjorie from Great Asby, Rosemary from Carlisle and Stephen, Kirby Lonsdale

David attended the village school and then went on to Appleby Grammar

A wedding party photograph taken outside Glebe House. Left to right - Tony Dent (now Revd), Kathleen Bellas, David Dent groom, Audrey Dent (nee Bellas) and Dorothy Bellas.

The marriage of John Henry Dent to Lena Brunskill

school. When he left school he went to work with Tommy Longstaff, town clerk for Appleby to train to become an accountant.

On return from doing National service he saw an advert in the *Herald* for the job of secretary to Carlisle United football club. The advert asked for someone interested in sport and with some knowledge of book keeping. He felt that the job would suit him and applied for it. He was successful and at only 23 years he became the youngest secretary in football league. He remained at Carlisle United for 18 years.

He married Audrey Bellas who lived at Glebe House and the couple had two children, Joanne and Lindsey. Whilst he was at Carlisle the club had its most successful time. The club was promoted from the fourth division in 1964 and this was followed by the third division championship. In 1974 the club won a place in the first division, now the Premier League.

In 1978 David went to work with Coventry City who at that time were being managed by Jimmy Hill. After six years there David saw another opportunity, this time administering the Football League at their headquarters in St Annes. He now had a much broader view of the business as he looked after the interests of all the clubs instead of one.

PEOPLE OF BOLTON

TONY DENT

Tony Dent, David s brother is well known by those who have lived in the village a long time. Tony or to give him his full title the Revd Tony Dent is a Methodist minister in Settle. He says other people appeared to know before him that he would have a career in the church. He remembers Jack Stockdale working at Elm House when it was hay time. Jack was helping Tony s dad to trample the hay down so they could get more into the barn when Tony appeared round the barn door. Here comes the little parson , said Jack Stockdale.

Whilst Tony was in the sixth form at school he did consider being a teacher of geography but instead of pursuing his idea he went home to work on the farm for two years. It was when he was nineteen that he applied to become a minister and started the rounds of interviews and entrance examinations. He went to theological college, Wesley House, in Cambridge in 1961 and was ordained in 1964. Tony has worked in both rural and urban areas such as Lincoln, Staffordshire, Shropshire, Lancashire, Bradford, and finally Settle.

The Dent family came to Bolton from Kings Meaburn when Henry Dent moved to Gilflosh or Elm House, as it is known today in 1742. Henry married a Barbara Bowness whose home Gilflosh may have originally been. However there is also a record in the Court Rolls stating that Henry Dent today took over Mary Broughams.

ALISON & FRANK BAXTER

During the war Frank was evacuated to Penrith from the north east and, when his mother bought a house at Newby, he would spend most of his spare time on a neighbouring farm. It was here his interest in agriculture was inspired. After school he went to Kings College, Newcastle University, to study agriculture and, following his studies, he went to work at Newton Rigg.

In 1951 Frank moved to Bolton Lodge farm with his parents. Previously the farm was known as Bolton Moor and had been farmed by the Savage family and then the Thwaites. In 1947 it was bought by Percy Metcalf who sold the Baxters the farmhouse and half the land. Mr. Metcalf built a new house called Eden Fields for himself and his family.

Alison also studied agriculture at Newcastle but did not meet her future husband until she went to work in the dairy at Newton Rigg. They were married in 1954 and lived at Bolton Lodge with Frank s parents living in nearby Edenholme. Frank and Alison have five children. Their second son David and his family now live and farm at Bolton Lodge. The farm has grown over the years to around 300 acres.

Frank and Alison bought Holly House from the Dents in the late 1960s as a farm hand s house. Fifteen years ago they moved to Holly House and semi-

Holly House

retirement - Frank says he has come full circle and is now the farm lad again.

During their many years in Bolton the couple have given of their time for the community. Frank has been a magistrate at Appleby for more than 30 years. He is also a member of a Ministry of Agriculture advisory committee and a Willows committee member. The Willows committee let the Willows and parish field every two years and then distribute the money collected to Bolton parishioners.

Alison has been a member of the WI for many years and has been both president and treasurer of Bolton WI. She has been a churchwarden and a member of the Women s Voluntary Service, delivering meals on wheels to people in the village. In 1999 Bolton WI members voted Alison Jewel of a Member. Her name was forwarded to the Federation in Kendal where she was selected for the presentation of the award.

BRIAN STOCKDALE

Gerald Brian Stockdale, known as Brian, was born at Slee Croft on 17 June 1934. His parents were Jack and Evelyn, nee Walker. Evelyn was born at Hanging Bank, now known as Eden Bank. Brian went to Bolton School from the ages of five to eleven and then went to Appleby School.

When he was ten years old he was rewarded for rescuing baby John Smedley from the River Eden. Mrs. Keitch, then headmistress of Bolton School, felt his action was worthy of public recognition and village residents raised the sum of £6 for him. Brian left school at fourteen and went to work on Percy Metcalfe s farm at Bolton Lodge, followed by several other local farms. He met Edith, who

Reward.

Regardless of his personal safety, Brian Stockdale, at the age of 9 years, performed Life Saving in the River Eden, June 30th, 1943.

The deed was one of the utmost bravery and entirely worthy of this Presentation of the sum of £1. 0. 0 (which is to be invested) and which is the gift of the Bolton Parishioners.

M. A. Keitch.
Schoolmistress.

Bolton Red Cross Fête,
August 14th, 1943.

came from Gamblesby, at a Young Farmers dance when he was working for Dolphenby Farm, Edenhall estates. They were married on 10 June 1967. After short periods at farms at Armathwaite and Carlisle, they became tenant farmers at Adenthwaite, Ravenstonedale.

Brian was a keen Rough Fell sheep breeder. He loved the outdoor life and was very observant of wild life and weather patterns. He enjoyed stone walling but, not being a competitive man, he did not enter competitions.

Edith bred and sold Fell ponies as a hobby. She also enjoyed caring for the sheep and used some of the wool for spinning. Another pastime was breeding and rearing poultry. The ponies Edith bred were often prize winners at local shows and both Brian and Edith made many friends through the Fell Pony Society.

While they lived at Ravenstonedale, Edith started a bed and breakfast business which she continued when the couple moved to Bolton. Their very first customers still come to stay with Edith in Bolton. They moved back to Bolton

168

Brian with his sheep at Ravenstonedale

in 1985 to Croft House because Brian had been ill and wanted to take things easy. He went to work for British Steel, Shap for eleven years, a very different type of work which he did not take to easily.

Brian continued to breed sheep as a hobby and they bought two fields behind Croft House and rented the Memorial Hall field. One of Brian s other interests was the Romany Society. As a young boy he spent every opportunity with his brother Des at Old Parks, Glassonby, where Romany, alias the Revd. Bramwell Evans was a frequent visitor. Out with Romany had a massive following and was perhaps the most famous of children s programmes. Edith continued to breed Fell ponies and brought two of her favourites to Bolton - Gypsy and Dinah. One of Gypsy s daughters went to the Royal Mews and was used to compete with by the Duke of Edinburgh in his Fell Pony driving team.

As an extension to the bed and breakfast business the couple converted some old barns into holiday accommodation. This was Brian s proudest project and Edith says she is so pleased he was able to see it completed before his sudden death in September 1999. Brian was a kind, gentle, man who befriended so may people, especially new comers to the village. Edith is carrying on with the many projects they had planned together.

DAVID HAYTON

David and Eleanor Hayton live at Prospect Cottage, a house built around 150 years ago from the materials from a much older house built down the field at the back. The couple have three sons - Christopher, Mark and Philip.

The marriage of Jim Laycock and Roberta Brunskill from Prospect Farm Cottage. Left to right, back row - Chris Butterworth, Tommy Hornesby, John Henry Dent, Joseph Butterworth, and Robert Allonby, vicar.
Row 2 - Annie Brunskill, Mary Butterworth, Evelyn Horn, ?, Molly Butterworth.
Row 3 - Lena Dent, Lizzie Laycock. Jim Laycock groom, Roberta Laycock nee Brunskill bride, Willie Bellas, Eleanor Laycock
Front row - John Laycock (Eleanor Hayton's father), Amy Allonby, Dorothy Allonby, ?.

Eleanor comes from Bolton where her parents bought Prospect Cottage farm as it was known in the 1930s. Eleanor's uncle, Jim Laycock, had lived in the house before this. Her father, John Laycock, who was known as Jack, operated a livestock haulage business from the property. He had several wagons taking livestock all over the country and employed several people to help him. Jack and his wife Maggie also farmed around 150 acres.

David Hayton comes from Bleatarn and he and Eleanor were married in February 1966. David was working as a motor mechanic with J. Burne, Appleby, at the time. They set up home at Hillcrest and later that year David started his own business on the site. He carried out repairs on all types of vehicles and occasionally sold vehicles. His first employee was Alan Fleming from Bolton.

In 1977 after trading ten years, David was offered a retail franchise for

Hillcrest Garage, Bolton in 1980.

Peugeot which led to a direct dealership two years later. The business continued to grow and more staff were employed to cover the increased work shop and sales activity. Eventually the garage at Hillcrest became too small for the growing business and in 1989 moved to Gilwilly Estate, Penrith, and was later extended to Kendal in 1999.

It is very much a family business with Christopher and Philip working with David and Eleanor also working part-time. Mark is following a career in farming, following in the footsteps of both his maternal and paternal grandparents.

Prospect Cottage

THELMA & PHILIP JACKSON

Thelma, nee Nicholson, has lived in the village all her life. As a child she lived in Chapel Street. Her mother was a Bell from Street Farm. She attended school in Bolton and Appleby and when she left went to work with Mr George Ellwood as his farm lad. She had wanted to be a Land Army girl but by the time she left school the war was over. At least I got to wear the breeches, says Thelma.

Philip moved to Eden Bank from Kendal with Mr Tom Carrick as his herdsman and stayed with him for 39 years. Tom and his wife Jean bred Holstein Friesian cattle at Eden Bank for 30 years. The herd had an international reputation and Mr Carrick judged the breed at shows all over the world.

Philip and Thelma met when Philip had been in the village just two days. They were married when Thelma was just 19 and have been married for 44 years. Their married life began in one of the farm cottages at the top of the lane from Eden Bank on the right to Penrith. Their first child Jeremy was born a year later.

Philip has been a member of the Friesian Society for many years and was picked by the society to go to Russia for the British Exhibition in 1964. All kinds of animals went. He took six cows from the Ullswater herd one of the top herds in the country and three times champion at the Royal Show. This had

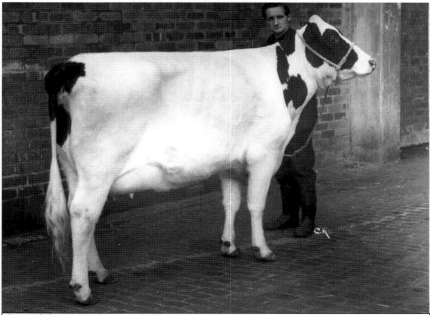

One of the Friesian cows taken to Russia by Philip Jackson

Philip with Jeremy and Ian wearing the hats Philip brought back for them from Russia. Photograph courtesy of the Herald.

never been achieved before or since.

Philip was away for six weeks and says it was a wonderful experience. It was a very poor country and the women appeared to do all the work. He watched the May Day parade and thought it ironical that the country could be so poor and yet have plenty of money for all the armoury. The party was well and truly wined and dined and they met many very interesting people including president Khruschov and Sir Christopher Soames MP. The authorities watched them closely and when they went to the embassy they were counted in and counted out again. When travelling by train soldiers with guns would climb on board at the borders and search the train. It could feel very intimidating. Philip went with the group to see a football match and the Bolshoi Ballet.

Thelma and Philip's second son Ian was born in 1962. Thelma's role was very much that of homemaker and caring for her family. She says that that was what was expected of married women in those days. The only professions for women were teaching or nursing or you could work in a shop or a factory. If you got married you had to leave work. When Tom Carrick became ill Thelma went to care for him.

Jeremy their eldest son became interested in cattle when as a teenager he went to shows with Philip. Jeremy went to Myerscough Hall agricultural college in Lancashire and then worked for Mr Geoffrey Wilson and his wife Marjorie at Low Field Farm, Appleby. In 1986 he exhibited the champion British Friesian winner at the Great Yorkshire show. As a result he was awarded a trophy The Ian Jackson Memorial Trophy donated by Mr Tom Carrick in memory of Jeremy's brother Ian. Ian aged 22 had exhibited the champion British Friesian the year before and shortly afterwards had been killed. His employer, Tom Carrick had given the money for the Yorkshire British Friesian Club to award an annual memorial trophy to be presented to the herdsman or woman in charge of the champion Friesian at the Great Yorkshire Show. It was a proud if emotional moment when Philip and Thelma presented the trophy to Jeremy.

In 1991 Jeremy set up his own business preparing cattle for sale and photographs. Jeremy has now got his own farm in Gloucestershire with his wife Trica, nee Wharton, from Temple Sowerby and three children Tom, Harry and Jo. When Ullswater Royal Sovereign was sold the price was far too high for Jeremy but he was delighted to be able to buy the beast some time later.

The house Philip and Thelma live in today they built about 15 years ago. When Tom Carrick sold Eden Bank Philip went to work for a semen company for 11 years. He says this gave his friends the opportunity to make him the butt for many a good joke.

Thelma was elected to the parish council in 1979 the same year that Mrs Thatcher got into Number 10 says Thelma with a laugh. Thelma stayed on the parish council longer than Mrs Thatcher did in Number 10, retiring in 1998. Thelma went to work at Eden Grove for the Coles after Ian's death for 11 years. She says she just loved being with the children and they helped her at a very sad time. Thelma is very interested in handicrafts and is a very good needle woman. Philip has now retired and top of their list of priorities are their grand children who they try to see as much of as possible.

PAT & DAVID HEATH

Pat and David came to Bolton in 1991 from Sywell in Northamptonshire. David had taken early retirement from Social Services where he had been area director and Pat had secured a job working as a mental health social worker with the community mental health team in Penrith. The couple had spent many holidays in the Lake District and Yorkshire Dales and were planning to retire to the area. They found their house, the Conifers, here in the village and liked it as it was in a lovely unspoilt area.

David continued to do some part time work as a guardian ad litum for three years. He joined the Appleby Bowls Club and a fellow bowler who was a member of the Anglican church in Appleby drew his attention to an article in the local newspaper telling of the plight of the people of Albania the poorest country in Europe. The Anglican Church members were planning to build a hospital in Sarawanda and were asking for supplies. The church both organised fund aid and fund raising and David became involved in helping.

In 1993 and early 1994 he lead a team of 14 people out to Albania with three lorries and one support vehicle. This started a period of several years either taking aid or arranging aid projects. What started as Appleby Albania appeal grew to be the Westmorland Albania appeal. The focus for the aid started to change from hospitals to schools. One of the projects was to arrange for an ambulance to be modified by British Leyland with a Rover Discovery engine to go to a remote hill town in southern Albania. Another was to construct a playground for

The modified ambulance being handed over to David to be painted bright yellow before being taken to its destination in Albania.

children to be able to play on from an enormous heap of rubble. These are just two examples from the many projects that were executed.

David decided to retire from active service when he reached 65. The work was very stressful and his health was beginning to suffer. David has played an American harmonium since he was a child although he describes himself as a piano player really. He is often to be found playing the organ at All Saints for funerals and weddings and plays for the Methodist Chapel every Sunday. He also plays for Long Marton church and plays twice a month for the Methodist church at the Sands in Appleby. David does all this on a voluntary basis and feels he gets more back than he gives.

Pat ran the Sunday school supported by the village church and the chapel in her home for three years. Twelve children attended on a regular basis, which was very good for a small village. Initially the children played small roles in the annual nativity and carol services. Later under Pat s direction they progressed to a full production of nativity and carols in the Memorial Hall. Pat says the success of the school and the nativity was very much due to the support and commitment of the parents. Sadly the children started to go to different schools and had other school and family commitments and the numbers slowly dwindled.

Pat supported David in his involvement with the appeals for Albania in many ways but mostly by helping to sort wash and repair the clothing that were donated from all over the county. She says her home was more often like a Chinese laundry than a home. Pat now has more time to enjoy her garden and care for their dog and the cats that seem to adopt them.

NATHAN SIMPSON ~ Village Blacksmith

Bolton s Smithy was situated about 50 yards east of the cross roads and had been in the Simpson family for generations before it was closed on Nathan Simpson's retirement in 1938. The closure was brought about because of a decline in business caused by the increasing use of the motor car. Farmers were using tractors rather than horses for farm work and horses not used to road work were being allowed to go unshod. Another invention was the use of rubber tyres for farm carts reducing the need for hooping.

The smithy appeared to have been a friendly meeting place and features often in peoples memories of Bolton. People would stand and pass the time of day whilst watching the horses being shod and wheels being fitted with red hot tyres for the village wheel wright to collect later. Many people using the Ribble service to travel between Appleby and Penrith would have been able to savour some of the atmosphere of the smithy when the vehicle stopped outside to set down passengers and pick others up.

Nathan was the first registered smith in the district obtaining a qualification from the Worshipful Company of Farriers in1892. He was very much respected in the area and had a good deal of veterinary knowledge. He was married to Mary Fisher from Appleby and they had three sons Joseph, Harold and John and a daughter. John was a poultry farmer in Bolton. Joseph and his father Nathan opened a shop in Temple Sowerby two days a week but when Nathan retired Joseph left the shop and began farming at Knock.

Nathan's twin brother was a retired road worker living in Bolton and another brother John had the smithy at Long Marton. In the 1850s Henry Dent immigrated to Australia and he wrote to John Dent to ask him to order two ploughs from Bolton s blacksmith for him. Nathan was a member of the parish council taking a term as chairman and clerk and a trustee to the Memorial Hall and Bolton Willows Land. See Simpson family tree page 268.

THE BUTTERWORTHS OF BOLTON MILL

The Butterworths have been in occupation at Bolton Mill since the early 1850s, Graeme and Barbara and their family being the sixth generation to live there. Graeme s father Chris milled himself until after the war, but the necessity for this declined from about 1945. The reason for this was that farmers started to buy tractors for the farm work instead of using horses and the tractors were equipped with a pulley wheel to drive crushes, so farmers could now crush their own meal.

Prior to this time the surrounding farmers brought their oats to the mill to be

CHANGING TIMES

crushed for animal feed. The oat-meal was also used for humans. No flour was milled in Chris time but it had been before. The milling of flour was stopped during the war because the government found it impossible to control the rationing of it.

The oats were dried out in a kiln and then passed through a light set of stones to crack the shell. They were then put through a shelling mill where the husks were blown one way and the kernels the other. The shells were not required by the farm-ers but rather than throwing them away they were fed to the pigs kept in a row of stys in the yard. The ker-nels were put through another set of stones and broken into the size required, rough or fine. The oats were then roasted in a kiln according to taste. Wheat could also be treated

Christopher Butterworth and his wife who were the first Butterworth millers to occupy Bolton Mill.

Bolton Mill

Hay making at Bolton Mill, left to right, Christopher Butterworth (the fourth), Rob Rands, Ted Cragg, Jennie Butterworth and Chris Butterworth (the third).

in this way but no barley was used, as the climate was unsuitable to grow it for milling.

Bread made of wheat would only have been eaten on very special occasions such as christenings and funerals. At funerals small loaves were given to be taken home by the guests to be eaten in remembrance of their deceased neighbour. This bread was known as arval bread. In the poorer homes and farms a bread was made using barley mixed with rye. By the mid 19th century every one was eating wheat bread. Another way of eating oatmeal was to mix it with water and eat it with butter, milk, treacle or beer. It was called hasty pudding and was the principal part of the morning and evening meal.

When Chris' son Graeme and

The third Christopher Butterworth to mill at Bolton. Many old Boltonians will have known his son, the fourth Christopher Butterworth, who was an active member of the Bolton Players.

178

Barbara, Graeme s wife renovated the mill recently a large oven was found in the house. Chris thinks it was used to make bread for the visiting farmers and was probably used by his great great grandfather. Another memory is of water being piped to the house in the early 1930s. Prior to that the family had to go down the lane over the bridge and then over the stile to a spring 50 yards below the bridge. The water came from an overflow piped to the river bank. There was a windmill close by pumping water up to Redlands Bank. The millstream ran down near to the house. The electricity supply was connected to the Mill in 1950.

What of the times before the Butterworths moved in? In 1784 it is recorded in the church register that a daughter born to Peter Reed of Crekenthrop (sic) miller was baptised. It is reasonable to suppose that he could have been miller at Bolton. In 1798 Hugh Heelis MA owned the freehold of Crooks Island upon which Bolton Corn Mill operates. And in 1851 William Mitchell aged 35 years was living there with his family wife Elizabeth, sons John, William, Thomas, Matthew and daughter Elizabeth.

The fifth Christopher Butterworth who milled for a short time, pictured with his son Graeme. The milling has been replaced by farming and two caravan sites - one for static caravans and the other for touring vans.
Graeme and his wife Barbara have renovated the mill to make a very comfortable home. They have incorporated some of the old workings of the mill into the fabric of the building and Chris now lives in a bungalow next door.

Mary Robinson was a house servant and John Connor was a miller. It was after Mr Mitchell's time at the Mill that it passed into the Butterworth s occupancy.

Red Cross support for work in the Great Wars

In 1917 the ladies of the village decided to hold a fund raising event in aid of the Red Cross. It was held in the grounds of Eden Grove loaned for the day by Colonel Palmer. There was a sale of produce and work, a baby show and a tea. £10 was made on the stalls and this was donated towards the benefit of local soldiers on active service. The main event of the day appears to have been the baby show. The judging took place by ballot and the result was a tie between Vera Alice Wilson aged 5 months and Dorothy Sowerby 4 months. A concert was held in the evening at which £30 was made. The proceeds were divided between the committee s fund and Appleby Military Hospital.

A similar event was organised during the 1939-45 war. Records exist for the years 1943, 44 and 45. The fetes were on a much grander scale than the previous one and they were organised by Bolton s WI in association with Crackenthorpe. The committee were - Revd W. Lindop as chairman, Miss M. Allison as secretary (now Mrs Padget Richardson) and Mr J. Bellas as treasurer. There were sub committees for fancy dress parade and sports, baby show, tea, concert and dance, stalls, collecting and for donations. There was a great selection of livestock for auction, some people donated money and others items such as cakes, chocolate, cushions, a hundred weight of oats and a hundred weight of coal.

The 1943 fete was a most successful one raising over £500. Revd Lindop

Commandant, staff and patients at the Red House Military Hospital, Appleby, August 1918.

180

The baby show at a fund raising event for the Red Cross in 1917.
Left to right - Mrs. Graham, Mrs. Arnison, Mrs. Sowerby and Mrs. Wilson.
The fifth lady is unknown.

performed the opening ceremony coupled with this was the presentation of the bravery award to Brian Stockdale for saving baby John Smedley from drowning in the river Eden. The days programme opened with a fancy dress parade judged by Mrs Jackson Dawson and Dr and Mrs Ainscough. The afternoon closed with a football match between two army teams and a concert by the Blackberries . In the evening a dance was held in the Memorial Hall.

The annual fete has evolved into the crowning of the Rose Queen. This was included in the programme for the first time in 1956 and the first Rose Queen was Dorothy Bellas from Sunny Bank (Glebe House). Dorothy wore a white dress with a net over lay and velvet cloak. Dorothy had four attendants Mary Jackson, Eleanor Laycock, Mary Harrison and Judith Metcalf and Barry Bowman, Alan Bainbridge, Brian Nicholson and Joseph Harrison acted as page-boys. Crown bearer was Margaret Fleming. Miss Gentry of the Poplars performed the crowning ceremony. Many Field Days have taken place since that day and every one continues to enjoy them and the facilities the field and hall offer.

Bolton Women s Institute

The year 2000 has been a busy and happy one in the Institute. There have been 24 members with an average attendance of 15. Many Federation events and classes have been attended as well as two group meetings and visits to our neighbouring institutes.

Undoubtedly the highlight of the year was the Millennium Field Day when we entered the cooperative class in the fancy dress. Twelve members dressed (or undressed) as the Yorkshire Calendar Ladies, we didn t win but it was great fun. Again we entered the cooperative class at Appleby Show — this was the mad hatter s tea party - we didn t win but again we enjoyed it.

The Federation Link up day in June was fine, six members donned their fine hats and took the bus to Colby where they were entertained to coffee and refreshments, they then walked home. Two of our members stayed back home and welcomed two ladies dressed in Victorian costume who travelled by horse and carriage from Kings Meaburn to Bolton.

The programme for the year has been interesting and erudite we have had interesting speakers who have introduced us to the Galapagos Islands and the Falklands we have been shown the ancient art of quilling and a few of us had a go at doing it. Undoubtedly the best speaker was Amanda Bell a paramedic who spoke with great knowledge and obviously loves her work. The summer outing was to Oasis the holiday village in Whinfell Woods.

Members of Bolton s Women's Institute in the 1930s.

Some of Bolton Women's Institute who visited Liverpool in May 1940.

The WI members have always been very active and have presented the village with trees for planting on the village green and daffodils to be planted at various places within the village. A seat has been donated for the use of the people of the village. Members have picked up litter in and around the village to keep it tidy.

The WI started the carol singing around the village. Social evenings are organised and the members do most of the entertainment and catering. The Silver Jubilee Party was organised by the WI and the senior citizens party became an annual event for a number of years but has recently not taken place because the number of senior citizens has declined.

We have decorated floats for entry at Appleby Castle and the village fete. Crafts, knitting, cookery and flower arrangements are entered into Appleby and Kendal shows and other county events. We have an annual Christmas dinner and this year it was held at the Corner House in Penrith and this was very successful.

Records of our Institute go back to 1934, but it was started about 1922, the 75th anniversary was in 1997. Some of the founder members were:
Mrs Walker from Crackenthorpe, Mrs Walton, Miss Russell and Miss Longmire.

Bolton's Women's Institute celebrating 35 years in 1962. Photograph courtesy of the Herald.

Our longest serving members are: W. Wills 1952 and T. Jackson, nee Nicholson, 1954.

Presidents from 1975 have been: Mrs P Lynes, Mrs C Wills, Mrs A Baxter, Mrs J Hunter, Mrs T Jackson, Mrs A Shepherd, Mrs B Price, Mrs B Davis.

On average there are 22 members and in the year 2000 there were 24. The Federation is now seeking those people who have been members for a minimum of forty years. Long-standing members in the village are Charlotte Wills, Ena Pigney, nee Laycock, Winnie Wills who joined in 1952 and Thelma Jackson who joined in 1954. New members are always welcome.

Bolton Mothers Union
by Mrs Ann Shepherd

Bolton Mothers Union was re-formed on 13 October 1975. Twelve ladies met in All Saints, Bolton, when Revd Ambrose Southward led the service. Mrs Janet Haythornthwaite, diocesan president was the speaker. Mrs Ann Shepherd was elected enrolling member, Mrs Annie Greenwood secretary and Mrs Jenny Bell treasurer.

Mrs Eleanor Hayton and Mrs Ann Shepherd are two remaining founder members in the year 2000. Meetings are held on the third Thursday of each month in the members homes, unless there is an open meeting, then members and guests meet in the Church or the Memorial Hall. Membership has averaged 12 over the past 25 years.

There are presently 14 members in the branch. The enrolling member is Mrs Helen Harrison and her assistant is Mrs Margaret Wilson. Secretary is Mrs Judith Winter, assisted by Mrs May Forrester. Treasurer is Mrs Ann Shepherd assisted by Mrs Mary Allison. Scrapbook secretary and media representative is

Bolton Mothers Union 25th Anniversary, November 2000. Pictured Helen Harrison (front centre), enrolling member of Bolton Mothers Union, cutting the cake to celebrate the 25th anniversary of the groups re-launch. Guests and past and present members joined in the celebration and the cake was cut by diocesan president Mrs. B. Johnson, Mrs. Harrison and the enrolling member of 25 years ago, Mrs. A. Shepherd. Photograph courtesy of the Herald.

185

BOLTON MOTHER'S UNION

Mrs Eleanor Hayton. The deanery representative is Mrs Barbara Kingston.

The Mothers Union banner stands in Bolton Church and was dedicated in 1987. Mr. & Mrs Len Barham designed the banner and Mrs. Jenny Bell and Mrs Eleanor Hayton embroidered it. Mr. Harry Jones made the oak stand. The Mothers Union supports the church in so many ways:-

Mrs Margaret Wilson - churchwarden.

Mrs Eleanor Hayton and Mrs Ann Shepherd - deputy church wardens.

Mrs Barbara Kingston and Miss Linda Thomas - open and close the church each day.

Mrs Doreen Ridehaugh - assistant organist.

Mrs Kathleen Bainbridge - needlework repairs.

Other members are on the flower and cleaning rotas, also helping with coffee mornings, cream teas and harvest suppers.

The 25th anniversary celebration was held on 16 November 2000 in the WI room, when 20 members and guests sat down to a three course meal. Mrs Barbara Johnstone, diocesan president, toasted the Mothers Union branch, Mrs. Ann Shepherd cut the cake that had been made and decorated by Mrs Mary Allison and Mrs Thelma Jackson. Mrs Annie Kirkup entertained everyone with her dialect poetry.

During the year the vicar, Revd David Wood, enrolled four members. They were Mrs Kathleen Bainbridge, Mrs Barbara Kingston, Miss Linda Thomas and Mrs Doreen Ridehaugh. The annual outing was a visit to St. Michael s Church, Shap. An interesting tour was finished off with a meal at the Brookfield Hotel, Shap.

The highlight of the year was a visit to Orton in April, when the worldwide president, Lady Christine Eames, gave a wonderful address, during which she described some of her fascinating visits overseas.

In November, four members went to Carlisle Cathedral to a millennium service to celebrate Mothers Union in the Carlisle Diocese. Mrs Helen Harrison proudly carried the branch banner. The Bishop of Penrith officiated the communion service. A Christmas party at the home of Mrs Ann Shepherd, finished the year s activities.

Bolton Players

During the 2nd World War, when Birmingham Wagon Repairs took over Eden Grove as their headquarters, their staff and local people formed many friendships. It was during this period that the Bolton Players started their productions and many of these were very successful.

Chris Butterworth can remember doing the milking with his father and making up songs and dittys to sing in the productions. The following was composed and sung by Mr Christopher Butterworth to the tune of Widdicombe Fair, at the farewell supper given to the Wagon Repair members of the Bolton Players on 30 May 1945.

> When Herr Adolf Hitler started bombing at Brum
> All along down, along out, along lee
> A few lads fra that district to Bolton did cum,
> *Chorus:*
> *Harry Hine, Ken Dunn, Bert Whitehouse,*
> *Bill Muirhead, Roy Brown, Ewart Nash*

Bolton Players in 1951. Left to right, back row - Chris Butterworth (senior), Fred Tatters, Maud Jackson, Chris Butterworth (junior), Harold Forrester, Marion Allison, Jackson Bellas, David Dent, Margaret Gaddas, George Ellwood, Roy Forrester, Tommy Huck, Mabel Steadman, Harrison Forrester. Front row - ? Baxter, Audrey Bellas, Ena Laycock, Sylvia Stockdale, Amy Simpson, Celia Butterworth.

BOLTON PLAYERS

and Bill Williams t larl Welshman and all,
Bill Williams t larl Welshman and all.

Noo at first when we saw them they leuked a rum lot
All along down, along out, along lee
And we wondered hooiver we wad keep them in their spot,
Chorus

First a Home Guard was formed and t main on em joined that,
All along down, along out, along lee
Except some at was over old and some over fat
Chorus

They aw hed bits of hobbies and when t neets were leet
All along down, along out, along lee
You d see them in their gardens amangst onions and beet
Chorus

Some liked to play tennis, others greyhounds preferred,
All along down, along out, along lee
Some fancied bee-keeping or fishing my word
Chorus

Some fished with maggots like any local guy
All along down, along out, along lee
But there was one real sports man, he just fished dry fly
Chorus
But we aw gat together when it cum winter days
All along down, along out, along lee
Than sumbody suggested well let s hev some plays
Chorus

So we aw pulled togither, and wed a jolly good run
All along down, along out, along lee
Giving other folks pleasure and oorselves some good fun, wid
Chorus

Noo I think that s enough chaps, I d better lap up
All along down, along out, along lee
So here s to them aw lads, just stand up and sup to
Chorus
Harry Hine, Ken Dunn, Bert Whitehouse,
Bill Muirhead, Roy Brown, Ewart Nash
and Bill Williams larl Welshman and all,
and all of their families and all.

Village Sports

THE DARTS TEAM

Ken Shepherd became involved with the darts team when he first came to Bolton 38 years ago and is still a team member. The team meet in the Eden Vale Inn every Tuesday and Friday evening from September to April each year. There are two sides the Penrith and District Darts League and the Fellside Darts League. Both sides had a very successful time in the early 1970s.

The team took their name of the Crown Aces from the name of the village inn at the time - the New Crown Inn and when Mr John Wilson was the licensee. Mr Wilson had been there for 42 years and was thought at 90 plus to be the oldest licensee in the country.

By the time Ken joined the team Mr Wilson did not serve very much behind the bar, Ella his daughter had taken over that part of the business. Mr Wilson originated from Clithero and came to Bolton as a child. He married Eliza Strong who lived at the Masons Arms, Long Marton. They had three other children Vera who became a teacher, Florrie and William.

Penrith and District Darts League, 1972-1975, left to right, back row - Ken White, Dennis Tatters, Eddie Sowerby, Frank Taylor. Front row - Gordon Shaw, Ken Shepherd (captain), Len Lightburn and Mike Wilson.

Appleby & Fellside Darts League, 1971-72. Left to right, back row - Dennis Tatters, Colin Sowerby, Tom Savage, Alan Bainbridge, Tom Clarke, Frank Taylor. Front row - Mike Wilson, Ken Shepherd, Doug Wills (captain), Len Lightburn, Gordon Shaw.

BOLTON CARPET BOWLERS CLUB

In 1989 the Bolton Carpet Club was set up by Lindsay and Barbara Price at the instigation of the hall committee who provided a set of carpet bowls and the appropriate mat.

At first there were two meetings per week, on Thursday afternoon and Monday evening, the latter being run by Charlotte Wills and Mac MacNulty who also made many of the fittings to go with the mat. Sadly, the evening meeting folded but the afternoon meeting goes from strength to strength.

Currently (2000) there are 18 members; some of these play dominoes instead of bowling. Members pay a nominal sum and provide their own milk, sugar, tea and coffee to decrease expenses. Aggregate competitions in bowling and dominoes result in the presentation of engraved cups, Easter eggs and plants to the winners, according to the season.

Members provide the goodies for their own Christmas party and there is a free monthly raffle. The annual summer trip has taken members to places as far a field as Scarborough and southern Scotland.

An interesting link has been forged with the village primary school who twice a term bake and serve cakes and biscuits for the members. In return the mem-

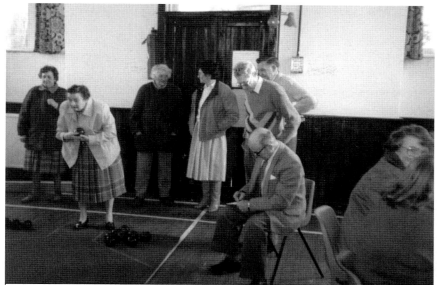

Bolton Bowls Club, 1990. Left to right - Noreen Charlton, Rita Ellwood. Bowling Grace Meadows, June Hunter, George Ellwood, Lindsey Price. Sitting Maurice Stables and Pat McNulty.

bers attend school productions and give each child in the school a small gift at Christmas.

Recently the Bowls Club members bought a second hand mat and bowls set to improve facilities. The Carpet Bowls Club has encouraged members to belong to outdoor bowls clubs in the area, during the summer season. It is also a focus for members who come, meet each other and enjoy the crack.

Barbara Price

BOLTON BADMINTON CLUB

In the two seasons covering the year 2000 there were two teams playing in the Penrith and District Badminton League. There were 25 senior club members paying a £25 membership fee and nine junior members paying £5 each. Membership fees covered the hall rent, purchase of shuttles and insurance.

Senior club nights were held in Bolton Memorial Hall on Tuesday and Thursday nights with juniors on Tuesdays only. Club chairman was Joe Bennett, secretary Alan Fleming and treasurer Richard Forrester. District committee representative and vice chairman of the Penrith & District Badminton League was Alan Fleming.

1st team members were Peter Dent, Ann Coward, Alan Fleming, Barbara Potts, Richard Forrester & Claire Hudson.

2nd team members were John Dent, Martin Fleming, Philip Hayton, Debra Mullen, Sarah Coward, Carolyn Smith and Paul Fleming.

Both teams won several games during the two seasons. An example of a results sheet shows that on Monday 13 November, Bolton A played Shap B in a league game and secured a convincing home win.

Both teams entered into the Ken Shaw Cup. In 1999/2000 the A team lost in the first round to Langwathby B. The B Team also lost in the first round to Stainmore B. Several members have entered into the district tournaments in both seasons.

The Christmas party was held at the Eden Vale Inn on 7 February 2000. All club members were present and a very enjoyable evening was had by all. The party games that followed the meal included the birthday game, Pictionary and the card game. The annual district awards dinner was held at the Conservative Club, Penrith and many members attended. A disco and raffle followed the meal.

Bolton Ladies Football team. Left to right, back row - Maud Jackson, Dot Hutchinson, Ena Laycock, unknown, Doreen Taylor, Mary Sowerby, Sally Ellwood.
Front row - Christine Laycock, Jean Butterworth, Eleanor Laycock, Thelma Nicholson, Kath Bellas.

Millennium Celebrations

In 1999 a committee was formed to oversee activities to celebrate the year 2000. The committee members were: Alan Kingston, chairman; John Bainbridge, secretary; John Cotter, treasurer; Derick Cotton; Claire Hudson; Thelma Jackson; Charlotte Wills and Andrew Allison.

The first event to take place in December 1999 was the planting of a yew tree provided by East Cumbria Countryside Project. The yew is believed to have a spiritual status and is a symbol of life. It is also known to live for many years so perhaps Bolton s yew tree will still be growing in the next millennium. The tree has been cared for by Mona Forrester and Andy Jackson. A stone, provided by former resident Mr. Padget Richardson of Appleby, was erected to mark the occasion. Mr. Michael Graham provided the commemorative plaque.

In February 2000 a ceilidh led by Chris Bland was held in the Memorial Hall. Village people supported the event and everyone had an enjoyable time. In March, Rob and Sylvia Dinsdale, owners of the Eden Vale Inn were hosts for a quiz night with Mr. Brian Lamont organising the event and acting as quiz master. The inn was also the venue for a domino competition in May organised by Mr. Ken Shepherd.

The weekend of 15 and 16 July provided brilliant weather for Bolton Field

The new Memorial Hall clock presented to the village by David & Eleanor Hayton as a thank you to all Bolton residents who gave them support when they had their business in the village.

193

MILLENNIUM CELEBRATIONS

The unveiling of the millennium stone by Billy Howe assisted by the Millennium Committee chairman Alan Kingston (right).

Day. The procession started at North End and was led by the Millennium Rose Queen, Laura Brown, with her attendant flower girls Zara Awde, Sophie Forester and Erin Taylor. The crown bearer was Iona Young and the gift presenter Kirsty Young. The retiring Rose Queen was Joanne Dinsdale with Joanne Mounsey as her attendant and Hollie Tolley as the flower girl.

Richard Birkbeck used his vintage tractor to pull the Queen s trailer to the Memorial Hall field. Revd. Tony Dent, who was born and brought up in the village, opened the event. He now lives in Settle where he works as a Methodist minister. Revd. Dent presented the millennium book-marks to the village children and also judged the competitions. David and Eleanor Hayton donated a clock in appreciation of the support given to them when their garage was in the village. The inauguration of the clock took place in the village hall. The clock was later fitted into the round window at the front of the village hall by Andrew Nelson and Colin Dawson.

In previous years the Field Day has closed with a domino drive in the Memorial Hall but in 2000 a great village party began at 7pm. Chris Bland led the ceilidh in the marquee and the traditional dancing was followed by Andrew Allison s disco. Committee members and villagers cooked and served a barbecue supper. Once again Rob and Sylvia Dinsdale came to the fore providing staff for the evening bar.

The following day Revd Tony Dent led a thanksgiving service in the church. It was a moving occasion and one where Revd. Dent expressed his love for the village and told stories of his childhood. Afternoon tea was served in the marquee.

Boltons Rose Queen 2000. Left to right, back row - Joanne Mounsey, Hollie Tolley, Laura Brown, rose queen, Joanne Dinsdale, retiring queen. Front row - Erin Taylor, Zara Awde, Sophie Forster.

Richard Birkbeck passing the Millennium stone and yew tree on his B.M.C. mini tractor.

Bolton Women's Institute joined the fancy dress parade for the 2000 Field Day, with their float ably driven to the Memorial Hall field by Richard Birkbeck.

Many people worked hard to make the weekend a success for everyone. The events were made possible by donations from the parish council, the Willows Trust and individuals.

The final objective of the millennium committee was the production of this book, an historical record of the village of Bolton. There have been some delays in the work, sadly including the outbreak of foot and mouth disease, but if you are reading this you will realise the committee did achieve its objective!

A circular was distributed to each household in 1999 asking for suggestions to celebrate the millennium. Anne Shepherd replied to the parish council with the idea to flood light the church of All Saints, Bolton.

The parish council negotiated with the vicar Revd David Wood and the Parochial Church Council. A faculty had to be granted by the Carlisle Diocesan Board and the intention to flood light the church had to be displayed in the church porch for people to see.

Mr John Allison donated one of the lights in memory of his son Martin and the parish council provided the other two. A mini-digger was organised to dig a trench. Mrs Claire Hudson parish clerk, Mrs Barbara Davis and Mrs Eleanor Hayton who are Parochial Church Council members assisted Mr Colin Dawson, electrician to lay the wires in the trench and then cover them over. Eden District Council granted £278-55p towards the cost of £309-50p. Mrs Ann Shepherd switched on the lights on 28 May 2000 after a service of dedication.

CREAM TEAS

On a sunny warm afternoon on the 23 July 2000 cream teas were served in the garden of Glebe House by kind invitation of Barbara and Derick Cotton. Members of the parochial council were kept busy serving teas, manning stalls and organising games.

Claire Hudson and Val Bromley preparing for the cream teas at Glebe House.

CAR TREASURE HUNT

In May 2000 approximately 20 cars left the village to travel around the countryside looking for clues which had been set by David and Judith Barker. After two hours or more the participants returned to meet in the Eden Vale Inn to hear the result. These two events are held annually and raise much needed money for the up keep of the Church. On this occasion £103.50.

WALK TO BEWLEY CASTLE

In June 2000 Barbara Davis organised an evening walk to Bewley Castle by invitation of Don and Val Bromley. The castle stands in a beautiful area hidden from the road to Colby. The return walk covered approximately seven miles and raised £30 for church funds.

MILLENNIUM BABY

Sally Elizabeth Barker was born at Penrith Maternity unit on the 21 January 2000 at 10-35am weighing 7lb 3oz. Her parents are Alan and Elizabeth Barker and her brother is Thomas who was born on 12 November 1997.

Alan, Elizabeth and Thomas moved to Bolton at the beginning of 1998 when Alan started work as herdsman for David Baxter at Bolton Lodge Farm. They lived first at Whiteriggs and moved to Whinfell Road in 1999. Thomas attends Bolton Nursery Group and both Sally and Thomas attend the playgroup with their mother. Sally was christened in Bolton Church on Mothering Sunday, 2 April 2000.

Ann Shepherd & Barbara Davies with the Millennium Banner.

MILLENNIUM BANNER

To celebrate the Millennium at Mayburgh near to Eamont Bridge a banner was made by a group of village ladies. Mrs Marjorie Gill was the designer; the banner now hangs in Bolton Church.

Kathleen Bainbridge, Doreen Ridehaugh, Eleanor Hayton, Barbara Davis, Val Bromley and Ann Shepherd carried the banner from the Penrith show field through Eamont to Mayburgh where an open air service and picnic was enjoyed by a large gathering of Christian people from throughout the deanery. The Bishop of Penrith unveiled the Millennium Stone, which had been made from Shap granite.

Bolton Parish Council

In May 1999, following local elections, a new council was formed comprising of Harry Bell, Richard Birkbeck, Barbara Butterworth, Richard Forrester and Mark Holliday with Claire Hudson as parish clerk.

At the annual general meeting, Richard Forrester was elected chairman. The precept for 1999/2000 was set at £3000 and the clerk s salary at £322. The number of residents on the electoral role was 300 and Cumbria County Council had the grass-cutting contract.

During 1999/2000 the Parish Council arranged, in conjunction with the Parochial Church Council, for All Saints Church to be floodlit. The idea came from a suggestion from Mrs. Ann Shepherd when the Parish Council was looking for ideas to commemorate the millennium. A grant was obtained from Eden District Council to assist with the costs and Colin Dawson installed the lights. Mr. John Allison and Mr. Richard Forrester donated the floodlights.

The new childrens play area was commenced in summer 2000 on the Memorial Hall field with the assistance of volunteers including Alan Bainbridge, Alan Barker, Harry Bell, Joe Bennett, Richard Birkbeck snr., Richard Birkbeck jnr., Richard Forrester, Harry Hancock, Keith Hogg, Mark Holliday, Claire & Richard Hudson, Colin Kinnear, Stuart Lees and Ken Shepherd. Some of the hard core for the base was kindly donated by Eden Grove School and play equipment was erected in November 2000.

There had been some debate regarding the siting of the play area as it was ini-

tially planned for the village Pinfold on South Road. However, after further deliberation, it was agreed to site it where the old play area had been some years ago. A grant of £9,200 was obtained from Eden District Council s Time Parishes scheme and a further £250 from Voluntary Action Cumbria. The equipment was supplied by Playdale of Ulverston.

Ownership of the village Pinfold area adjacent to Violet Bank was being sought as the site was not registered with the Land Registry. Plans were being made for a sculpture to be erected by Andy Goldsworthy through an initiative by Cumbria County Council education department.

Negotiations with county highways department were undertaken in order to secure the change in speed limit on South Road from 40mph to 30mph to bring it in line with the rest of the village.

Bolton Nursery Group

Bolton playgroup was re-established at Bolton Memorial Hall in 1994 by a group of parents who realised that their children deserved a good pre-school foundation in the form of a Mother s and Toddlers Group.

The success of the Mother and Toddler Group (now called playgroup) enabled the development of another group for over threes which is now the Nursery group. The Nursery began by using equipment that had been donated by parents and friends, but more recently it has received funding through grant aid and fund raising events (organised through the hard work and goodwill of parents, friends and the local community). This has enabled the group to expand its work and bring it into line with other nurseries, helping it to provide a safe environment where children are stimulated and are encouraged to develop their full potential physically, emotionally and intellectually.

The Nursery staff is comprised of a fully qualified teacher and her assistant who has a diploma in playgroup practice. The group often welcomes students into their nursery.

The children are drawn not only from the village of Bolton itself, but from Appleby, Colby, Cliburn, Kirkby Thore, Kings Meaburn and Great Strickland. At the beginning of the year the nursery was made up mostly of little girls, but by September the members were in the main, boys.

Activities are not confined to the hall itself. Other activities often include

Bolton Nursery Group party time.

Bolton Nursery Group dressed as Millennium bugs for Bolton Pageant

walks to explore the environment and visits to the friendly postmaster. The group are now looking forward to being able to use the recently completed playground which is presently not available due to the foot and mouth epidemic — some infected animals having been found there.

The year 2000 started with a topic on sounds. This started off with a walk around the village to discover the everyday sounds in the locality, followed by moving on to matters more musical.

The Easter term was rounded off with an Easter bonnet parade and Easter craft morning for all children, mums, and grandmothers. Youngsters made decorated eggs, Humpty Dumpty from a balloon and some cards with chicks or bunnies on. The morning finished in the traditional manner - a good picnic!

The summer term was rounded off with a pirates picnic. All the children came dressed up appropriately and made treasure chests and pirate glove puppets. In the summer holidays the traditional outing to Lowther Park for all members of the playgroup and nursery took place.

Morning sessions were a mixture of the formal and informal. One of the most popular activities was baking, and the finale to the year was to make a Christmas cake and decorate it. Youngsters enjoyed a lot of music and drama as well as PE type activities. At the tables play-dough or clay modelling, puzzles, writing and drawing and construction toys are enjoyed. The playhouse and dressing up are always popular.

BOLTON NURSERY GROUP

During the year, Eden Grove School very kindly took some posters and made them into lovely large floor jigsaw puzzles for the group. As they are pictures of farming machines and animals mainly they have proved a great success. The group has been fortunate to attract students on the NVQ course, and therefore benefit from an extra pair of hands once a week.

One of nursery s biggest purchases during the year was a computer and printer - largely the children have been teaching the leaders. The children have no fear of computers and enjoy this as much as activities at the craft table. The leaders have been prompted into attending courses locally!

Bolton School Diary 2000

Another busy year has flashed past at Bolton School. Here are a few of the main events that have taken place during 2000.

SPRING TERM - January

On 11 January the children returned to school after the Christmas holidays. The total number of pupils on roll being 38 with the arrival of Melissa Richardson in December. Staffing remains two full-time teachers, one part time teacher Mrs Adey - for one afternoon per week and a supply teacher - Miss Jorysz for two days a week to give the headteacher administration time. Mrs Young started giving booster maths lessons on four mornings each week to the Year 6 children. Mrs Gilbertson continues to teach music one afternoon a week. Mrs Overy gives flute and clarinet lessons to nine children. We also have part time infant and junior classroom assistants.

Mrs Hope attended a course on student mentoring. The topics for this term were the human body and senses for the Juniors and senses for the Infants. The whole school started swimming at Appleby pool. Extra-curricular French started with Mr Stephen Thompson and drama club with Mrs Richards resumed for the term. Our students were in school for the first of their visits.

School had to close for the day as we had no oil for the heating. It turned out that our oil had been stolen. New oil was ordered and the system checked to ensure that there was no leak.

February

Year 6 children took part in an oral health discussion organised by the Community Dental Service. Mr Parkin was in school to carry out risk assessment. The students paid two more visits to school.

The Lottery came to the end of its sixth successful year during which the sum of £1,560 was raised for school funds. We would like to thank everyone who has helped in the running of the lottery.

Mrs Hope and Mrs Richards attended literacy courses. Mrs Hope attended a two-day course on student mentoring and Mrs Young attended a course on numeracy training.

March

The Annual Governors meeting with parents was held on 1 March. Our infant classroom assistant, Mrs Radcliffe, left us for pastures new at the beginning of the month.

A heating engineer called to make a thorough check of the heating system. Two students began their teaching practice. Football training began for the older children.

Bolton School 2000. Left to right, back row - Adam Wignall, Rachel Farnham, Paul Chappelhow, Joanne Mounsey, Kirsty Young, Harry Baxter. Row 3 - Joan Massicks, secretary; Barbara Hope, infant teacher; Matthew Threlkeld, Ben Farnham, Kimberly Allinson, George Dadley, Thomas Hodgkinson, Thomas Dadley, Richard Dawson, Jane Ullyart, non-teaching assistant.
Row 2 - Kathy Mounsey, Amy Brown, Melissa Richardson, Katheryn Sharpe, Amanda Chappelhow, Sally Butterworth, Kate Cinis, Will Addison, Vanessa Richardson, head teacher.
Row 1 - Louise Huddart, Alexander Sharpe, Zara Awde, Emma Threlkeld, Sophie Forster, Stephanie Baxter, Catriona Young, Sammy Smith, Erin Taylor. Front row - Iona Young, Hannah Wignall, Matthew Hodgkinson, Stephen Cinis, April Threlkeld.

Mrs Carol Brennan came to see the Year 6 children about Appleby Grammar School. A group of children took tea to the Bowls Club, after which they enjoyed a game of bowls. The Year 6s went to the dress rehearsal of *A Midsummer Nights Dream* at Appleby Grammar School and enjoyed it.

Mrs Richards attended a lap-top computer course - the computer supplied crashed several times and a new one eventually arrived on 24 March. Our inspector/advisor, Diane Grant, came into school to discuss school review and self-evaluation.

Mr Martin Stitch, head of mathematics at Appleby Grammar School, came to talk about numeracy and the structure and content of both the Primary and Year 7 numeracy strategies. He watched Mrs Young teaching and was impressed with the content.

CHANGING TIMES

April

Lee Page, building and design came to look at the veranda conversion with a view to completion of this project in the near future. Mrs Hope attended a course on Key Stage 1 SATs assessment training.

The Junior children took part in a Manchester United Football Tournament at Long Marton. The Year 5 and 6 children, and Mr & Mrs Hope accompanied children and staff from Calthwaite School on a residential visit to York. A good time was had by all.

Our midday assistant, Mrs June Hodgson, retired at the end of term after more than 13 years. A special lunch was held for her and Mrs Radcliffe when many of the people they had worked with over the years were invited. Presentations were made to both Mrs Hodgson and Mrs Radcliffe. Mrs Sue Allinson took over from Mrs Radcliffe as classroom assistant in the Infant class. After an end of term service in the Church school closed for the Easter holidays.

SUMMER TERM
May

The summer term started on 2 May with 38 children on roll. Mrs Sally Dryden took over as midday supervisor. The topics for this term were the Second World War for the Juniors, and minibeasts for the Infants. Rounders club started.

Carol Brennan was in school again to talk to the Year 6 children who are transferring to Appleby Grammar School in September. A team of doctors and nurses from the School Medical Service were in school to carry out meningitis immunisation.

Mr Phil Cheesley, RSPCA, came into school to give a talk to the children about the work of the organisation. Mrs Richards attended performance threshold training in Kendal. Many of our children took part in the Swimming Gala at Appleby Pool. Once again they were the winners.

The Junior children went on a visit to Eden Camp as part of their study of the War. While the Juniors were at Eden Camp the Infants had a fun day in school. We said goodbye to Joanne and Katie Wiseman who are moving to Long Marton School.

June

The new starters made several visits to school. The photographer visited school and took individual photographs and eventually found a suitable day to take whole school photographs outside.

The children took part in many football and netball matches during the second half of the term, winning the Manchester United Football Tournament and the King s Meaburn Football Tournament. The netball team won their League. Many thanks to Mrs Dawson and Mrs Farnham for organising and taking charge of the many sports events.

The Infant children visited the Ashton Memorial Butterfly House at Lancaster as part of their topic on Minibeasts. Mrs Hope attended courses in literacy and first aid. The children in Year 5 took part in the maths trail at Appleby Castle organised by Appleby Grammar School.

The Juniors held two performances of *The Pirates of Penzance* to great critical acclaim. After the evening performance Millennium mugs were presented to all children by our local councillor, Mr Tim Evans. This was followed by a cheese and wine party. This event raised £170.

Jilly Jarman came into school to help the children practice the songs for the Eden Millennium Party. Cannan & Brown carried out electrical testing of the portable equipment in school and we were given a clean bill of health.

A sponsored spell was held which raised a total of £633-67 for school funds. A parents evening was held to discuss the children s work with the teachers. The children enjoyed a visit from *Travelling By Tuba* who entertained them with their many musical instruments.

Mrs Richards, along with the heads from Asby, Crosby Ravensworth and Temple Sowerby put in a bid for a shared video conferencing facility. This was successful and should get underway next term.

July

The Eden Millennium Festival, attended by most of the primary schools in the Eden area was held in Penrith. This was followed by a picnic for all the children. It was a most enjoyable day.

The children were again successful at the Westmorland Area Sports Day at Appleby Grammar School. The school fun sports afternoon was finally held two days late but was enjoyed by everyone.

Mrs Richards attended a meeting with Andy Goldsworthy about the sheepfold project which will happen during the next year.

Year 6s attended the induction day at Appleby Grammar School. Mrs Angela Sidey was in school for the last week of term to cover for Mrs Richards. A barbecue was held in the school grounds. This was thoroughly enjoyed by everyone, especially the cricket and football played after the food had been eaten. The event raised £160.

A Maths 2000 Day, organised by Mrs Young, was held in place of a school visit as several had already taken place. This showed that maths can be fun! Following the leavers service in church, when they were presented with books, the school closed for the summer holidays.

Mrs Allinson left us at the end of term as she has been offered a full time post at Eden Grove School. The final day of term was a staff training day for threshold and performance management. There were no unauthorised absences dur-

Bolton School play 2000 - The Pirates of Penzance. Left to right, back row - Harry Baxter, Joanne Mounsey, Rachel Farnham.
Middle row - Thomas Dadley, Hugo Addison, Richard Dawson, Paul Chappelhow, Kirsty Young, Kimberley Allinson, Ben Farnham, Matthew Threlkeld, Thomas Hodgkinson, Will Addison.
Front row - Kate Cinis, Emma Threlkeld, Amanda Chapelhow, Catriona Young, Kathy Mounsey, Stephanie Baxter, Amy Brown, Sally Butterworth, Adam Wignall.

ing the year. The percentage of authorised absence was 4.9%.

During the summer holidays the new junior cloakrooms were completed. A big thank you to Mrs Williams for all her hard work during this very difficult time.

AUTUMN TERM
September

School re-opened for the new academic year on 6 September with 37 children on roll. The reception children began coming to school part time. Unfortunately Mrs Richards did not return to school after the holidays. Mrs Sidey was in school for the first few weeks. Mrs Ullyart has moved into the Infant class in place of Mrs Allinson until we can appoint a replacement. Mrs Pincombe joined us to teach the Junior class in Mrs Richards absence.

The Juniors studied the Greeks and the Infants studied books. Football training sessions began with coaching from Graeme Butterworth and Chris Addison. Netball training was held at lunchtime on several occasions.

One of the lovely church banners made by Bolton School children to commemorate the Millennium. The banners are now hanging in All Saints Church, Bolton.

A Harvest Festival took place in school when the children brought in harvest gifts to make up a display.

October

We agreed to take part in Operation Christmas Child. The children were asked to fill a shoe box with small gifts, toys, sweets, hats and gloves for a child in a war torn country. The boxes would be collected by the organisers who would check the boxes to see that the items were suitable and they would then be taken abroad and distributed in time for Christmas.

Mrs Hope held a meeting with the parents of the reception children to explain about numeracy and literacy. Mrs Hope attended a two day numeracy course, a teaching assessment course and a student mentoring course.

The older children took tea to the Bowls Club. The Year 4, 5 and 6 children played football and netball at Morland. Mrs Pincombe left us to take up a teaching post at Appleby Primary School.

November

The reception class joined the school full time. Mrs Christine Rudkin began teaching the Junior class in the absence of Mrs Richards. Thirty-four shoe boxes for Operation Christmas Child were collected from school.

Two Year 3 students were in school for their teaching practice, while two Year 4 students were in school for a week before their teaching practice next term. The whole school were entertained by a Musical Ensemble.

The Year 5 and 6 children went to the Sands Centre at Carlisle to see a performance of *Macbeth* by Shakespeare 4 Kidz. Two painting sessions were held to paint the outside of the school as it had got into a bit of a state. The Willows fund agreed to make a donation towards the cost of the paint, as did Mr Alan Chapelhow.

A ballot was held among parents about whether they would prefer their children to have milk or biscuits at morning playtime. The result was 50/50 so it was agreed to give milk a try next term.

The children were given a talk on railway safety by PC Duncan Wardlow. The Year 4, 5 & 6 children played football at Kirkby Thore along with Crosby Ravensworth.

A parents evening was held for the Infants. Mrs Dot Bell was away from school until the end of term after an operation and her position was ably filled by Mrs Dryden. Mrs Sue Mounsey stood in for Mrs Dryden.

December

The Year 7s from Appleby Grammar School returned to talk to the Year 6s about their new school. Mrs Hope attended a course on preparing pupils for writing test.

The student teachers left us on 8 December. As always December was very busy with the many events leading up to Christmas. Christmas lunch was served on Thursday 14 December. We had not held a craft afternoon for several years but we held one this year and it was enjoyed by everyone. A big thank you to everyone who helped.

The Christmas party was held on 18 December when a surprise visitor was in school! The term and year closed on 19 December with a carol service at All Saints Church.

COMMUNITY LINKS

Sports - The children have enjoyed taking part in a variety of sports, including football, netball, cricket, swimming and athletics. These are played against pupils from schools in both the Appleby and Penrith area. We are very grateful to all those whose help enables the children to participate in such a wide variety of sports.

Collective Worship - As well as regular assemblies led by Mrs Richards and Mrs Hope, Revd Wood also comes into school weekly to lead worship.

Music- Mrs Barbara Gilbertson still comes in to do **a** regular Tuesday afternoon music session. Mrs Linda Overy teaches flute and clarinet to **a** small group of children who wish to learn. Many of these children were successful in music exams during the year.

Bowls Club - Once each half term a group of children take tea to the village Bowls Club. The food they take is prepared by the children guided by Sue Mounsey, Pat Wignall and June Chapelhow.

Staff Development - As is the case every year, the staff have attended many staff development courses, too many to list, in order to stay up to date with all developments. These courses have taken place both in and out of school time.

School Prospectus - Our new school prospectus has had only minor changes made to it since it was last published.

Special Educational Needs - We have **a** policy on our provision for Special Educational Needs which is available for anyone who wishes to read it. Also, we wish it to be known that although we have no special facilities for disabled pupils, should the need arise and financial support be available, we would wish to make such provision.

SATs - As there were ten or less pupils taking the tests at both Key Stages we will not publish our results this year to ensure that the results of individual pupils remain confidential.

Target Setting - We are required by the Local Education Authority to set targets for the number of children achieving Level 4 or above in the Key Stage 2 maths and english tests in the year 2002. We have once again set these at 100%.

Security - The aims of the school policy on security are to ensure that children and staff can work in a secure and crime free environment. We will endeavour to make the school premises as secure as is feasible, allowing for structural difficulties, cost constraints and location. When necessary we will always seek advice from local authorities (LEA, police etc.) to ensure that these aims can be met.

In the event of any security incident, various procedures are in place in order that the staff can deal with it as quickly and as safely as possible. A review of security is carried out annually or when the need arises.

During the last year the security lighting has been extended around the school. This was paid for by security funding from the LEA. That is the end of the school diary for 2000.   *David Baxter, Chairman of Governors*

GOVERNOR S NAME	APPOINTED BY	SPECIAL RESPONSIBILITY	END OF CURRENT TERM OF OFFICE
Mr D Baxter (chairman)	LEA	Finance	September 2004
Mrs C Addison (vice-chair)	Parents	Link. Governor	June 2002
Mrs A Threlkeld	LEA	Fund raising/ Special Needs	September 2004

CHANGING TIMES

Mrs S Allinson	Co-opted	Buildings & Security/Literacy	September 2004
Mr A Chapelhow	Cliburn Parish	Staffing/Cliburn Meeting	February 2002
Mrs F Young	Parents	Numeracy	September 2003
Mr G Butterworth	Parents		October 2004
Mr G Sharpe	Co-opted		October 2004
Mrs V Richards	Headteacher		As long as employed
Mrs B Hope	Teacher		at this school

Chairman of Governors - Mr D Baxter, Bolton Lodge, Bolton, Appleby
Clerk to the Governors - Mrs J Massicks, 2 Slee Croft, Bolton, Appleby
All Governors have a four year term of office. The next time we will have a vacancy for a parent governor will be in September 2002. Governors meetings are held every half term. Any parent wishing an issue to be raised at a meeting can contact any governor and they will ensure it is included on the next agenda.

YOUNG PEOPLE LIVING IN THE VILLAGE IN 2000

Joanne Mounsey aged 12 years lives in Whinfell View and says: I really like living in Bolton because it is fairly quiet and has a nice river running through it, which is good to walk beside. Also you can go biking on the back roads through Appleby, round by Dufton and back through to Bolton. It also has a village shop where you can by bits of food. The parish council are building a play area and if you are interested in sport there is a badminton club on Tuesday evenings.

Some of my dislikes for living in Bolton is that if you have to go to the super-market or the doctors you have to go into Appleby or Penrith which is even fur-ther away. Probably I will have to get up earlier for school than people who live in Appleby because I have to catch a bus at 8-20am. Another thing is that you have to have a car unless you catch the bus into Appleby which only stays for two hours from 10-00am to 12-00pm.

There are some problems with living in Bolton. One is that there is only one village shop and no bigger shops. There are people making pollution because you have to have a car to get anywhere. If you buy any petrol or food in the vil-lage it is dearer than in Penrith or Appleby.

My village could be improved by building another shop e.g. New Look, where I could buy clothes instead of going all the way to Carlisle. I would stop every body building more new houses and I would bring back the tennis courts that used to be in the village field. It would be good to have a bus shelter made so that when I am waiting for the school bus to come, I won t get wet when it is

Joanne Dinsdale and Helen McWilliam, teenagers in 2000.

raining and I won t get cold.

Joanne Dinsdale aged 15 years, lives at the Eden Vale Inn and Helen McWilliam lives in Eden Fold. They are both friends. Joanne moved from Sedburgh to live in Bolton in February 1996. She attended the village school for 18 months before going to Appleby Grammar School. She has an older brother and sister.

Joanne will be starting to study for year two of her GCSE examinations and wants to be a graphic designer but if she is not able to do this she wants to work some where in the design area. Her best subjects at school are art and maths. She hopes to go on to further education and afterwards to be able to get a job that will enable her to build up some financial security. She has no intention of settling down and having children until she is at least thirty. She would like to travel. This year she is going to Wales for a holiday but in previous years has been abroad travelling by air to Tenerife, Portugal and Lanzarote. She has been to France travelling by ferry and by the Channel Tunnel.

Joanne sometimes helps her parents with their work at the Inn. She would like to have a different job but she would have to rely on her mum and dad for transport. She enjoys reading and reads modern teenage fiction and science fiction. She also enjoys watching television and listening to her music - she likes most types of dance music but not pop or classical.

Joanne says she has tried all sorts of other activities but soon tires of them. She feels she is a bit of a defeatist sometimes and gets impatient if she does not master a new activity quickly. She really just prefers the quieter pastimes.

CHANGING TIMES

Helen has lived in Bolton since 1998 and moved here from Wales. She started her education at Appleby Grammar School and wants to be a dietician when she leaves school. She is interested in cooking, is good at food technology and wants to have a career where she can help people. She needs two science A-levels to enter college or university to study. Helen starts the first year of GCSEs in September 2000.

Helen says that one good thing about living in Bolton is that she feels safe. She doesn t have to worry about strangers and the roads are comparatively free of traffic. She goes on holiday to places in Britain. This year she went to Devon. She has never been abroad.

Helen plays tennis at Kirkby Stephen and goes to Guides in Appleby on a Monday evening. She also plays squash. She says she has to rely on her parents to take her to these activities. The two friends walk and talk together often. Helen often cooks at home but likes to be adventurous in her cooking rather than cooking plain family food. She also wants to experience life before settling down and having children.

She attends the Catholic Church in Appleby with her parents. Joanne says she does not go to church. She is not against it but just does not go. They both have friends living in other villages who they sometimes see. T hey are both very much against the alcohol and drug scene, which seems to dominate some young people s lives. It is very difficult they say at their age not to be drawn into it because as teenagers they want to be part of the group. It can also be very difficult not to be drawn in when there is so much peer pressure to do so.

Both girls say their parents are strict and although it can be a nuisance sometimes they feel it is important and helps to guide them through difficult choices. If their parents were not strict they would feel they did not really care about them or were just too lazy to be bothered with them. They say if other parents were strict with their children there would not be so many problems with drink and drugs.

Helen and Joanne would both like a better transport service to and from the village so that they do not have to be so dependent on their parents. They would like to be able to get to the bigger shopping centres to look for clothes. Carlisle is the nearest but it would also be fun to be able to go to the Metro Centre at Gateshead or the Trafford Centre in Manchester sometimes. Penrith and Appleby do not have the fashion they are interested in.

Leo Houlding spent the first six months of his life in Colby before moving to Violet Bank, Bolton. He attended the village school and Appleby Grammar where he achieved some good GCSE results. He completed his first year in the sixth form before moving to Bangor in North Wales where he hoped to complete his secondary education. However his passion for climbing started to take precedence and he began climbing full time.

YOUNG PEOPLE

Leo s father says he was climbing as a youngster. He climbed trees and onto roofs, anything that could be climbed was climbed even if it did get him into a few scrapes. Edith Stockdale remembers Brian her husband having to rescue him from one of the apple trees on one occasion and his father remembers Dr. Tim Young having to put stitches in his leg.

Leo started climbing seriously with his dad when he was about ten years old, when they would go to the meadow at Hoff and climb the sandstone cliff there. They then climbed Jackdaw Scar at Kings Meaburn before moving to more difficult locations in the Lake District.

Leo had a glorious moment in 1995 when he won the World Junior Championship at the national indoor arena in Birmingham. However he lost interest in competitions after this and started taking on increasingly hard routes, some considered to be too advanced for this age.

After a difficult two years at Bangor he started to get a few lucky breaks. Some of his climbs were featured in climbing magazines and he was filmed climbing for BBC 2 for the programme Wild Climbs which went out at the prime viewing time of 8pm. Since this his achievements have grown and through sponsorship from Berghaus, DMM Climbing Gear and 5-10 Climbing Shoes he is able to pursue a climbing career full time.

In *Climbing Magazine* he has had written about him: the one man rave scene with a boom box and anything s possible attitude and the *Climbing* millennium edition said: The best traditional rock climber in the world.

For someone who is just 21 years old, Leo has much to be proud of. He has now decided to return home to Violet Bank where he has set up his office. From there he will continue to climb and write articles for the climbing magazines. He will also be busy making audio visual presentations to use when giving talks. In 2001 Leo and his climbing achievements have been given a high profile with articles appearing in the Carlisle evening paper, the *Observer Magazine*, *Telegraph Magazine*, the *Sunday Sun* and he has been featured on the front of several climbing magazines. In all probability he will also be doing some more television programmes - surely a name to watch in the future.

Thoughts on Life in Bolton from on off comer
by Derick Cotton

*C*ome to Bolton in the Eden Valley and share the experience of winding the *clock back 40 years or so.* This is how we wrote to our friends shortly after moving to Glebe House in 1992. The sentiment was not that the good folk of Bolton were years behind the rest of the country; it was more a reflection that life in the village continued to contain some wonderful virtues that had long been lost by other less fortunate communities. This is perhaps only noticeable to those new to the area; those who have lived in the village for many years will not necessarily have experienced any other way of life and would certainly not view life in Bolton as being so special.

Perhaps one of the most notable experiences to me as an off comer was to learn that there were those in the village who had never ventured beyond the county borders. Indeed for some travel within the county was a rare event, and who could blame them, given the scenery and setting which surrounds Bolton. With the Pennines on the doorstep and the Lakeland fells to the west, the village enjoys its own micro-climate and shares the thankfully largely undiscovered attributes of the most aptly named Eden Valley. I have no idea how the name evolved, but what other name could be so evocative and yet so accurate? I certainly enjoy sharing the peaceful experience with family and friends but would be horrified if we suddenly had to cope with bus loads of tourists like other parts of Cumbria. That said, tourism has to be part of our way of life and if carefully managed it can help the area thrive and survive. It would also perhaps be rather selfish not to allow others to visit this special place.

So what is so special about Bolton? Unlike many other villages it has somehow managed to retain most, if not the entire, key features of villages of 40 or so years ago. It not only has its 12th century church, but a Methodist chapel as well. Not only one school but two, with Eden Grove School helping youngsters with its own brand of education. A shop, post office, garage and public house - some communities would kill for only one of them! A village hall, recreation ground, village green, Women s Institute, Mothers Union, Bowls Club, Badminton Club, Parish Council, visiting tradesmen.... the list is not endless but nonetheless when completed is impressive. Add to this the history including the array of old buildings and dwellings, the horse troughs, the Willows Fund and others, Bolton becomes a special place with a rich diversity of people and places.

Until the recent and very sad outbreak of foot and mouth disease, another endearing feature has been the stone fenced fields full of wonderful and varied breeds of livestock. This is a situation long forgotten in other parts of England

217

Farming 2001 - Alan Barker with his son Thomas.

where former grazing lands, and indeed hedges, have been lost to enormously large fields of cereals and other crops. Finally, add the sensible pace of life and the values of life found especially in rural Cumbria, and only a cynic could claim that Bolton was not a special place to live and to visit. A now nearly automatic comment by our many visitors to Glebe House is that I have not slept so well or so peacefully for many years. Naturally we would like to think that our hosting has a role to play, but our surroundings in Bolton play by far the larger part.

To the off comer life in Bolton gives additional cause to reflect on how lucky we all are to be living not only in the village but also in the historical period of time that we have so fortunately and individually been allotted. Within my family, I have often had cause to reflect that of the times in history I could not think of a better time to have lived. Looking to the future, neither can I foresee a time that will surpass experiences or developments that have happened in living memory. In my case this is clearly helped by moving into a house that has been around since 1660, even older than most items now classified as antiques! In living in such surroundings it is also impossible not to be aware of how life has changed and the likely experiences of those who have lived there before - if only the walls could talk!

Even though the walls cannot talk, there is always a distinct feeling of being able to remain very much in contact with some of the ways of life often referred to as the good old years . How nice it is, and how much it reminds me of my childhood, to smell the smoke of coal fires, a distant memory for other parts of England. Today our hearth and range is shared not only by the dog and cat but with the nearby television. The room is certainly warmer thanks to additional central heating, but otherwise life in our front room is certainly much richer and more relaxing than in our former estate house in commuter land.

The winter power cuts, to some unwelcome, also give chance to live life as it was in childhood. Out come the Tilley lamp and the candles and who can better the toast made by the glowing embers of the fire? Quite recently we had to turn the lights off again once power had been restored as our guests were so enjoying their ability to live as their parents did - not that many years ago. How grateful we are for modern conveniences in every sense of the word. Not for us the trip outside to the privvy hidden from view and for other sensory reasons. That said, no doubt many of us can still remember the peace of the visit to the little house at the bottom of the garden, the newspaper squares and for those with better equipped facilities the two holer . Even more memories if you had been involved with the chore of disposing of the contents!

Another outside chore that we are spared - especially today s mothers - is that of the laundry washing and the big copper boilers. Here before washing could start, the fire had to be lit and the boiler filled with water from the nearby well; the latter a feature throughout Bolton with some still as functional as they were not that many years ago.

These same parents could never have dreamt that at the turn of the millennium we would have witnessed such amazing developments in every part of life. On the health front we now take so much for granted. Gone

Frank Baxter and Christine Birkbeck passing the time of day at South End, the ominous warning of foot and mouth disease pinned to the gate. The disease devastated the county in 2001.

are the days when antibiotics were undiscovered and when a visit to the dentist did not involve injections. I can remember my early visit to a dentist when he foot pedalled even the drill - and not at a constant speed! At the same time period - in the late 1940s - memories recall grandfather tuning in his cat s whisker crystal wireless. He also had a valve driven set powered by accumulator and which grandmother had to take to the local town to be recharged - electricity had not yet reached the farm let alone running water or main sewers.

Now we scarcely blink an eye as we watch and witness world events on the other side of the globe - and if we wish to, we can travel there to see things first hand thanks to modern transport. What would our grandparents make of modern communications? In their time, they were considered fortunate, and perhaps well to do if they had their own telephone. For most, keeping in touch was by letter and if this was to friends and family overseas, this could take days and perhaps weeks. Now we can speak directly - even from he middle of nowhere thanks to mobile phones. We can even send written correspondence by e-mail around the world and get replies within minutes. What would grandma think of shopping from her own front room?

On the school front, life is again much changed and our expectations of upcoming generations so much greater. Long gone are the days when our generation learned to write on slates and left school for a job for life at 15 - even then quite older than our own grandparents. Now for most, education stretches through until their twenties and sadly for Bolton means that many youngsters will have to leave the area if they are to fulfil modern careers. In fact life has changed so very much for children and their families. Now families are much smaller. Gone are the days, for most of perhaps four or five children, top to tailed in beds and sharing rooms sometimes even with their parents. Even the time when we produce our families has changed.

Many more couples are opting to wait until their thirties and even forties before starting a small family of perhaps one or two children. In other cases we see - perhaps like years gone by - youngsters starting families even before they have left school. However, unlike years ago at least the young woman does not have to disappear to distant parts for the birth. Mobility has seen the break up of extended families with no grandma on hand around the corner or even next door. We also now have to accept that family make up is so variable with long term marriages no longer the norm and split families much more the case. But who is to say which was or is right or wrong?

Remember those summers when full families helped in the fields to get the harvest in? Now youngsters find it hard to find things to do in the long summer holidays. Farms are deemed to be unsafe places and we have stringent laws about employing school children. This cannot be said about women today, many following successful full time careers and even some commuting away from

CHANGING TIMES

home with dad becoming house husband .

With homes now needing two wages, parents also have problems in providing adequate care for their families especially during long summer holidays; no longer can they be found in the same field perhaps picking potatoes. There never used to be cries of there s nothing to do around here! That said, we still produce youngsters to be proud of and who would now swap with the other pressures that we put on them today?

On the community front Bolton also has a record of which to be proud. the Field day has run for many years, both churches and other groups and facilities survive and most activities and events are very well supported. Shortly after arriving we had cause to find help for nursing my mother who had ben taken quite ill. The support we were given was quite outstanding and within a few minutes of identifying a need for a commode, we had offers of three - and with prospects of more should we need them! In short, we knew we had arrived at a friendly place, albeit it would be some time before we might be invited round for tea!

So what does the future hold for Bolton and its residents? And here our crystal ball is certainly no better than that of our own grandparents. Hopefully in the fairly near future the ravages of foot and mouth will become a memory and the fields will return to normal with flocks of sheep and herds of cows. There will be changes as the years pass, but hopefully successive generations will try to hold on to all that is good. It would be nice to think that our church, which has survived since the 12th century can survive for another millennium. Its already impressive history would surely be outstanding in the year 3000! Perhaps the world of science fiction might hold some clues. Perhaps our successors might be beamed around as they are on Startrek. Perhaps they will be in contact with beings on other planets. Perhaps they might have found the eternal youth pill. In space perhaps our successors will venture to distant planets or even constellations in solar powered spaceships. Who know what might be found or invented? Looking at the human being, I suspect that we still have lots more to discover. I for one am sure that we have more than five senses - premonition and thought transfer come to mind. How many like me suffer the fate of a wife who claims to read my mind - so inaccurately!

As an otherwise contented individual, I very strongly suspect that life int he year 2100, let along 3000, is unlikely to surpass the richness of our present experiences here in Bolton. I wonder how many of us would want to trade life now with those of the generations yet to come?

My conclusion is much the same as my opening quotation. For those of us that live in Bolton, we must treasure and maintain all that makes it such a special place. For those that visit us, please enjoy and share that experience. And let s hope that the place retains its undoubted beauty and benefits for many, many years to come.

CHILDHOOD REVISITED

Once upon a time, not so very long ago
A child live in a village, a village that I know
And oft my mind goes wandering back
 to the childhood of my dreams
Where our play ground was the green fields,
 our paddling pools, blue streams.

And now if I could have a wish for every child on earth
I d let it live, for a year at least, in the village of my birth
And there throughout the seasons, summer, autumn, winter, spring
They d find the joy and wonder the different seasons bring

Audrey Dent, nee Bellas, February 1999

The Rolls of Honour

The Rolls of Honour to those who served and died in the First and Second World Wars. The Rolls hang in the Memorial Hall.

ROLLS OF HONOUR

The Rolls of Honour to those who served and died in the First and Second World Wars are hung in the Memorial Hall. Agriculture was a protected occupation during war time and so many of the men of the village were required to stay at home and produce the food for the nation. However they still played their part by joining the Home Guard.

Padget Richardson remembers that they had as their head quarters a hut at the side of Orchard House in Dents field. They would light a fire there when they had their meetings and Padget and his little band of warriors would climb onto the roof and put a sod of turf over the chimney to smoke them out. Apparently it was great fun to see them all dash outside coughing.

Bolton s Home Guard, left to right, back row - George Ellwood, Joe Thompson, Ronnie Robinson, Tom Smedley, Alan Robinson
Middle row - Jackson Bellas, Bill Birkbeck, Harry Hine, Joe Allison, Fred Atkinson, Les Shaw, Walter Balmer
Front row - Hewit Nash, Arthur Tatters, Fred Tatters, Fisher Simpson, Roy Brown, Maurice Williams

THE MAKING OF CHURCH BELLS

Wigan is known to have been a notable centre for the manufacture of non-ferrous church bells from the late 16th century to the middle of the 18th century. The skill and method may have been handed down from the 12th century. Wigan appears to have been a long established centre for the brazier trade, manufacturing all types of brass ware, from which bell founding developed as a speciality.

The bells were either cast in the proprietor s own foundry and then delivered to the site, or the materials were taken to the site and the bells made in the churchyard or near by. The Wigan bell founders preferred to work at home and then transport the finished bells to their destination. This must have been a task of mammoth proportions considering the poor roads and transport facilities.

Robert Orwell was the first of three local Wigan families to carry on the trade for over 150 years. The other families were the Scotts and the Ashtons. The bells can have a very long life and usually bear the initials of the maker and where they originated. There may also be an inscription to record the name of a benefactor or churchwarden

It is known that Robert Orwell worked on site some times and so his premises may have been quite modest He made or recast bells in the years 1587 1592, 1594, 1600, 1604 and 1614. His son Richard is described as a bell maker in the Kings Pleas for 1619.

The Scott family then became dominant in the trade. John and James Scott are recorded as braziers and bell founders. However from the records it appears that James was more involved in the pewter trade and John concentrated on producing the bells.

Both brothers were appointed bailiffs in 1627, which suggests that they had some status in the town. The only known bell work to be attributable to John Scott is up to 1635 and 1646. He died in 1647 and the trade was carried on by Jeffrey Scott born in 1605. It is believed that Jeffrey was John s nephew. Records of Jeffrey s work exist between 1647 and 1664. He died in May 1665 and his eldest son William took over.

His first known work was for Chetham s Hospital in Manchester indicating that although the vast number of bells were made for churches, commissions could also come from charitable institutions and civic authorities. It appears that much of William Scott s work was recasting rather than making new bells. It is known that he made bells for Eskdale in Cumbria in 1687. To date no records have been found for the bells in All Saints. He cast his last bell in 1710 three years before his death. William Scott had no one to succeed him and the business came to an end after three generations.

William was the owner of a water mill called Pepper Mill used to grind corn, and he was very active in public life being a burgess in 1670 and elected an

Alderman in 1699. In 1701 he became Mayor of Wigan.

The foundries of William Scott and Ralph Ashton were both working in the town at the beginning of the 18th century. Ralph may have been an apprentice to William Scott before setting up business on his own. Ralph Ashton supplied bells through out North Wales and the north west of England just as the other bell makers before him. He retired in 1722 and his son Luke took over. He is known to have made bells for most years from 1723 to the early 1750s. He is also known to have made bells for North Meols in 1750 and Toxteth chapel in 1751. Then there are no records until 1756 and in 1758 it is thought that he may have supplied a bell to Peel on the Isle of Man. His son Ralph succeeded him on his death in 1767.

The only bells known to have been made by Ralph were those supplied to churches in Denbighshire in 1752 and 1753.

CURATES OF BOLTON

November 1663 Beek - On 17 November of this year he obtained a license to teach school and read prayers in the chapel of Bolton.

September 1668 - Robert Wayte was ordained as Deacon on 20 September 1668 and there is some doubt as to whether he was ever Curate at Bolton

1687 Christopher Wright

1692 John Breeks - Licensed to teach school and prayers. Ordained as Deacon in 1693. He had a daughter baptised in Bolton Chapel in 1694 and went to live at Watermillock. In 1705 as curate he was refused Priest s orders by Bishop Nicholson.

James Hanson
About 1724 Joseph Summers
1728 Daniel Hudson
1729 Thomas Castley
June 1732 George Alderson
June 1739 Thomas Smith
Thomas Blaymire died 1745
June 1748 William Kilner
1753 Hugh Stokoe

1754 Joseph Tickel - Caused some scandal when he suddenly left the parish and was found in Virginia in America where he founded an Episcopalian Mission. He was for ever after referred to as the runaway curate

1758 John Earl
1768 Thomas Kilner
John Walton 1776 William Rumney
1795 John Jackson

PERPETUAL CURATES

1799 Edward Jackson was always very interested in the life of his parishioners and made several representations to the vestry meeting on their behalf.

1834 William Shepherd

VICARS

1868 William Shepherd
September 1872 William Henry Hughes
1873 John Dobson M.A.
1876 Charles Dowding
1876 William Morgan Stoate M.A.
November 1880 Philip Pinnington
December 1891 Robert Burn
April 1895 John Taite Suttie
December 1912 Thomas Arthur Carmichael
1929 Lowes Foster
1937 William Lindop
1944 John Steel Smith
1946 George Edward Ferrers day
1957 Thomas William Harry Rutherford
1967 Arthur Brooker
1974 Douglas Ambrose Southward
1982 Richard Harptree Curney.

Rev. T. A. Carmichael

The chapel appears to have been leased to a Lancelot Dawes in 1162 vicar of Barton. Could he have been a descendent of Marget Dawes of Bewley fame? A John Fenwicke reader of Cliburn and Barnabus Sympson testify to the burial of certain persons in about 1680. It appears that they may have had some sort of supervision over the chapel.

There was evidence of a Christopher Knight at Bolton. He may have been a neighbouring clergyman officiating at the following event:

June the 13 1687 was Edward Stodart and Isabell Wilkinson married by Mr Christopher Knight as appears by his certificate.

CHURCH PLATE AND BRASSES

Revd Carmichael was vicar of Bolton in the early 1920s and he appears to have been interested in researching the history of the church and village. He wrote articles about his findings many printed in the *Penrith Observer*. In one dated 16 May 1922 he identifies the church plate and brasses in the church at the time.

The oldest vessel. A silver plated chalice seven and a half inches high, marked Richard Constantine, revealing some evidence of repair and inscribed: The gift of George Harrison, of Whitfield Brow (Eden Grove) 1786 — 1813.

Three old pewter vessels made in the reign of William IV, 1830-1837. Consisting of a mug six and a half inches high and marked with a lion four times under X and WR under a crown. On the reverse side it is marked with WB and IG. A flagon six and a half inches high marked on the lid WB, IG and ID and a dish nine and a half inches in diameter marked on the bottom with a lion s head four times under X and a crown, WB and IG and EdUBLY London.

A chalice eight and a half inches high, flagon twelve and a half inches high, paten ten and a half inches in diameter and four and a half inches high and alms dish. The first three marked James Dixon and Sons. Revd Carmichael does not know what the alms dish refers to. It is 8 inches high by five and a half inches and the space where the coins should be deposited measuring five and a half by five inches.

A silver chalice presented to the church by William Graham believed to have formerly belonged to the private chapel of George III (1760-1820). It is six and a half inches high and marked TL, a lion, a crown N and the head and bust of a man. It is inscribed round the base In Memory of his mother who died September 22nd 1901, Presented by William Graham.

The silver paten in regular use was presented to the church in 1918 by Revd E. F. Pinnington the son of a former vicar. It was used for many years in the Mission of Powassan, in the Diocese of Algoma, Canada, and also in the Canadian Expeditionary Force, during the Great War. It is six and a half inches in diameter and marked MEBIDEN, a pair of scales in between, B.COMPANY. Quadruple Plate. USA.

Revd Pinnington also presented at the same time a solid silver communion set for use of sick communicants in their homes. The chalice is four inches high and the paten is three and a half inches in diameter. It is inscribed In Memoriam Philip Bertram Pinnington Born in Bolton, October 28th 1887. Died in Ontario Canada July 1st1906. R.I.P.

THE CHURCH BRASSES

A plain cross 2ft high standing on an oak table.

Two flower vases used at the chief festivals, 6 inches long presented in 1913.

Two more 9 inches long presented In Memoriam in 1918.

The book-rest or table lectern 13.5 by 11 inches was presented in 1914 with the accompanying service book as an Easter gift to the church.

The alms dish, fixed on a small oak table, a gift, standing on a credence table, another gift, was presented in 1913. It is 12.5 inches in diameter, in the centre the sacred monogram and round the border the inscription: Freely ye have received, Freely give.

The bar or telescopic slide replaced a gate like opening in the Communion rails. It was a gift in1914.

The font ewer resting on a square oak stand, has a cross on top and the sacred monogram in the centre and was given In Memoriam 1918.

The mural tablet was erected to the memory of eight local men who fell in the Great War and placed in the church July 1920. The inscription and border of laurel leaves are deeply engraved and the tablet is mounted on a marble slab.

THE DERWENTWATERS

Derwentwater — Sir Thomas Derwentwate 1240-1303 of Derwentwater alias Castelton and Keswick in Cumberland and of Bolton and Ormside in Westmorland. M.P. for Westmorland 1295-1298. Son and heir of William de Derwentwater married to Margaret.

Sir Thomas received letters of protection 17 September 1265 and was one of the Cumbrian Jurors who testified at the Castle of the Maidens in the Kings Forest of Englewood 18 August 1268, in regard to the Perambulations of Englewood Forest.

He was knighted before 13 July 1276 when he was licensed to have a market and fair at his Manor of Keswick. He was appointed a Justice of Gaol Delivery at Carlisle 20 November 1290 and at Appleby 1291-2.

He brought a suit in Westmorland against John, son of Thomas de Goldington 1291 and in 1292 was amerced of ten marks for fine for land in that county. Michael de Haron acting as his surety; he was also ordered to pay 40/- in 1292 on account of having been in a Jury at Appleby, which had unlawfully allowed Dame Iodine de Layburne to alienate certain property without obtaining The Royal Licence to do so.

At some time Sir Thomas was one of the Jurors to decide certain claims of the Abbot of Shap concerning the Manor of Reagill and he claimed against John de Lancaster 200 acres of pasture in Castelrigg, Co Westmorland of which Roger de Lancaster (John s father) had unjustly dissesied William de Derwentwater (father of the petitioner) whilst said petitioner a minor. The case was later dismissed as the Jury found Castelrigg was not in Westmorland but in Cumberland in the west assize roll.

Thomas de Derwentwater, John de Reagill and Hugh de Murton justices at Appleby had condemned and hanged Alan Dugget a notorious malefactor on Friday after S. T. Barnabus the Apostle 1291 but they were brought to judgment as they acted without the knowledge or consent of their fellow justice Henry de Staveley in 1291 and 92 Sir Thomas was named as elector for Westmorland.

He was appointed assessor and collector of subsidy in Westmorland 4 December 1295 and collector of Cumberland 14 October 1297, he was witness to numerous charters in Cumberland and Westmorland between 1285 and 1300 on 30 April 1300 he was made Commissioner of array in County Westmorland to raise 1000 foot against the Scots.

In 1301 he was elected by the communities of Cumberland to be one of the assessors and collectors of the 15th empowerment of the 24 October. The Sheriff of Cumberland was ordered to assist him on the 9 February 1302 and it would appear that his assistance was needed because 28 April it was noted that Sir Thomas has become a broken imbecile.

On the 7 November 1303 he was named in a commission to buy an aid from the Knights fees in county Cumberland but he died 29 April 1303 leaving a son and heir John aged 33 and more a widow Margaret who had grant of dower on the 26 May.

His inquisition post mortem took place at Aspatrick 15 May 1303 and records that he held the Manor of Derwentwater plus Hamlets of Keswick and Castlerri Co Cumberland of the King in chief as the honour of Cockermouth by homage and suit of court.

The Westmorland properties of Bolton and Ormeside are mentioned in the inquest taken in 1323 after the death of his son Sir John de Derwentwater who died 1317 when they are recorded as being held by Carnage of the Barony of Appleby.

Bolton Census Returns

Constables Census Westmorland 1787

Morland Parish, Constablewick of Bolton

1 - Chrisr Parkin, husbandman, M
Mary Parkin, F
Mattw Parkin, M
Mary Bellas, F
Margt Bellas, F
Jos Hall, servant, M
John Farrer, servant, M
Margt Holm, servant, F

2 - Joseph Roper, mason, M
Brid Roper, F
Ann Roper, child, F
Jos Roper, M
Willm Roper, M
Hannah Roper, F

3 - Edw Addison, mason, M*
Mary Addison, F
Esabile Addison, F
Mary Addison, F
* Died since census added over his name in MS. He was buried on 19 December 1787, aged 72. See Bolton parish register (WPR/25/2)

4- Ricd Bellas, husbandman, M
Hannah Bellas, F
Eliza Bellas, F
Joseph Bellas, M
Hannah Bellas, F
Jas Boanson, servant, M

5 - John Hoarsley, basket maker, M
Mary Hoarsley, F
John Hoarsley, M
Wm Hoarsley, M
Thos Hoarsley, M
Ricd Hoarsley, M

6 - Thos Burney, labourer, M
Jane Burney, F
Mary Burney, F
Jane Burney, F
Joseph Burney, M
Mary Martindale, spinster, F

7 - Hannah Burney, spinster, F
Mary Bowness, F

8 - The Revd Mr Rumney, M
Mrs Rumney, F
Elisa Rumney, child, F
Joseph Rumney, M
John Rumney, M
Deb Pearson, servant, F
Henry Clemmet, M

9 - John Lambert, husbandman, M
Esable Lambert, F
Jos Lambert, M
John Lambert, M
Grace Lambert, F
Robert Lambert, M
Ralph Lambert, M
John Lambert, M
Mary Jackson, F

10 - Natn Simpson, blacksmith, M
Ann Simpson, F
Jos Simpson, child, M
Elizth Simpson, F
Jos Nicholson, servant, M

11 - Wm Gibson, husbandman, M
Elizath Gibson, F

12 - Ricd Addison, husbandman, M

BOLTON CENSUS RETURNS

Esable Addison, F
Tho Addison, servant, M
Mary Spedding, F

13 - Ester Nixon, spinster, F
Susan Nixon, F
Jane Nixon, F

14 - Wm Stephenson, labourer, M
Eliza Stephenson, F
John Stephenson, child, M
Eliz Stephenson, F
Hugh Stephenson, M

15 - John Stephenson, labourer, M
Bridgt Stephenson, F

16 - Mr Dent, gentleman, M
Mrs Dent, F
Wm Nixon, servant, M
Mary Grant, F
Nichols Dent, M

17 - John Salkeld, miller, M
Dinah Salkeld, F
Jane Salkeld, F
Joseph Salkeld, M
John Salkeld, M
James Salkeld, M
Elizath Salkeld, F

18 - John Nicholson, tailor, M
Letty Nicholson, F
Heny Nicholson, child, M
Sarah Nicholson, F
Mary Nicholson, F

19 - Henery Nicholson, poor man, M
Mary Nicholson, F

20 - Willm Wolf, labourer, M
Esable Wolf, F

Elizath Wolf, child, F

21 - Willm Longmire, carpenter, M
Barbra Longmire, F
James Longmire, child, M
Grace Longmire, F
Ann Longmire, F
Wm Longmire, M
Geo Longmire, M
Jane Longmire, F
Barbra Longmire, F

22 - John Longmire, labourer, M
Margt Longmire, F
Ricd Longmire, M
Stephen Longmire, M
Margt Longmire, F

23 - John Longhorn, shoemaker, M
Eley Longhorn, F

24 - Josiah Corry, husbandman, M
Barbra Corry, F

25 - Bridgt Tuer, F
Bridgt Allen, F

26 - Elizabeth Corry, spinster, F

27 - Stephen Bellas, schoolmaster, M
Barbra Bellas, F
Mary Bellas, child, F

28 - Samuel Gibson, husbandman, M
Ann Gibson, F
Jontn Gibson, child, M
Christr Gibson, M
Margt Gibson, F
Samuel Gibson, M

29 - Mr Geo Longhorn, schoolmaster, M

30 - Willm Allen, husbandman, M
Jane Allen, F
Thos Savage, M
Margt Savage, F

31 - John Horn, husbandman, M
Ann Horn, F
Mary Horn, child, F
Wm Horn, M
John Horn, M
Jane Horn, F

32 - John Spedding husbandman, M
Alice Spedding, F

33 - John Jamson, shoemaker, M
Jane Jamson, F
Mary Jamson, F
Jane Jamson, F
Sarah Jamson, F
Ann Jamson, F

34 - Mary Parkin, F

35 - Henery Dent, husbandman, M
Ann Dent, F
Wm Dent, child, M
Margt Dent, F
Barbra Dent, F
Thos Dent, M
Ann Dent, F
Henery Dent, F
Jane Dent, F
Thos Wright, servant, M
Elizabth Lowis, F

36 - Willm Savage, husbandman, M
Amelia Savage, F
Wm Savage, M
Ann Todd, servant, F

37 - Thos Chapelhow, husbandman, M

Elizabth Chapelhow, F
Barbra Chapelhow, child, F
Willm Chapelhow, M

38 - Willm Bowness, yeoman, M

39 - James Parkin, husbandman, M
Elizabeth Parkin, F
John Dodd, servant, M
Margt Hanson, F

40 - Samuel Oglethorp, cooper, M
Margt Oglethorp, F
Joseph Oglethorp, M
Jos Addison, servant, M

41 - Franceis Chapelhow, M
Esable Chapelhow, F
Sarah Rittson, F

42 - Joseph Egleston, weaver, M
Ann Egleston, F
George Egleston, child, M
Wm Egleston, M
Michael Egleston, M
Ann Egleston, F
Isaac Wilkinson, servant, M

43 - Isaac Dodd, labourer, M
Margt Dodd, F
Mary Dodd, child, F

44 - Thos Lambert, husbandman, M
Esabel Lambert, F
Hannah Lamber, child, F
Joseph Lambert, M

45 - John Chapelhow, husbandman, M
Jane Chapelhow, F
Mary Chapelhow, child, F
Jane Chapelhow, F
Frances Chapelhow, F

John Chapelhow, F
Jefy Bowness, servant, M

46 - Rd Bartholw Dacre, curate, M

47 - Joseph Barton, carpenter, M
Mary Barton, F
Thos Barton, child, M
Margt Barton, F
Willm Barton, M
Mary Barton, F
Jane Matinson, servant, F
Thos Goodburn, M

48 - Caleb Mason, breeches maker, M
Ann Mason, F
Jane Mason, child, F

49 - Mary Asbridge, single woman, F

50 - Bowness Harrison, labourer, M
Mary Harrison, F
Jos Harrison, child, M
James Harrison, M
Wm Harrison, M
George Harrison, M

51 - John Burro, husbandman, M

52 - Willm Corry, husbandman, M
Elizabeth Corry, F
Jos Corry, child, M
John Corry, M
Francis Corry, F
Elizabeth Corry, F

53 - John Browell, husbandman, M
Ann Browell, F

54 - Nichls Lunson, husbandman, M
Jos Toppin, child, M
Esable Toppin, F

Isaac Toppin, M
Jane Lunson, servant, F

55 - James Savage, husbandman, M
Mary Savage, F
Willm Savage, child, M
Ann Savage, F
James Savage, M
Mary Savage, F
Hannah Savage, F

56 - John Attison, husbandman, M
Margt Attison, F
Isaac Attison, child, M
Robt Attison, M
John Attison, M
Mary Attison, F
Dinah Attison, M

57 - Isaac Stephenson, husbandman, M
Margt Stephenson, F
Margt Stephenson, child, F
Isaac Stephenson, M
Dinah Stephenson, F
Jane Stephenson, F
Willm Stephenson, M

58 - George Steel, carpenter, M
Mary Steel, F
Willm Steel, child, M
Elizth Steel, F
Thos Steel, M
George Steel, M

59 - Nichols Temple, husbandman, M
Elizabith Temple, F
Robert Temple, child, M
John Temple, M
Ann Robinson, servant, F

60 - Christr Bird, husbandman, M
Margt Bird, F

Ralf Bird, child, M
Daniel Bird, M
Christr Bird, M
Sarah Bird, F
Nelly Bird, F
Margt Bird, F
Jos Hodgon, servant, M

61 - John Farrer, poor man, M
Esable Farrer, F
Mary Farrer, child, F
Ann Farrer, F

Esable Farrer, F
62 - Samuel Oglethorp, husbandman, M
Mary Oglethorp, F
Ann Oglethorp, child, F
Joseph Oglethorp, M

63 - Thos Idle, weaver, M
Margt Idle, F
Willm Idle, child, M
Christr Idle, M
Elizabeth Idle, F

Morland Parish Index Constables Census Index 1851 Census

No. of separate occupiers 80
Inhabited houses 80
Uninhabited houses 2
Male 200
Female 184
Total 384

1 - William Savage, head, 58, farmer of 18 acres employing one labourer, born Bolton.
Elizabeth Savage, wife, 53, born Elston, Northumberland.

2 - John Dent, Head, 58, Farmer of 180 acres, born Bolton
Agnes Dent, wife, 53, born Bolton
Ann Dent, daughter, unmarried, 26, born Bolton
Henry Dent, son, unmarried, 24, born Bolton
John Dent, son, unmarried, 19, student, born Bolton
William Dent, son, unmarried, 17, born Bolton
Joseph C. Dent, son, 10, scholar, born Bolton
Margaret Smith, visitor, married, 60, born Morland
Margaret Young, servant, 17, born Hawes, Yorkshire
Anthony Sawyer, servant, unmarried, 28, farm servant, born Bolton
Jonathan Watson, servant, 17, farm servant, born Bolton

Gargate House - Elizabeth Wilkinson, head, widow, 79, parish relief, born Asby.

4 - Richard Heslop, head, 83, retired farmer, born Kirkoswald

Margaret Heslop, wife, 83, born Ormside
Ann Bownson, servant, widower, 70, born Kirkby Stephen

5 - Richard Horn, head, 32, farm labourer, born Morland
Agnes Horn, wife, 31, born Milburn
John Horn, son, 8, scholar, born Milburn
Agnes Horn, daughter, 3, born Morland

6 - George Smith, head, 77, retired farmer, born Ormside
Agnes Smith, wife, 74, born Kirkby Stephen
James Smith, grandson, 10, scholar, born Bolton
Margaret Smith, daughter, unmarried, 27, house servant, born Appleby
Elizabeth Smith, granddaughter, 6, scholar, born Appleby
Thomas Smith, grandson, 4, scholar, born Cliburn

7 - John Savage, head, 55, farm labourer, born Morland
Ruth Savage, wife, 45, born Ainstable
Joseph Savage, son, 8, scholar, born Morland
Elizabeth Savage, daughter, 5, scholar, born Morland
Ann Savage, daughter, 3, born Morland
Thomas Savage, son, 5months, born Morland

Bolton Hall - Thomas Todd, head, 63, farmer of 70 acres, born Skelton
Margaret Todd, wife, 39, born WLS
Agnes Todd, daughter, 16, scholar, born Morland
Barbara Todd, daughter, 14, scholar, born Morland
John Todd, son, 10, scholar, born Morland
Elizabeth Todd, daughter, 8, scholar, born Morland
Sarah Todd, daughter, 3, born Morland.
Thomas Warwick, unmarried, 25, farm servant, born Kirkby Thore

Eden Grove House - Richard Tinkler, head, unmarried, 53, magistrate & landed proprietor, born London
Jane Robinson, cousin, unmarried, 53, housekeeper, born Soulby
Mary Loadman, unmarried, 27, house servant, born Milburn
James Richardson, married, 32, groom, born Crackenthorpe
Alice Richardson, married, 30, house servant, born Long Marton
Henry Richardson, 3, born Crackenthorpe

10 - Joseph Jackson, head, 46, shoemaker, born Cliburn
Jane Jackson, wife, 49, born Morland
John Swithin Jackson, son, 12, scholar, born Morland

William Jackson, son, 10, scholar, born Morland
Jane Jackson, daughter, 8, scholar, born Morland
Grace Jackson, daughter, 6, scholar, born Morland

11 - Richard Allen, head, unmarried, 58, farmer of 33 acres, born Morland
Mary Allen, sister, unmarried, 71, annuitant, born Morland
William Thompson, unmarried, 30, husbandman, born Long Marton
Isabella Nicholson, unmarried, 26, house servant, born Morland

12 - James Dodd, head, widower, 62, farmer of 71 acres, born Asby
William Dodd, son, married, 30, farmer s son, born Morland
Mary Dodd, daughter-in-law, married, 32
James Dodd, grandson, 2, born Bolton
Joseph Dodd, grandson, 1, born Bolton
William Brunskill, unmarried, 18, farm servant, born Westmorland
Hannah Wilson, 15, house servant, born Westmorland.

13 - Isaac Clark, head, 59, farm labourer, born Kirkland
Barbara Clark, wife, 61, born Shap
Elizabeth McDonnell, niece, 9, scholar, born Liverpool

14 - Thomas Simpson, head, 61, farmer of 90 acres, born Bolton
Dinah Simpson, wife, 51, born Bolton
Joseph Simpson, son, widower, 24, smith, born Bolton
Thomas Simpson, son, unmarried, 21, farmer s son, born Bolton
Ann Simpson, daughter, 16, born Bolton
Daniel Simpson, son, 11, born Bolton
Margaret Simpson, daughter, 4, born Bolton

15 - William Ellwood, head, 38, grocer & draper, born Bolton
Elizabeth Ellwood, wife, 39, born Bolton
Elizabeth Ellwood, daughter, 16, scholar, born Bolton
John Ellwood, son, 14, scholar, born Bolton
Joseph Ellwood, son, 11, scholar, born Bolton
Mary Ellwood, daughter 9, scholar, born Bolton
William Ellwood, son, 6, scholar, born Bolton
Sarah Ann Ellwood, daughter, 4, born Bolton

16 - Thomas Sawer, head, 65, farm labourer, born Warcop
Eleanor Sawer, wife, 45, born Kirkby Stephen

17 - William T. Bousfield, head, 45, farm labourer

BOLTON CENSUS RETURNS

Sarah Bousfield, wife, 46, born Morland
William Bousfield, son, 6, scholar, born Morland

18 - John Longmire, head, 54, smith, born Morland
Isabella Longmire, wife, 47, born Warcop
Isabella Longmire, daughter, unmarried, 24, dressmaker, born Morland
William Longmire, son, 11, scholar, born Morland
Jane Longmire, daughter, 7, scholar, born Morland
Betsy Longmire, daughter, 6, scholar, born Morland
James Longmire, son, 3, born Bolton

19 - John Fothergill, head, 27, carpenter, born Dufton
Mary Fothergill, wife, 29, born Morland
Thomas Fothergill, son, 2, born Kirkby Stephen
Barbara Fothergill, daughter, 5 months, born Bolton
Robert Slee, apprentice, 18, carpenter, born Long Marton

20 - Margaret Parkin, head, unmarried, 55, farm labourer, born Morland
Matthew Parkin, son, 16, scholar, born Morland

21 - Ann Longmire, head, widow, 74, annuitant, born Dufton
John Dent, lodger, unmarried, 23, carpenter, born Morland

22 - Thomas Jackson, head, 29, farm labourer, born Lowther
Jane Jackson, wife, 35, born Bolton
William Jackson, son, 2, born Bolton
Thomas Jackson, son, 2, born Bolton
Jane Jackson, daughter, 1, born Bolton

23 - William Dixon, head, 75, farmer of 65 acres, born Croglin
Jane Dixon, wife, 75, born Morland
Ann Robinson, unmarried, 21, house servant, born Greystoke
William Gibson, 15, farm servant, born Morland

24 - William Horn, head, unmarried, 71, farmer of 30 acres, born Bongate
John Horn, brother, unmarried, 68, landed proprietor, born Morland
George Horn, brother, unmarried, 61, landed proprietor, born Bolton
Jane Horn, sister, unmarried, 65, housekeeper, born Morland
Matthew Savage, nephew, married, 33, butter merchant, born Morland
Mary Savage, niece, married, 34, born Morland

25 - Michael Stephenson, head, 58, stone mason, born Bolton

CHANGING TIMES

Bridget Stephenson, wife, 57, born Ainstable
William Stephenson, son, unmarried, 23, mason, born Morland
Michael Stephenson, son, unmarried, 18, mason, born Bolton
Ann Stephenson, daughter, 12, born Bolton

26 - Elizabeth Lambert, head, widow, 38, annuitant, born Warcop
Thomas Lambert, son, 10, scholar, born Morland
William Lambert, son, 9, scholar, born Morland
John Lambert, son, 5, scholar, born Morland

27 - John Thompson, head, 39, farmer of 30 acres, born Melmerby
Mary Thompson, wife, 30, born Bolton
Frances Thompson, daughter, 5, born Bolton
Ann Thompson, daughter, 3, born Bolton

28 - Mary Thompson, head, unmarried, 21, labourer, born Morland

29 - Ann Stephenson, head, unmarried, 72, annuitant, born Morland
William Simpson, nephew, 13, farmers son, born Morland
Mary Ann Shaw, niece, 9, born Long Marton

30 - James Nelson, head, 76, farm labourer, born Edenhall
Ann Nelson, wife, 76, born Yorkshire
Ann Fawcett, step-daughter, unmarried, 37, dressmaker, born Winton

31 - John Steel, head, 66, farm labourer, born Bolton
Margaret Steel, wife, 70, born Hayton,
Thomas Steel, grandson, unmarried, 17, apprentice carpenter, born Bolton
John Foster, boarder, 10, scholar, born Morland
Mary Foster, boarder, 9, scholar, born Morland
Jane Foster, boarder, 3, born Morland

32 - Lancelot Bellas, head, widower, 58, farmer of 8 acres, born Bolton
Stephen Bellas, son, unmarried, 34, farm labourer, born Bolton
Barbara Bellas, daughter, unmarried, 32, housekeeper, born Bolton
Margaret Bellas, daughter, unmarried, 20, dressmaker, born Bolton
William Bellas, grandson, 4, born Bolton

33 - Margaret Bellas, head, unmarried, 66, dressmaker, born Bolton

34 - Samuel Oglethorpe, head, unmarried, 38, cooper, born Temple Sowerby
Jane Edmondson, unmarried, 20, housekeeper, born Morland

35 - Margaret Bellas, head, widow, 69, annuitant, born Warcop
Mary Bellas, daughter, unmarried, 42, born Colby
Thomas Bellas, grandson, unmarried, 19, farm labourer, born Bolton
Joseph Bellas, grandson, 9, scholar, born Bolton

36 - Thomas Ellwood, head, 68, farmer of 6 acres, born Brampton
Jane Ellwood, wife, 72, born Bolton

37 - William Bland, head, 41, tailor, born Blencow
Ann Bland, wife, 34, born Bolton
Elizabeth Bland, daughter, 9, scholar, born Bolton
Mary Bland, daughter, 8, scholar, born Bolton
Margaret Bland, daughter, 7, scholar, born Bolton
John Bland, son, 5, scholar, born Bolton
Ann Bland, daughter, 4, scholar, born Bolton
William Bland, son, 1, born Bolton

38 - George Wilson, head, 27, farmer of 30 acres, born Cumnew
Isabella Wilson, wife, 22, born Bolton
William Wilson, son, 2, born Bolton
Ann Wilson, daughter, 6 months, born Bolton
Elizabeth Shaw, 13, house servant, born Bolton
Mary Thompson, mother-in-law, 53, annuitant, born Bolton

39 - Mary Bella, head, unmarried, 35, dressmaker, born Bongate

40 - James Jennings, head, 28, flesher?, born Little Strickland
Ruth Jennings, wife, 29, born Penrith
Mary Jennings, daughter, 4, born Bolton
Jane Jennings, daughter, 1, born Bolton

41 - Robert Jackson, head, 37, agricultural labourer, born Henshaw, Westmorland
Jane Jackson, wife, 30, born Newbiggin
James Jackson, son, 9, scholar, born Bolton
William Jackson, son, 7, scholar, born Bolton
Robert Jackson, son, 4, scholar, born Bolton
John Jackson, son, 1, born Bolton

42 - Margaret Hodgson, head, widow, 38, grocer & draper, born Bolton
Isabella G. Mitchell, daughter, 15, born Bolton
John M. Hodgson, son, 10, scholar, born Bolton
Margaret Hodgson, daughter, 8, born Kings Meaburn

CHANGING TIMES

George Hodgson, son, 6, scholar, born Bolton
William Hodgson, son, 3, born Bolton
Margaret Mitchell, visitor, widow, 73, born Carlisle.

43 - Thomas Ellwood, head, 34, farmer of 30 acres, born Bolton
Eleanor Ellwood, wife, 32, born Dufton
Thomas Ellwood, son, 7, scholar, born Long Marton
Jane Ellwood, daughter, 3, born Bolton
William Ellwood, son, 1, born Bolton

44 - Samuel Gibson, head, unmarried, 70, landed proprietor, born Bolton
Ann Gibson, niece, unmarried, 39, housekeeper, born Bolton

45 - Thomas Lowthian, head, 47, tailor, born Temple Sowerby
Mary Lowthian, wife, 54, born Bongate
Robert Howe, step-son, unmarried, farm labourer, born Morland
John Howe, step-son, unmarried, 23, farm labourer, born Morland
Hannah Lowthian, daughter, 13, born Morland
Allen W. McDonald, lodger, 11, scholar, born Liverpool
Alexander McDonald, lodger, 5, born Liverpool

46 - Matthew Mitchell, head, 33, farm labourer, born Bolton
Margaret Mitchell, wife, 31, born Long Marton
Elizabeth Mitchell, daughter, 8, born Bolton
Mary Mitchell, daughter, 4, born Morland
John Mitchell, son, 2, born Morland

47 - John Steel, head, 28, farm labourer, born Bolton
Elizabeth Steel, wife, 30, born Kirkby Thore
Margaret Steel, daughter, 4, born Bolton
Sarah Steel, daughter, 2, born Bolton

48 - Hugh Stephenson, head, 65, riddle maker, born Bolton
Jane Stephenson, wife, 57, born Bongate

49 - John Johnstone, head, 50, labourer, born Bolton
Sarah Johnstone, wife, 48, born Cliburn
Sarah Johnstone, daughter, 13, scholar, born Bolton
Christiana Johnstone, daughter, 11, scholar, born Bolton
Philip Johnstone, son, 9, scholar, born Bolton
Eleanor Johnstone, daughter, 6, scholar, born Bolton
Margaret Johnstone, daughter, 4, scholar, born Bolton

Ann Tinswood, daughter, married, 26, born Bolton
Sarah Tinswood, grand-daughter, 6 months, born Bolton

50 - Robert Lamb, head, 41, gardener, born Blencarn
Elizabeth Lamb, wife, 31, born Bongate
Fergus Lamb, son, 6, born Bolton
Jane Lamb, daughter, 2, born Bolton

51 - William Goodburn, head, 38, carpenter, born Bolton
Mary Goodburn, wife, 34, born Warcop
William Goodburn, son, 4, born Bolton
Betsy Goodburn, daughter, 1, born Bolton
Thomas Jackson, nephew, 18, apprentice carpenter, born Bolton

52 - Jane Sewell, head, widow, 81, receiving parochial relief, born Castle
Sowerby
Hannah Sewell, daughter, unmarried, 47, labourer, born Ousby
Isabella Sewell, grand-daughter, 12, born Morland
Elizabeth Sewell, grand-daughter, 10, scholar, born Morland
Thomas Sewell, grandson, 3, born Bolton

53 - Barbara Sewell, head, widow, 87, receiving parochial relief, born Morland

54 - Mark Ellwood, head, 54, farmer of 10 acres, born Bongate
Mary Ellwood, wife, 51, born Culgaith
George Ewin, son-in-law, 29, born Ousby
Mary Ewin, daughter, 25, born Long Marton
Mark Ewin, grandson, 9 months, born Bolton

Eden Grove Lodge - Esther Horn, head, widow, 77, lodge keeper, born Penrith
Thomas Horn, son, unmarried, 49, receiving parochial aid, born Kirkby Thore
Joseph Horn, son, unmarried, 41, labourer, born Bolton

56 - Joseph Jennings, head, 38, malster & victualler, born Little Strickland
Jane Jennings, wife, 31, born Morland
Thomas Nicholson, step-son, 6, scholar, born Bolton
William Jennings, son, 4, born Bolton
Isabella Jennings, daughter, 1, born Bolton
Jane Robinson, unmarried, 19, house servant, born Cliburn
William McQuity, guest, unmarried, 32, draper & tea dealer, born Scotland

57 - Margaret Edmondson, head, married, 51, dressmaker, born Bolton

William Edmondson, son, 13, scholar, born Bolton
Isabella Edmondson, daughter, 7, scholar, born Bolton

58 - Joseph Nicholson, head, 25, farm labourer, born Bolton
Ann Nicholson, wife, 23, born Long Marton
John Brunskill, son, 5, scholar, born Long Marton
Thomas Nicholson, son, 1, born Long Marton
Robert Brunskill, cousin, 16, scholar, born Long Marton

59 - Josiah Corry, head, 70, landed proprietor, born Bolton
Isabella Corry, wife, 30, born Crosby Ravensworth
Thomas Holmes, step-son, 9, scholar, born Crosby Ravensworth

60 - Mary Nicholson, head, widow, 68, victualler, born Warcop

61 - Isaac Thompson, head, widower, 72, farm labourer, born Great Salkeld

62 - John Richardson, head, 31, farm labourer, born Cliburn
Martha Richardson, wife, 32, school mistress, born Bongate
Elizabeth Richardson, daughter, 9 months, born Bolton

Bolton Mill - William Mitchell, head, 35, miller, born Morland
Elizabeth Mitchell, wife, 32, born Bolton
John Mitchell, son, 7, scholar, born Bolton
William Mitchell, son, 6, scholar, born Bolton
Thomas Mitchell, son, 4, born Bolton
Elizabeth Mitchell, daughter, 2, born Bolton
Matthew Mitchell, son, 4 months, born Bolton
Mary Robinson, 15, house servant, born Long Marton
John Connor, unmarried, 29, miller, born Lowther

Bewley Castle - Rowland Slack, head, unmarried, 51, farmer of 200 acres, born
Warcop
Margaret Slack, sister, unmarried, 54, housekeeper, born Appleby
Margaret Burn, unmarried, 19, house servant
Joseph Wilson, unmarried, 25, farm servant
Matthew Sanderson, unmarried, 20, farm servant
Thomas Wappet, 16, farm servant, born Appleby

Bolton Lodge - John Thompson, head, 46, hind, born Temple Sowerby
Mary Thompson, wife, 46, born Musgrave
John Thompson, son, 17, farmers servant, born Kirkby Thore

George Thompson, son, 14, farmers servant, born Bolton
Ann Thompson, daughter, 12, scholar, born Bolton
Mary Thompson, daughter, 9, scholar, born Bolton
Thomas Thompson, son, 7, scholar, born Bolton
William Wilson, unmarried, 22, farm servant, born Kirkby Stephen

Hill Top - John Stamper, head, 42, farmer of 14 acres, born Kirkby Thore
Betty Stamper, wife, 46, born Appleby

Mansgrove House - John Airey, head, 31, farmer of 80 acres, born Morland
Frances Airey, wife, 25, born Morland
William Airey, son, 4, born Bolton
John Airey, son, 1, born Bolton
Agnes Ion, 13, house servant, born Bolton

Street Side House - John Ion, head, widower, 59, farm labourer, born Appleby
Sarah Ion, daughter, unmarried, 23, born Bolton
Elizabeth Ion, daughter, unmarried, 21, housekeeper, born Bolton
William Ion, son, 11, scholar, born Bolton
Hannah Ion, daughter, 4, scholar, born Bolton

Sion Hill - Joseph Ion, head, 25, farm labourer, born Bolton
Margaret Ion, wife, 32, born Morland
John Brownrigg, step-son, 12, scholar, born Morland
Elizabeth Ion, daughter, 1, born Morland

Bolton Lane End - John Goulding, head, 31, farmer of 82 acres, born Lazonby
Mary Ann Goulding, wife, 24, born Castle Sowerby
William Goulding, son, 3, born Lazonby
Robert Goulding, son, 1, born Bolton
William Wells, unmarried, 21, farm servant, born Cliburn
Grace Reay, 15, house servant, born High Hesket

Bolton Lane End - John Walker, head, 49, farmer of 40 acres & keeper of beer shop, born Bolton
Sarah Walker, wife, 45, born Penrith
Mark Walker, son, 16, farmers son, born Newbiggin
Elizabeth Walker, daughter, 15, born Newbiggin
George Walker, son, 10, scholar, born Bolton
John Walker, son, 9, scholar, born Bolton
Nicholas Walker, son, 7, scholar, born Bolton
Thomas Walker, son, 5, scholar, born Bolton

Robert Walker, son, 2, born Bolton
Sarah Ann Walker, daughter, 10 months, born Bolton

Birdby House - William Byers, head, 61, farmer of 50 acres, born Morland
Elizabeth Byers, wife, 71, born Asby
Elizabeth Sewell, unmarried, 18, house servant, born Morland
(not to be confused with Birdby)

Crossrigg Hall - Robert Addison, head, unmarried, 75, farmer of 203 acres
employing 12 labourers, born Kings Meaburn
Margaret Addison, unmarried, 19, house servant, born Long Marton
Sarah Atkinson, unmarried, 33, house servant, born Long Marton
Thomas Richardson, unmarried, 21, farm servant, born Ormside
Robert Gare, unmarried, 20, farm servant, born Bolton

Briggam Bank - Joseph Taylor, head, 42, farmer of 80 acres, born Walton
Margaret Taylor, wife, 40, born Ousby
Joseph Taylor, son, 12, scholar, born Ousby
Christopher Taylor, son, 10, scholar, born Ousby
William H. Taylor, son, 5, born Bolton
Elizabeth Taylor, daughter, 14, born Ousby
Christopher Barker, visitor, unmarried, 30, joiner, born Ousby

Oxen Stands - Edward Cherry, head, 48, farm labourer, born Morland
Isabella Cherry, wife, 43, born Morland
Henry Cherry, son, 16, farm labourer, born Morland
Mary Cherry, daughter 13, born Morland
Isabella Cherry, daughter, 10, born Morland
Agnes Cherry, daughter, 7, born Morland
Edward Cherry, son, 4, born Morland
Elizabeth Cherry, daughter, 11 months, born Morland

Oxen Stands - Robert Fawcett, head, widower, 44, tea dealer, born Warcop

Brackenrigg Hill - William Oldcorn, head, 38, farmer of 100 acres, born Greystoke
Mary Oldcorn, wife, 35, born Sedbergham
Ann Oldcorn, daughter, 17, born Bolton
Thomas Oldcorn, son, 15, farmers son, born Bolton
John Oldcorn, son 12, farmers son, born Bolton
Hannah Oldcorn, daughter, 9, born Bolton
Robert Oldcorn, son, 6, born Morland
William Oldcorn, son, 3, born Morland
Isaac Oldcorn, son, 6 months, born Bolton

BOLTON CENSUS RETURNS

Peatgate House - Thomas Nicholson, head, 74, farmer of 109 acres, born Bolton
Elizabeth Nicholson, wife, 66, born Milburn
Mary Nicholson, daughter, unmarried, 36, born Bolton
John Nicholson, son, unmarried, 30, born Bolton
Thomas Woof, grandson, 15, farm servant, born Morland
Mary Woof, grand-daughter, 14, house servant, born Morland

Bolton Willows - William Dixon, head, 38, farmer of 4 acres, born Bolton
Ann Dixon, wife, 31, born Helton
Jane Dixon, daughter, 2, born Kirkby Thore

Hanging Bank - John Savage, head, 32, farmer of 100 acres, born Bolton
Elizabeth Savage, wife, 37, born Bolton
William Savage, son, 4, born Bolton
John Savage, son, 1, born Bolton
James Parkin, unmarried, 22, farm servant, born Bolton
William Thompson, 13, farm servant, born Bolton
Isabella Sowert?, unmarried, 26, house servant, born Cliburn
John Stubbs, visitor, married, 71, farmer, born Orton

Lathey House - William Slack, head, 75, farmer, born Newbiggin
Mary Slack, wife, 65, born Gamblesby
Sarah Slack, daughter, unmarried, 39, born Long Marton
John Slack, son, unmarried, 37, born Long Marton
Thomas Slack, grandson, 14, scholar, born Bolton
Robert Nicholson, unmarried, 20, farm servant, born Morland

Morland Parish Index Constables Census Index
1881 Census

216 Males 188 Females Total 404
77 Houses Inhabited
3 Houses Uninhabited
1 Caravan

Mansgrove - William Airey, head, farmer 87 acres
Thomas Airey, brother, shepherd
Francis Margaret Airey, sister, dairy maid

Street House - William Dent, head, farmer 130 acres
Elizabeth Dent, wife

Mary Jane Dent, daughter
Agnes Emily Dent, daughter
John Henry Dent, son
William James Dent, son
Annie Elizabeth, daughter
James Tuer, domestic servant
Alexander James, farm servant
James Bellas, farm servant

Lane End Cottages - George Bainbridge, head, farm labourer
William Bainbridge, son
John Bainbridge, son
Mary Wappe, servant, housekeeper

Hanging Bank - William Savage, head, farmer 453 acres
Martha Savage, wife,
Martha Savage, daughter
Thomas Chester, farm labourer
John Egleston, farm labourer
George Brunskill, farm labourer
Ann Roper, domestic servant
Ann Clematson, domestic servant

Laithes - John Dixon, head, farmer 103 acres
Ellen Dixon, wife
Antony Dixon, son
John Dixon, son
Lancelot Dixon, son
Alice Dixon, daughter
Robert Dixon, son
John Richardson, farm servant
Harry Jackson, farm servant
Isabella Longmire, dairy maid

Birdby - John Thompson, widower, head, farmer 128 acres
George Thompson, son
Margaret Ann Thompson, daughter, domestic servant
Ann Elizabeth Thompson, daughter, domestic servant

Oxen Stands - William Farrer, head, farm labourer
Joseph Farrer, son
Mary Ann Farrer, daughter
William Farrer, son

Peatgates - George Walster, head, farmer
Elizabeth Walster, sister
Mary Baily, cousin
Isobella Wilson, domestic servant
George Bellas, farm servant
William Stewartson, farm servant

The Willows - Hannah Sewell, head, retired domestic servant
Thomas Sewell, senior, farm labourer

10 - Samuel Oglethorpe, head, retired cooper
Edward Cherry, lodger, shoe maker

11 - Mary Anne Edmondson, annuitant

12 - William Steel, head, farmer 30 acres
Anne Steel, sister, housekeeper

Bewley Castle - George Hewetson, head, farmer
Jane Hewetson, wife
William Hewetson, son
Margaret Hewetson, daughter
William Hewetson, brother, gentleman
Thomas Sewell, farm labourer
Nathan Routledge, farm labourer
Elizabeth Witter, domestic servant
Violet Nicholson, domestic servant

14 - John Hood, head, agricultural labourer
Isabella Hood, wife
Mary Hood, daughter, domestic servant
Isabella Hood, daughter, domestic servant
Robert Hood, son, scholar
John Hood, son, scholar
Joseph Hood, son
Henry Hood, son
Arthur Hood, son

15 - William Dodd, head, agricultural labourer
Mary Dodd, wife
James Dodd, son, agricultural labourer
John Dodd, son, agricultural labourer

Jane Dodd, daughter, dress maker
Joseph Ball, visitor

16 - Thomas Longmire, head, agricultural labourer
Mary Longmire, wife
Mary Bellas, daughter
Margaret Longmire, daughter
John Longmire, son
Sarah Longmire, daughter
Henry Longmire, son

17 - John Longmire, head, retired blacksmith
Isabella Longmire, wife

18 - William Clarke, head, agricultural labourer
Christine Clarke, wife
Joseph Clarke, son, agricultural labourer
John Clare, son, agricultural labourer
John Richardson, head, agricultural labourer
Martha Richardson, wife
Martha Richardson, daughter

Crossrigg Hall - Hugh Rigg, head, gentleman, JP
Margaret Rigg, mother
? Addison Rigg, brother, Lt Artillery
Fanny Rigg, sister
Jemima Rigg, sister
Jonathan Rigg, brother
Frederick Rigg, brother
Elizabeth Custance, cook
Mary Milner, parlour maid
Margaret Ward, house maid
Sarah Bell, laundry maid
Annie McDonald, kitchen maid
Sidney Gibson, footman

Brigham - John Bullock, head, farmer 133 acres
Margaret Bullock, wife
William Bullock, grandson, farm servant
Anna Bullock, son s wife
George Bullock, son
Mary Anne Bullock, daughter

Richard Bullock, son
Elizabeth Bullock, daughter
Sarah Bullock, daughter
Jane Bullock, daughter
Margaret Bullock, daughter
Joseph Bullock, son

21 - George Wilson, head, farmer 7 acres
Isobella Wilson, wife
John Wilson, son
Dinah Wilson, daughter
Elizabeth Wilson, daughter
Mary Thompson, mother-in-law

22 - William Bland, head, tailor and draper
Ann Bland, wife
Emma Bland, daughter, dairy maid
Henry Bland, son, tailor
John Richardson, grandson, scholar
Isobella, grand-daughter, scholar

23 - George Jennings, head, shoe maker
Elizabeth Jennings, daughter

24 - William Bland jnr., head, tailor
Jane Bland, wife
William Bland, son
Anne Bland, daughter

Bolton Lodge - Catherine Backford, housekeeper
James Watt, farm servant
James Miller, farm servant
Nicholson Richardson, farm servant
John Jenkinson, farm servant

Old Bewley Castle - Thomas Johnson, head, farmer 28 acres
Sarah Johnson, wife
Annie Johnson, daughter
Robert Johnson, son
John Parkin snr., farm servant
Elizabeth Longmire snr., domestic servant

CHANGING TIMES

27 - John Airey, head, agricultural labourer
Mary Anne Airey, wife
Thomas Atkinson, nephew, scholar

28 - William Wilson, head, mason
Mary Wilson, wife
John Wilson, son, scholar
George Wilson, son, scholar
Alice Wilson, daughter, scholar
Joseph Wilson, son, scholar

29 - Nicholas Weoff, head, farmer 7 acres
Ann Weoff, wife
Eleanor Weoff, grand-daughter
Ann Thompson, retired domestic
Mary Weoff, niece

30 - William ?, head, retired farmer
Anne ?, wife
Sarah ?, daughter

31 - Elizabeth Lambert, head, farmer 39 acres
William Lambert, son, farmer
John Lambert, son, farmer
Robert Armstrong, visitor
Ann Armstrong, visitor
William Armstrong, visitor

32 - Jane Weoff, head, housewife
Wharton Weoff, son, butcher
William Weoff, son, labourer
Margaret Wharton, mother
James Weoff, son, railway labourer
Joseph Weoff, son, railway labourer

33 - Antony Metcalf, head, farmer 27 acres
Isobella Metcalf, wife
Hannah Buick, servant, dairy maid

34 - John Armstrong, head, game keeper
Sarah Anne Armstrong, wife

BOLTON CENSUS RETURNS

35 - One Unknown in Caravan

Waldridge Cottage - John Wall, head, farm servant
Hannah Wall, wife
Thomas Wall, son, errand boy
John James Wall, son
Margaret Wall, daughter
George Wall, son
Cristion Wall, son

37 - James Parkin, head, farmer
Margaret Parkin, wife
William Parkin, son

38 - Leonard Robinson, head, farm labourer
Betsy Robinson, wife
Thomas Robinson, son

39 - Michael Stephenson, head, stone mason
Jane Stephenson, wife

40 - Elizabeth Steel, head, laundress

41 - George Jackson, head, farm labourer
Mary Jackson, wife
Adam Jackson, son, scholar
Robert Jackson, son
George Jackson, son
Joseph Jackson, son
Clark Jackson, son

42 - Joseph Ousby, head, general labourer
Sarah Ousby, wife
Frederick Ousby, son

Elm House - John Dent, head, farmer 188 acres
Sarah Richardson, housekeeper
Ambrose Davidson, farm labourer
Joseph ?, farm labourer

44 - Dinah Simpson, widow, head, farmer 28 acres
William Simpson, son, farmer
Margaret Sewell, domestic servant

252

Grocers Shop - William Ellwood, head, grocer
Elizabeth Ellwood, wife
Thomas Ellwood, son
Thomas Ellwood, grandson, apprentice
Francis Nicholson Ellwood, son, general servant

46 - William Graham, head, farmer 44 acres
Annie Graham, wife
William Graham, son, farmer
Elizabeth Birches, mother-in-law
Catherine Birches, sister-in-law
Edward Brunskill, nephew
Isobella Reay, servant

47 - Thomas Robinson, head, stone mason
Elizabeth Robinson, wife
Charlotte Robinson, daughter
Mary Robinson, daughter
Sarah Robinson, daughter
George Robinson, son
Thomas Robinson, son
Margaret Robinson, daughter
Agnes Robinson, daughter

48 - William Thompson, head, labourer
Sarah Thompson, wife
Mary Wilson, daughter, joiner s wife
Robert Wilson, grandson

49 - Jane Brunskill, head, retired domestic servant
Joseph Sewell, boarder, scholar
Robert Sewell, boarder, scholar
James Sewell, boarder, scholar

50 - Joseph Simpson, head, blacksmith
Grace Simpson, wife
Nathan Simpson, son
Joseph Simpson, son
William Simpson, son
Margaret Simpson, daughter
John Simpson, son

51 - Elizabeth ?, head, grocer & draper
Sarah Bailey, dress maker

52 - Joseph Watson, head, corn miller
Sarah Watson, wife
Annie Watson, daughter
Mary Watson, daughter
Sarah Watson, daughter
Emma Watson, daughter
John Watson, son

53 - John Savage, head, farm bailiff
Agnes Savage, wife
Adam Savage, son
Elizabeth Savage, daughter
Mary Savage, daughter
Elsie Savage, daughter
Elsie Savage, daughter
Margaret Savage, daughter
Sarah Savage, daughter
Robert Savage, son
Matthew Savage, son

54 - William Goodburn, head, carpenter
Thomas Clark, son-in-law, labourer
Jane Clark, daughter
Mary Clark, grand-daughter
Tom Clark, grandson

Eden Grove - William Graham, head, magistrate
John Chester, servant, farm bailiff
Jane Dalton, housekeeper
James Goodman, indoor servant
Margaret Hall, nurse maid
William Chester, gardener
William Stephen, groom

New Crown Inn - William More, head, stone mason & innkeeper
Ellen More, wife

Malt and Shovel - Thomas Hodgeson, head, innkeeper & farmer
Barbara Hodgeson, wife

Leonard Hodgeson, son, farmer s son
Bridget Hodgeson, daughter, scholar
William Hodgeson, son, scholar
Timothy Hodgeson, son, scholar
Elizabeth Hodgeson, daughter
Joseph Hodgeson, son, scholar

58 - Joseph Conners, head, butcher
Frances Conners, wife
Ann Conners, sister
Mary Conners, sister, annuitant
Francis Nicholson, niece

Vicarage - Philip Pennington, head, vicar
Alice Edgar, domestic servant
Mary Moore, visitor

The Lodge - Joseph Weoff, head, gardener
Isabella Weoff, wife
Annie Weoff, daughter, scholar
Elizabeth Weoff, daughter
Mary Weoff, daughter
John Weoff, son
William Weoff, son

Bolton Mill - Christopher Butterworth, head, miller & farmer 28 acres
Christopher Butterworth, son
Elizabeth Butterworth, son s wife
Ellen Butterworth, son s daughter
Joseph Butterworth, son
Rufus Butterworth, son
Elizabeth Sewell, domestic servant

No1 Lane End Cottages - George Mackeretty, head, husbandman
Rachel Mackeretty, wife
James Mackeretty, son
Mary Mackeretty, daughter
Elizabeth Mackeretty, daughter
Frederick Mackeretty, son

No3 Lane End Cottages - David Ferguson, head
Pam Ferguson, wife
Mary Jane Ferguson, daughter

BOLTON CENSUS RETURNS

No 4 Lane End Cottages - William Bewley, head, farm labourer
Mary Bewley, wife
John Bewley, son
William Bewley, son
Master Bewley, infant

No 5 Lane End Cottages - Rob Savage, head, general labourer
Mary Savage, wife
William Savage, son, groom
Sarah Savage, daughter
Margaret Anne Savage, grandmother
Matthew Savage, grandson

Bolton Hall - William Horn, head, farmer 400 acres
Annie Horn, wife
Mary Horn, daughter
Barbara Horn, daughter
John Horn, son
Annie Horn, daughter
William Horn, son
Joseph Horn, son
Anthony Malone, uncle, labourer
Elizabeth Robinson, domestic servant
Helena Shaw, visitor, scholar

67 - Stephen Bellas, head, agricultural labourer
Ann Bellas, wife
Joseph Bellas, son

68 - John Savage, head, cottager
Ruth Savage, wife

69 - William Cherry, head, joiner
Ruth Cherry, wife
Isobella Cherry, daughter
John Cherry, son, apprentice joiner
Ruth Cherry, daughter
William Cherry, son

Cross Rigg Farm - Richard Richardson, head, farm bailiff
Sarah Richardson, wife
Joseph Richardson, son

William Chester, farm servant
Mary Davidson, domestic servant

No1 Crossrigg Hall Cottage - Andrew Dent, head, gardener

No2 Crossrigg Hall Cottage - Thomas Holland, head, coachman
Sarah Holland, wife
Mary Holland, daughter
Edith Holland, daughter
George Holland, son
Alfred Holland, son
Jude Holland, son

1891 Census
1 - Joseph Simpson, head, 64, blacksmith, born Bolton
Grace Simpson, wife, 45, born Bolton
Nathan Simpson, son, 22, blacksmith, born Bolton
Joseph Simpson, son, 22, agricultural labourer, born Bolton
John Simpson, son, 14, agricultural labourer, born Bolton
William I. Simpson, son, 12, born Bolton
Margaret H. Simpson, daughter, 10, scholar, born Bolton
Mabel A. Simpson, daughter, 5, scholar, born Bolton

2 - Elizabeth Steel, head, widower, 70, born Kirkby Stephen

3 - James Lambert, head, 36, farmer, born Askrigg
Eleanor Lambert, wife, 33, born Warcop
Robert Lambert, son, 3, born Bolton
William J. Lambert, son, 3 months, born Bolton
Isabella Pearson, unmarried, 16, general servant, born Blencarn

4 -William Moore, head, 60, builder, born Morland
Eleanor Moore, wife, 54, born Belford
Charles E. Moore, grandson, 7, scholar, born Penrith

5 - James Hamilton, lodger, unmarried, 32, schoolmaster, born Scotland

6 - Wilfred E. Skaife, head, 29, storekeeper/commercial traveller, born Kirkby Thore
Isabella Skaife, wife, 24, storekeeper s assistant, born Appleby
Reginald H. Skaife, son, 8 months, born Bolton
Elizabeth Skaife, mother, widow, 61, living on her own means, born Kirkby Thore

7 - John Savage, head, 71, general labourer, born Bolton
Agnes Savage, wife, 54, born Scotland
Elizabeth Savage, daughter, 21, dressmaker, born Bolton
Robert Savage, son, 11, scholar, born Bolton
Matthew Savage, son, 11, scholar, born Bolton
James Savage, son, 9, scholar, born Bolton

8 - Samuel Richardson, head, 30, agricultural labourer, born Bongate
Sarah Richardson, wife, 27, born Greystoke
Mary A. Richardson, daughter, 6, scholar, born Kirkland
Thomas Richardson, son, 2, born Bolton
Martha Simpson, visitor, unmarried, 15, born Greystoke

9 - William Goodburn, head, widower, 78, joiner, born Bolton

New Crown Inn - John Furnass, head, 33, licensed victualler, born Sandford
Mary Furnass, wife, 26, born Long Marton
Henry M. Furnass, son, 4, born Appleby
Mary A. Furnass, daughter, 3, born Bolton
Agnes Jones, 14, general servant, born Bongate

11 - George Thompson, head, 54, farmer, born Bolton
Margaret Thompson, wife, 38, born Scotland
John G. Thompson, son, 7, born Bolton
Lizzie Thompson, daughter, 7, born Bolton
Arthur J. Thompson, son, 3, born Bolton
Isabella Gibson, visitor, married, 32, born Scotland
Frederick S. Gibson, visitor, 4, born Scotland
Isabella Waring, unmarried, 16, general servant, born Penrith

12 - William Chester, head, 29, gardener, born Cliburn
Mary E. Chester, wife 26, born Morland
Mary L. Chester, daughter, 1, born Bolton

Eden Grove - William Graham, head, unmarried, 36, JP, born London
Matthew Chester, unmarried, 36, butler, born Great Strickland
Sarah Edgar, widow, 42, housekeeper, born Cumberland
Elizabeth Strong, unmarried, 22, housemaid, born Great Strickland
Eliza Brown, unmarried, 22, kitchen maid, born Carleton

14 - Nicholas Woof, head, 30, groom, born Little Strickland
Sarah Woof, wife, 27, born Lowther

Elizabeth Woof, daughter, 4, born Bolton
Mary E. Woof, daughter, 2, born Bolton
Charles H. Woof, son, 1, born Bolton

The Vicarage - Philip Pinnington, head, 55, vicar of Bolton, born Cheshire
Alice M. Pinnington, wife, 41, born Runcorn
Elizabeth J. Pinnington, daughter, unmarried, 32, teacher of cookery, born Lancashire
Edward F. Pinnington, son,5, born Bolton
Philip B. Pinnington, son, 3, born Bolton
Edith M. Sanders, unmarried, 20, general servant, born London

Bolton Mill - Christopher Butterworth, head, widower, 81, corn merchant & miller, born Morland
Christopher Butterworth, son, 46, miller, born Brampton
Elizabeth Butterworth, son s wife, 43, housekeeper, born Sleagill
Joseph Butterworth, grandson, unmarried, 21, miller, born Bolton
Rufus Butterworth, grandson, unmarried, 19, miller, born Bolton

New Bewley - William Nicholson, head, 45, farmer, born Morland
Elizabeth Nicholson, wife, 44, born Hackthorpe
Joseph H. Nicholson, son, 12, scholar, born Culgaith
Frances L. Nicholson, daughter, 10, scholar, born Culgaith
Richard H. Nicholson, son, 7, scholar, born Culgaith
John R. Nicholson, son, 6, scholar, born Culgaith
Jonathan R. Nicholson, son, 4, born Culgaith
Frederick S. Nicholson, son, 2, born Culgaith
Litany Gowling, visitor, 10, scholar, born Kirkby Thore
Frances Proudfoot, unmarried, 15, general servant, born Carlisle
John Haugh, unmarried, 36, farm servant, born Sandsfield
William Jackson, unmarried, 19, farm servant, born Cumberland

New Bewley Cottage - William J. Thompson, head, 24, farm servant, born Bolton
Margaret Thompson, wife, 22, born Bolton
May H. Thompson, daughter, 1, born Bolton

Old Bewley Castle - Thomas Johnston, head, 48, farmer, born Ormside
Sarah A. Johnston, wife, 40, born Bolton
Annie E. Johnston, daughter, 14, born Bolton
Robert J. Johnston, son, 11, scholar, born Bolton
Sarah Johnston, daughter, 9, scholar, born Bolton
Maria Johnston, daughter, 6, scholar, born Bolton

BOLTON CENSUS RETURNS

Frank H. Johnston, son, 3, born Bolton
Margaret E. Johnston, daughter, 1, born Bolton

Bolton Lodge - Tom Grisdale, head, 26, farm manager, born Stainton
Mary J. Grisdale, wife, 28, housekeeper, born Penrith
Sarah J. Grisdale, daughter, 7 months, born Lazonby
John Lancaster, unmarried, 22, farm servant, born Shap
Hugh Abram, unmarried, 19, farm servant, born Brough

21 - Ann Steel, head, unmarried, 71, living on her own means, born Bolton

22 - Mary A. Edmondson, head, unmarried, 62, living on her own means, born Bolton

23 - John Airey, head, widower, 57, farmer, born Kirkby Thore

24 - William Bland, head, 41, tailor, draper, butter & cheese factor, born Bolton
Jane Bland, wife, 37, born Bolton
William Bland, son, 15, cabinet maker s apprentice, born Bolton
Ann E. Bland, daughter 10, scholar, born Bolton
Emily J. Bland, daughter, 7, scholar, born Bolton
Mary Bland, daughter, 4, born Bolton

25 - Ann Bland, head, widow, 74, farmer, born Bolton
Nathan Bland, son, unmarried, 31, tailor & draper, born Bolton
Emma Bland, daughter, unmarried, 30, dairy maid, born Bolton
Isabella A. Akrigg, grand-daughter, unmarried, 18, house maid, born Bolton
Joseph Cannon, visitor, married, 64, butcher, born Morland

26 - George Wilson, head, 67, contractor, born Cumberland
Isabella Wilson, wife, 62, born Bolton
Elizabeth Wilson, daughter, unmarried, 20, dressmaker, born Bolton
Thomas Wilson, grandson, 5, scholar, born Bolton

27 - William Wilson, head, 42, stone mason, born Bolton
Mary Wilson, wife, 41, born Lyth
James Wilson, son, 10, scholar, born Bolton
Ada M. Wilson, daughter, 8, scholar, born Bolton
Emma J. Wilson, daughter, 6, scholar, born Bolton
Edith E. Wilson, daughter, 5, born Bolton
Ernest Wilson, son, 3, born Bolton

28 - Margaret Jennings, head, widow, 47, born Bolton
Mary I. Jennings, daughter, 9, scholar, born Bolton
Cuthbert Jennings, son, 7, born Bolton
Margaret A. Jennings, daughter, 1, born Bolton

29 - Thomas Milner, head, 30, farmer, born Musgrave
Annie Milner, wife, 26, born Bolton
Elizabeth A. Milner, daughter, 7 scholar, Kings Meaburn
Alice Milner, daughter, 6, scholar, born Bolton
Mary V. Milner, daughter, 5, born Bolton
William L. Milner, son, 4, born Colby

30 - Mary Nicholson, head, unmarried, 76, living on her own means, born Bolton

31 - Thomas Robinson, head, 51, stone mason, born Burton in Holme
Elizabeth Robinson, wife, 50, born Whitehaven
Joseph Robinson, son, 9, scholar, born Bolton
John Robinson, grandson, 2, born Shap
Charlotte Hewetson, daughter, married, 24, born Cheshire
Joseph Hewetson, grandson, 1, born Staveley
Elizabeth J. Hewetson, grand-daughter, 4 months, born Kendal

32 - Elizabeth Lambert, head, widow, 81, living on her own means, born Warcop
William Lambert, son, married, 49, farmer, born Bolton
Mary Lambert, son s wife, 38, born Kirkland
Isabella Lambert, grand-daughter, 1, born Bolton
John Lambert, grandson, 1 month, born Bolton
Emma Birbeck, 13, general servant, born Westmorland

33 - William Brunskill, head, 59, farmer, born Long Marton
Margaret Brunskill, wife, 55, born Dufton
George Brunskill, son, unmarried, 24, coachman, born Bolton
Agnes Brunskill, daughter, 18, born Bolton
Frederic Brunskill, grandson, 5, born Bolton

34 - Robert Jackson, head, 59, agricultural labourer, born Shap
Isabella Jackson, wife, 57, born Appleby
John R. Jackson, son, unmarried, 34, agricultural labourer, born Appleby
Agnes E. Jackson, daughter, 14, born Bolton
Miles Bateman, nephew, unmarried, 43, living on his own means, born Appleby

35 - William Hall, head, 55, farmer, born Crackenthorpe

BOLTON CENSUS RETURNS

Ann Hall, wife, 50, born Stainton
Hannah Hall, daughter, 12, born Appleby
Thomas Hall, son, 11, born Appleby

36 - William Dodd, head, 70 agricultural labourer, born Kirkby Thore
Mary Dodd, wife, 74, born Morland
James Dodd, son, unmarried, 42, agricultural labourer, born Bolton
John Dodd, son, unmarried, 37, agricultural labourer, born Bolton

37 - Matthew Savage, head, 74, farmer, born Bolton
Mary Savage, wife, 75, born Bolton
Kate Holder, unmarried, 21, general servant, born Lowther
Thomas Graham, unmarried, 17, farm servant, born Skirwith

38 - Charles B. Haynes, head, 41, scaffolder/bricklayer, born Woodstock
Mary Haynes, wife, 45, born Bongate
Charles Albert Haynes, son, 15, scholar, born Bongate
Ada Anna Haynes, daughter, 13, scholar, born Bongate
Alexander Haynes, son, 11, scholar, born Bongate
William B. Haynes, son, 8, scholar, born Crackenthorpe

39 - Isabella Howe, head, widow, 51, char woman, born Unthank
Isabella Howe, daughter, unmarried, 27, born Bolton
Mary Ann Howe, daughter, unmarried, 28, born Bolton
Joseph Howe, son, unmarried, 17, schoolmaster s assistant, born Bolton
Henry Howe, son, 13, scholar, born Bolton
James Arthur Howe, son, 11, scholar, born Bolton

40 - Jane Thompson, head, unmarried, 36, charwoman, born Bolton
Frances Thompson, daughter, 8, scholar, born Bolton

41 - Isaac Garnet, head, unmarried, 34, shoemaker, born Hutton-in-the-Forest
42 - Alice Robinson, head, married, 67, living on her own means, born Durham

43 - William Clark, head, 59, farm labourer, born Long Marton
Christiana Clark, wife, 52, born Bolton
John Clark, son, unmarried, 27, farm labourer, born Bolton
Sarah Ellen Millican, visitor, unmarried, 22, born Morland

44 - Mary Steel, head, unmarried, 78, living on her own means, born Bolton

45 - Margaret Agnes Longmire, head, unmarried, 22, dressmaker, born Bolton

46 - Thomas Longmire, head, 56, farm labourer, born Bolton
Mary Longmire, wife, 49, born Warcop
Henry James Longmire, son, 13, scholar, born Bolton
Joseph Longmire, grandson, 6, scholar, born Bolton
Ada Longmire, grand-daughter, 5 months, born Bolton

Elm House - John Dent, head, unmarried, 59, farmer, born Bolton
Jane Tuer, unmarried, 38, housekeeper, born Ormside
Watt ? , 15, farm servant, born Kirkby Thore
Frederick Beetham, 14, farm servant, born Hilton

48 - Thomas Slack, head, 54, general labourer, born Bolton
Jane Slack, wife, 36, char woman, born Bolton
Mary Jane, daughter, 11, born Bolton
Tom Slack, son, 10, scholar, born Bolton
Joseph Slack, son, 7, scholar, born Bolton
Frederick Slack, son, 5, scholar, born Bolton
Frank Slack, son, 3, born Bolton
Henry Slack, son, 1, born Bolton

49 - Michael Stephenson, head, 57, stone mason, born Bolton
Jane Stephenson, wife, 53, dressmaker, born Morland

50 - William Cherry, head, 59, joiner & farmer, born Morland
Ruth Cherry, wife, 56, born Bolton
Elizabeth Cherry, daughter, unmarried, 21, born Bolton
William Edward Cherry, son, 16, joiner s apprentice, born Bolton
Ruth Savage, mother-in-law, widow, 85, born Plumpton
Ruth Cherry, boarder, 8, scholar, born Penrith

51 - John N. Richardson, head, 30, traction engine driver, born Bolton
Sarah Richardson, wife, 32, born Plumpton
Margaret Richardson, daughter, 3, born Penrith
Annie Richardson, daughter, 1, born Penrith

52 - John Richardson, head, married, 71, agricultural labourer, born Cliburn
Martha Richardson, daughter, unmarried, 28, born Bolton

53 - William Hugill, head, 26, agricultural labourer, born Dacre
Kate Hugill, wife, 18, born Blencarn
Isaac Hugill, son, 2, born Kirkby Thore
Thomas Hugill, son, 5 months, born Bolton

BOLTON CENSUS RETURNS

54 - John Hugill, head, 30, agricultural labourer, born Skelton
Elizabeth Hugill, wife, 23, born Milburn
John William Hugill, son 3, born Bolton
Robert Hugill, son, 3, born Bolton

Bolton Hall - Joseph Crosby Dent, head, 50, owner & occupier of farm, born Bolton
Eleanor C. Dent, wife, 50, owner & occupier of farm, born Appleby
Margaret Eggleston, unmarried, 16, general servant, born Great Strickland

56 - Thomas Hill, head, 32, farm servant, born Maryport
Rebecca Hill, wife, 27, born Crosby Ravensworth
?? Hill, daughter, 7, scholar, born Bongate
John James Hill, son, 5, scholar, born Bongate
Rebecca Jane Hill, daughter, 2, born Crosby Ravensworth

57 - Margaret Parkin, head, widow, 55, farmer, born Scotland
William Parkin, son, unmarried, 23, general labourer, born Bolton

58 - John Robinson, head, 37, agricultural labourer, born Newbiggin
Mary J. Robinson, wife, 40, born Bolton Gate
Elizabeth Thwaites, step-daughter, 12, scholar, born Kirkbampton

Laitha - Thomas Threlkeld, head, 32, farmer, born Long Marton
Mary Threlkeld, wife, 31, born Crosby Ravensworth
Elsie Threlkeld, daughter, 6, born Dufton
John Threlkeld, son, 3, born Dufton
Lavina Threlkeld, daughter, 2, born Dufton
Stanley Threlkeld, son, 7 months, born Bolton
Nanny Scaife, unmarried, 19, servant, born Crosby Ravensworth
John J. Parkin, unmarried, 17, farm servant, born Cumberland

Hanging Bank - Joseph Simpson Todd, head, 35, farmer, born Milburn
Eleanor Todd, wife, 33, farmer s wife, born Crosby Ravensworth
Robert John Todd, son, 9, scholar, born Crosby Ravensworth
Edward George Todd, son, 7, scholar, born Crosby Ravensworth
Jane Elizabeth Todd, daughter, 5, scholar, born Crosby Ravensworth
Margaret Eleanor Todd, daughter, 4, born Crosby Ravensworth
?? Thexton, visitor, unmarried, 16, farmer s daughter, born Crook
?? Watt, unmarried, 21, general servant, born Kirkby Thore
William Lancaster, unmarried, 16, farm servant, born Clifton
George Fairer, unmarried, 16, farm servant, born Crosby Ravensworth
John Southward, unmarried, 15, farm servant, born Bongate

61 - George Walker, head, unmarried, 50, farmer, born Bolton
Elizabeth Walker, sister, unmarried, 51, farmer, born Newbiggin
Mary Elizabeth Bailey, unmarried, 18, general servant, born Bolton
William Lowis, unmarried, 41, farm servant, born Penrith

62 - William Fairer, head, widower, 58, agricultural labourer, born Morland
Jane Fairer, daughter, unmarried, 28, born Penrith
Joseph Fairer, son, unmarried, 24, born Morland

Birdby - Joseph Bird, head, 30, farmer, born Kings Meaburn
Elizabeth Bird, wife, 29, born Orton
Margaret Bird, daughter, 6, scholar, born Yanwath
Joseph Bird, son, 3, born Barton
Betsey Bird, mother, married, 64, farmer s wife, born Bolton
William Robinson, visitor, unmarried, 22, fitter - steam ship, born Orton
Isaac Robinson, unmarried, 25, farm servant, born Penruddock
Priscilla Robinson, unmarried, 15, general servant, born Penrith

Brigham Bank - John Moffatt, head, 52, farmer, born Newton
Isabella Moffatt, wife, 52, born Plumpton
Henry M. Moffatt, son, unmarried, 28, farmer s son, born Newton
George Moffatt, son, unmarried, 26, farmer s son, born Newton
Mary J. Moffatt, daughter, unmarried, 21, farmer s daughter, born Barton

Crossrigg Hall - Hugh C. Rigg, head, unmarried, 42, JP, living on own means
Henry Wilkinson, married, 37, general servant, born Asby
Margaret Wilkinson, married, 29, housekeeper, born Asby
Thomas William Wilkinson, servant s son, 6, scholar, born Crosby Ravensworth
James Herbert Wilkinson, servant s son, 4, born Crosby Ravensworth
Walter Henry Wilkinson, servant s son, 2, born Crosby Ravensworth
Conni? Jenkinson, unmarried, 28, housemaid, born Culgaith

66 - Matthew Davidson, head, 61, gardener, born Kirkland
Isabel Davidson, wife, 58, born Appleby
Isabel Davidson, daughter, unmarried, 20, dressmaker, born Cliburn
Ethel Atkinson, grand-daughter, 5, born Bolton

Crossrigg Farm - John Wilson, head, unmarried, 33, farmer, born Yorkshire
Mary Fisher, unmarried, 23, general servant, born Appleby
Mary I. Brownrigg, unmarried, 15, general servant, born Lazonby

68 - Robert Savage, head, 68, agricultural labourer (deaf), born Long Marton

Mary Savage, wife, 73, born Morland
Sarah J. Dixon, grand-daughter, 11, scholar, born Barton

69 - John Frith, head, 34, farm labourer, born Great Strickland
Mary Frith, wife, 36, born Bolton
Margaret Thompson, step-daughter, 15, born Bolton
Dinah Thompson, step-daughter, 12, scholar, born Shap
Jane Frith, daughter, 4, born Kirkby Thore
Hannah Frith, daughter, 2, born Bolton
Elizabeth Frith, daughter, 2 months, born Bolton

70 - Richard Sowerby, head, 27, farm labourer, born Cliburn
Eliza Sowerby, wife, 22, born Shap
Sarah J. Sowerby, daughter, 1 month, born Shap

71 - John Atkinson, head, 50, agricultural labourer, born Hawes
Isabella Atkinson, wife, 41, born Cliburn
Joseph Atkinson, son, 13, scholar, born Brougham
George Atkinson, son, 10, scholar, born Brougham
John Atkinson, son, 7, scholar, born Brougham
Isabella Atkinson, daughter, 5, scholar, born Brougham

72 - William Savage, head, 30, groom, born Morland
Sarah Savage, wife, 30, born Kirkland
Margaret A. Savage, daughter, 10, scholar, born Morland
Thomas Savage, son, 8, scholar, born Morland
Edith Savage, daughter, 6, scholar, born Penrith
William Savage, son, 2, born Morland
Emily Savage, daughter, 1, born Morland

Street House - William Dent, head, widower, 57, farmer, born Bolton
Mary Jane Dent, daughter, unmarried, 25, farmer s daughter, born Bolton
Agnes Emily Dent, daughter, unmarried, 24, farmer s daughter, born Bolton
John Henry Dent, son, 21, farmer s son, born Bolton
William James Dent, son, 15, farmer s son, born Bolton
Annie Elizabeth Dent, daughter, 13, scholar, born Bolton
Esther Amy Dent, daughter, 5, born Bolton

Mansgrove - John Slee, head, 32, farmer, born Stainton
Annie Jane Slee, wife, 30, born Temple Sowerby
Harvey Slee, son, 4, born Temple Sowerby
Linda M. Slee, daughter, 3, born Temple Sowerby

Ethel Ada Slee, daughter, 1, born Bolton
Sarah Clementson, unmarried, 20, general servant, born Hutton-in-the-Forest
Isaac Thompson, unmarried, 19, farm servant, born Kings Meaburn

75 - William Simpson, head, unmarried, 23, farmer, born Bolton

76 - Joseph Bellas, head, unmarried, 38, agricultural labourer, born Bolton
Stephen Bellas, father, widower, 74, agricultural labourer, born Bolton

Post Office - Thomas Ellwood, head, 41, grocer & sub-postmaster, born Bolton
Sarah Ann Ellwood, wife, 27, postmaster s assistant, born Morland
William Ellwood, son, 3, born Bolton
Mary Jane Ellwood, daughter, 2, born Bolton

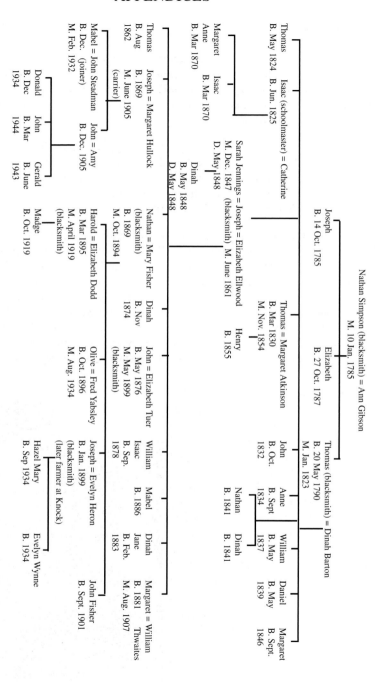

The Simpson family tree - blacksmiths of Bolton, Westmorland.

CHANGING TIMES

THE AUTHORS

John Maden took all the recent photographs. John became interested in photography in 1992 when he started walking in Wales. It was at that time that he bought his first Camera a Canon 1000F. In 1993 he joined a Camera Club in Redcar. He has entered just one competition and came second with a picture of an old lady taken in Rhodes.

John assisted by Elizabeth has enjoyed taking photographs in and around the village and both have enjoyed meeting the inhabitants. He probably has enough photographs to produce a pictorial diary of Bolton in the future. John and Elizabeth moved from Redcar to live in Eden Fold in August 1998. They really enjoy living in Bolton and say that it surpasses all their expectations.

Pam Metcalf has lived in the village all her life. She was born at Bolton Lodge Farm and is the daughter of Edith and Percy Metcalf. When she was about three years of age she moved to live at Eden Fields. Pam attended the village school and the County School in Appleby. Having a disability from birth made it difficult for Pam to take up a career or to have employment outside the home. She has always enjoyed writing, especially writing poetry. Because of these interests when she was asked by the members of the Millennium Committee if she would like to be involved with producing the book she was very keen to do so and has been of great assistance in helping to type the manuscript.

Pam had to learn how to use the computer and was very grateful to Cath Butterworth from Appleby Heritage Centre for her tuition and support. Pam says she has enjoyed every minute of her involvement with the project and it has led to other projects for her. For example, writing small articles for the South Eden Project newsletter and involvement in producing their book *Taking the Plunge*. She is also available to make posters to publicise village events. Her latest venture is to surf the net.

Annie Kirkup

Annie Kirkup was born at Sleagill and when she was very young moved to Whitestone Farm between Newby and Shap with her family. She came to

Pam Metcalf

Bolton when she married John Kirkup a builder and moved into the house she lives in today near the Memorial Hall. The house is next to the house where her mother-in-law ran the Post Office several years ago. Annie has one daughter and two grandsons.

Several years ago Annie entered her first dialect competition. It was organised by the Rotarians at Silloth and much to her surprise she won. A panel of judges gives points for content, delivery and if the contestant has written it they get a further point. Since that first competition Annie has entered and won many times.

Barbara Cotton came to live in Bolton with her husband Derick when he took early retirement from the RAF in 1992. Barbara has worked in Education and the Health Service and took early retirement from health visiting in the area in March 2000. She has always been interested in history particularly local history and family history. Her involvement in the book came about when she went to offer support to Pam in acquiring her word processing skills. She never dreamt she would become so involved with the production or that her work would eventually be so open to the public eye.

The experience of meeting so many people whom she would not have had reason to come into contact with has been humbling and interesting and many new friends have been made. Barbara feels that she now knows her adopted village very well and all the information she has gathered for the book confirms her reasons for wanting to live in the village of Bolton.

Hazel Bird was very pleased to draw and paint the pictures. Hazel was originally trained as an art teacher with an extra qualification in music. She has taught art and music in many of the schools in the area and draws and paints for pleasure when she has the time.

Glossary

Armigorous - An armiger is one who bears a coat of arms by lawful authority and is therefore armigorous

Ashlar - Masonry constructed of square hewn free stone. Also thin slabs of dressed stone used for facing walls over rubble. Ashlar is a characteristic of many sophisticated buildings.

Free warren - A franchise, obtained from the crown, granting rights to kill or keep beasts and game. Of particular significance in the context of Forest Law.

Mortmain - Dead hand meaning in the hand of the church. Land granted by laymen to ecclesiastical bodies became free of reliefs, thereby reducing the revenues of the Lord of the Manor. The Magna Carta prohibited the transfer of land without the lords consent. Further legislation added penalties for causing land to be transferred into Mortmain.

Ox gang - The eighth part of the carute or plough land varying from 10-18 acres or more. *Shorter Oxford English Dictionary.*

Speenhamland System - A system of supplementing poor relief first adopted in the Berkshire village of Speenhamland in c1795. Parishes tried to supplement low wages with an allowance which was related to the cost of bread. It was often abused by employers who reduced wages believing the parish would make up the difference. Instead of the numbers of poor claiming relief decreasing they increased.

Tenement - Land held of a superior or any rented land or dwelling.

Sumptuary Laws - Medieval Laws intended to restrict private expenditure.

References

Life and Tradition in the Lake District, William Rollinson, 1974.

A History of Cumberland and Westmorland, William Rollinson, 1996

The Shell Book of Cottages, Richard Reid, 1977

Encyclopedia of Dates & Events, revised by B. A. Phythian and edited by L. C. Pascoe

Westmorland Agriculture, 1800-1900, Frank W. Garnett, MRCVS

Old English Houses, Hugh Braun, 1962.

The Westmorland Protestation Returns 1641/2, edited with an introduction by M.A. Faraday, M.A. 1971, Cumberland and Westmorland Antiquarian and Archeological Society.

The Protestation The Magna Carta of the 17th century, Susan Pearl, Family Tree Magazine, January 1992 Vol, No 3.

Bolton in Westmorland — an Eden Valley Community 18th and early 19th centuries, Derek Longmire, County Archives, Kendal

Notes in Early Sculptured Crosses, Shrines and Monuments in the Present Diocese of Carlisle, Cumberland and Westmorland Archeological and Antiquarian Society, 1899.

Church wardens account book, County Archives. Kendal. Reference. WPR 25

Wigan Heritage Service

Later Records of North Westmorland of the Barony of Kendal, John F. Curnow

Appleby Quarter Sessions Indictment Book 1808/1807.

Around Eden, F. B. Chancellor, 1954

A History Of England, Keith Feiling, 1966

Poor Rate Assessment Bolton (Misc Records) WDX/530/4 and WPR 25 County Archives, Kendal.

Appleby Quarter Sessions 1741 WQ/SC/140, County Archives, Kendal.

Endowed Grammar Schools in Westmorland.

Westmorland Schools 1500-1700, J. H. D Bates M.A. (Cantab) Dip Ed.end

Eden Grove Estate papers, 1810-1915, WDX 807, Kendal Archives

Westmorland Census Returns

Cumberland & Westmorland Herald, 1937

Bolton Church Records.

Census of Westmorland 1787.

Court Manor Roll, Carlisle Castle Archives, D/LONS/L5/2/3/7.

Crossrigg Hall Estate Papers, County Archives, Kendal.

A Hired Lass in Westmorland, Isabella Cooke

Information supplied by Mr and Mrs David Woods.

The Place Names of Westmorland.

Morland Ecclesiastic Parish Records, (E & O E) by R G Thwaites.

CHANGING TIMES

Cumberland and Westmorland Archeological and Antiquarian Society Tracts.
The Westmorland Survey and Inventory Royal Commission on Historical Monuments.
The Batsford Companion to Local History, Stephen Friar
Information extracted from Family papers loaned by Mr Arthur Bird, Birdby.
Information supplied by Betty Fisher of Cliburn (late Crosby Ravensworth) Roberta Laycock nee Brunskill's daughter.
1851, 1881and 1891 census.
Bolton s Parish Church Records.
History and Directory of Westmorland, Bulmer, Sedburgh
Documents loaned by David Fox, Wayside Cottage.
Documents loaned by Richard Birkbeck, Whyber.
Deeds Glebe House, Barbara and Derick Cotton.
An Armorial for Westmorland and Lonsdale, Boumphrey, Hudleston & Hughes, 1976
Take a Pew, Joy Lodey, Family Tree magazine, November 1993.
Public Record Office Kendal Reference WD 1033 No 7
The ejected of 1662, Cumberland and Westmorland.
Cumberland and Westmorland Antiquarian and Archeological Society, Tract Series No XV.
Early Westmorland MPs 1258-1327, George S. H. L. Washington M.A. F.S.A.
Bells and Mortars, Wigan Heritage Service, The History Shop Wigan.

MORE BOOKS FROM HAYLOFT PUBLISHING

Better by Far a Cumberland Hussar by Colin Bardgett
(Hardback, £26.95, ISBN 09540711 2 3)
(Paperback, £16.95, ISBN 0 9540711 1 5)

The Northern Warrior by Adrian Rogan
(£8.95, ISBN 0 9523282 8 3)

A Riot of Thorn & Leaf by Dulcie Matthews
(£7.95, ISBN 0 9540711 0 7)

A Country Doctor by Dawn Robertson
(£2.25, ISBN 0 9523282 32)

Military Mountaineering by Retd. Major Bronco Lane
(Hardback, £25.95, ISBN 0 9523282 1 6)
(Paperback, £17.95, ISBN 0 9523282 6 7)

Yows & Cows by Mike Sanderson
(£7.95, ISBN 0 9523282 0 8)

Riding the Stang by Dawn Robertson
(£9.99, ISBN 0 9523282 2 4)

Secrets and Legends of Old Westmorland
by Peter Koronka and Dawn Robertson
(Hardback, £17.95, ISBN 0 9523282 4 0)
(Paperback, £11.95, ISBN 0 9523282 9 1)

The Irish Influence by Harold Slight
(£4.95, 0 9523282 5 9)

You can order any of the above books by writing to:

Hayloft Publishing, Great Skerrygill, South Stainmore,
Kirkby Stephen, Cumbria, CA17 4EU.
Please enclose a cheque plus £2 for UK postage & packing.
Tel. (017683) 42300
For more information see: www.hayloft.org.uk